*Studies in Writing & Rhetoric*

## Other Books in the Studies in Writing & Rhetoric Series

*Multiliteracies for a Digital Age*

# Multiliteracies for a Digital Age

---

Stuart A. Selber

SOUTHERN ILLINOIS UNIVERSITY PRESS

*Carbondale*

Publication partially funded by a subvention grant from The Conference on College
Composition and Communication of the National Council of Teachers of English.

*Library of Congress Cataloging-in-Publication Data*

Selber, Stuart A.
   Multiliteracies for a digital age / Stuart A. Selber.
      p. cm. — (Studies in writing & rhetoric)
   Includes bibliographical references and index.
   1. English language—Rhetoric—Study and teaching—Data processing. 2. Report
writing—Study and teaching (Higher)—Data processing. 3. English language—
Rhetoric—Computer-assisted instruction. 4. Report writing—Computer-assisted
instruction. 5. Computer literacy. I. Title. II. Series.
PE1404 .S365 2004
808'.042'0285—dc21
ISBN 0-8093-2551-9 (alk. paper)          2003011875

*For the Selbers, Liebermans, and Latterells,*
*but especially for Kate*

# Contents

# Preface

This book was written to help teachers of writing and communication develop full-scale computer literacy programs that are both effective and professionally responsible.

Readers might wonder why another book about computer literacy is even needed. After all, a search at Amazon.com finds around 750 books that have already been written on the subject, while the popular Internet search engine Google returns over 250,000 Websites that deal with computer literacy in one fashion or another. However, the vast majority of these texts tend to focus more on technological issues than on literacy issues. Furthermore, relatively few of them identify and directly address the difficult questions facing teachers of writing and communication in a digital age, questions such as: What should a computer literate student be able to do? What is required of English departments to educate such a student? What are the obstacles to this important task? What perspectives contribute to the current treatment of computer literacy in English departments? Given the fact that literacy is not a monolithic or static phenomenon, with predictable consequences for individuals and social groups, how can the profession conceptualize an approach that will hold up over time and that will illuminate the most important writing and communication issues? Given that students must learn to work with computers in hands-on ways, how can functional literacy be reimagined to align with the values of the profession? If computers have become a fact of life in writing and communication classrooms, by what means can a healthy dose of skepticism not only be preserved but strengthened? And by what means can students play a more active role in the construction and reconstruction of technological systems? These questions motivate the discussions in this book.

As the questions indicate, *Multiliteracies for a Digital Age* is

neither a how-to guide for the latest and greatest computer technologies nor a theoretical critique that remains on an abstract plane.
Although much of the discussion is conceptual in nature, it provides a framework within which teachers of writing and communication can develop comprehensive programs that draw together
functional, critical, and rhetorical concerns in the service of social
action and change. My view is that computer literacy education today is all too often a one-dimensional enterprise. How-to guides
teach useful information that can help students solve their most immediate and practical problems. Yet how-to guides succeed, in large
part, by ignoring the terms and conditions under which computer
technologies are imagined and created. And while theoretical critiques of computers point out their non-neutral aspects, these discussions typically look right through the complexities and uncer-
tainties of actual situations of use. In addition, they frequently fail
to provide realistic and constructive alternatives to the circumstances being analyzed. So the end result of either emphasis is one
and the same: students who are ill-prepared for the literacy challenges of the twenty-first century.

Such an outcome, however, is not inevitable. Although computer literacy is a complex area, this book provides heuristic approaches that combine practice and theory in ways that are meaningful to teachers of writing and communication. More specifically,
it shows teachers how to develop and nurture comprehensive programs through multilayered education, deep engagement, and micropolitical action. My hope is that this book offers flexible intellectual
structures that clearly lend themselves to implementation in pedagogical and programmatic contexts.

I wish to thank the many people who helped me with this
book. Robert Brooke solicited the project and provided wonderful
editorial advice at every stage in the process. I thank Robert for
his support, candor, great judgment, and prompt feedback. Robert
also appointed two reviewers: Pamela Takayoshi and Janice Walker.
Pamela and Janice provided numerous valuable suggestions and insights. In addition, my colleagues Jack Selzer and Cheryl Glenn
read the manuscript in various phases of development. I thank Jack

for his patience, wide perspective, and attention to detail, and I thank Cheryl for her comments on early drafts of three chapters, comments that helped me to speak better to my audience. John-dan Johnson-Eilola also read and commented on the manuscript, and his ongoing support and friendship have made a world of difference. I received research assistance from Brent Henze, Jodie Nicotra, and Jordynn Jack. I thank Brent, Jodie, and Jordynn for their hard work and for many useful conversations about literacy and computers. Anne Wysocki created the only figure in this book on very short notice, and because of her design talents, this figure is just right. I also want to thank my other colleagues who make Penn State such a terrific place to do scholarly work in rhetoric: Marie Secor, Keith Gilyard, Elaine Richardson, Margaret Lyday, Jon Olson, and Rich Doyle. Karl Kageff, Kathleen Kageff, and the staff at Southern Illinois University Press deserve special recognition for their efforts. Finally, I thank Kate Latterell, to whom I especially dedicate this book. For her help, faith in me, and affection, I am grateful.

A portion of chapter 3 was originally published in "Introduction: Computers in the Technical Communication Classroom," reprinted, with permission, from *IEEE Transactions on Professional Communication* 39 (1996): 179–82. Copyright © 1996 IEEE. A portion of chapter 4 was originally published in "Metaphorical Perspectives On Hypertext," reprinted, with permission, from *IEEE Transactions on Professional Communication* 38 (1995): 59–67. Copyright © 1995 IEEE.

*Multiliteracies for a Digital Age*

# 1 / Reimagining Computer Literacy

> Technology education is not a technical subject. It is a branch
> of the humanities.
>
> —Neil Postman,
> *The End of Education: Redefining the Value of School*

Since at least the 1960s, questions about computer literacy have
been asked and answered repeatedly in instructional settings, but
in ways that are often dissatisfying to teachers of writing and communication. Although academic institutions are investing in technology infrastructure and support at an astonishing rate—so astonishing, in fact, that it is futile to cite growth statistics, which
increase dramatically from year to year—these investments are
often driven by logics that fail to make humanistic perspectives a
central concern. Cultural critic Neil Postman has argued cogently
that a worthwhile education focuses on the consequences and contexts of technology rather than merely on the technology itself. But
just what would such an education entail?

Computers are indeed a fact of life in educational settings, yet
too few teachers today are prepared to organize learning environments that integrate technology meaningfully and appropriately.
There are several factors contributing to this state of affairs, including the popular if mistaken view that learning how to use—and
think about—computers productively is simply a matter of understanding, in operational terms, how computers work. Of course,
knowing how to operate a computer is one important aspect of
teaching and learning in contemporary instructional contexts. And,
increasingly, there is much to know about the online applications
developed to support writing and communication activities. But

1

simply understanding the mechanics of computing, particularly in decontextualized ways, will not prepare students and teachers for the challenges of literacy in the twenty-first century. For example, effective revision strategies for hypertext require a host of complex abilities, ranging from saving files as part of a shared network drive to restructuring the logical-deductive pattern of an essay. Unfortunately, students and teachers often find support for the former task but not the latter.

For that matter, computer literacy is a vexing and ongoing problem even for teachers who have good support systems. Many in the profession are understandably skeptical about getting involved in computer literacy initiatives. One explanation for this skepticism is that those who work with technology can quite easily find themselves in a number of precarious situations. Some are fortunate to have access to impressive computer facilities but find themselves operating in a culture that vastly underestimates what must be learned to take advantage of technology and to understand its social and pedagogical implications. Others function rather productively in relative isolation, organizing an active community of dedicated graduate students and part-time instructors, while bending over backwards to entice faculty colleagues to invest their time and energy in a new direction. Still others—the great majority of teachers, I would argue—are encouraged, even mandated, to integrate technology into the curriculum, yet no incentives are given for such an ambitious assignment, one that places an extra workload burden on teachers, adding considerably to their overall job activities.

Notwithstanding the genuine risks posed by such precarious situations, more than enough incentives for getting involved with computer literacy initiatives can be found in the educational realities of the current period. In the 1980s, teachers of writing and communication expended an enormous amount of effort in investigating whether computer programs could make students better writers (see Hawisher). This inquiry made perfect sense to a profession that was trying to decide whether or not to include computers in writing instruction. But, in this day and age, the need to make such a decision is moot. A new round in the old debate over computer literacy has begun, or at least the grounds of this debate have shifted in substantial ways. For better or worse, computer environments have become primary spaces where much education happens. It is indeed a rare university student who does not use computers—on a regular basis—for writing and research activities, for communicating with classmates and teachers, for organizing and scheduling tasks, and for many additional purposes. The Internet and other computer applications have succeeded in becoming an undeniable part of the instructional landscape across the entire curriculum. In English studies, computers are implicated in a wide range of crucial literacy issues no matter the view of any particular teacher or program. And the stakes could not be higher. For at issue is the future shape of writing instruction and its significance to students.

This chapter begins a detailed investigation into the nature of computer literacy programs in higher education. Its purposes are to characterize the consequences and contexts that so frequently get overlooked in such programs, to discuss at least some of the reasons for this neglect, and to make a few initial proposals about what might be needed in order to create better alternatives. Toward this end, I begin with a brief discussion of several obstacles to more productive literacy practices, including technology myths as well as pedagogical and institutional barriers that are difficult to deal with. I urge teachers of writing and communication to adopt a "postcritical" stance, one that locates computer literacy in the domain of English studies while operating under the assumption that no theories or positions should be immune to critical assessment. Next, I elaborate on the central problem driving this book by taking a closer look at computer literacy requirements in higher education, requirements that tend to overemphasize and draw attention to technical concerns. To conclude, I move from rehearsing the existing failures of technological literacy to introducing a more positive portrait of the ideal multiliterate student that teachers should be trying to develop.

*Obstacles to More Productive Literacy Practices*

Computer literacy is certainly a worthwhile project for teachers of writing and communication. Not only are teachers obligated to prepare students responsibly for a digital age in which the most rewarding jobs require multiple literacies, but students will be citizens and parents as well as employees, and in these roles they will also need to think in expanded ways about computer use. Teachers obviously have the potential to help enact productive change if they think about computer literacy in the right ways. And one thing that this means is removing themselves from several prevailing myths that compromise educational progress.

For example, all too often computer technologies are touted as the solution to all of our problems, an inclination deeply embedded in American culture and education. From a humanistic perspective, however, conversations about computers are often misguided by the cause-effect relationships they tend to assume, which typically attribute to computers alone the power to make deep-seated, positive transformations, above and beyond existing social, political, and economic constraints. The myth of the all-powerful computer is as vital in the classroom as it is in popular culture. But the fact is that although computer technologies can be one important part of an educational solution, they are almost always a relatively small part, and even then the solution is not a quick or necessarily sure one.

Other prevailing myths discourage targeted and insightful discussions of computer literacy. For example, there is the myth of equality through computers, the belief that computers will level the educational playing field. But although it is clear that the poor, people of color, and women too rarely enjoy equal access to technology and its opportunities and, in all likelihood, never will (Gomez; Grabill; Moran), teachers tend to forget that equal access, even if that were possible, does not guarantee parity for the ignored or disenfranchised. In order for equitable experiences to take place, these groups need access not only to networked computers that are reasonably current but also to extensive systems of pedagogical and social support. In considering how teachers might improve the education of at-risk children, Saul Rockman put it this way:

> Ensuring that schools have the same amount of equipment will not do. Providing schools with teachers who care and know enough about how to use computers effectively will help. Installing a technology infrastructure without reason for using it does not help. Refurbishing a building and making it beautiful and safe, does. Making certain that children have enough to eat and warm clothes to wear in the winter, is also a good starting point. (28)

But too frequently, computing infrastructures are established without the human resources required to make them just and productive for educational purposes, creating what Lawrence Tomei describes as the technology facade: a "false sense of activity and substance with respect to the uses of technology" in a learning environment (32).

One of the more compelling current myths encourages university administrators to assume that computers automatically make people more productive and thus are a cost-effective way of doing business. This myth, which is particularly appealing in a time of shrinking fiscal resources, inspires distance education initiatives that increase enrollments and workloads but not faculty positions; intranets and e-mail exchanges that unrealistically inflate communication expectations; and massive archives of online training materials that fail to contextualize software applications for students and teachers in departments of English. But there is very little evidence right now to suggest that computers actually reduce instructional costs in any significant manner, or that they enhance the research and teaching productivity of faculty members (Green and Gilbert; Martin). Indeed, given the intellectual and human dislocations that technology can produce, computers may even be counterproductive in many educational settings.

As might be expected, such a stark reality is not limited to academic settings. For example, in their review of the literature on business information systems, George Marakas and Daniel Robey cite numerous studies reporting the neutral or negative effects of computers on worker performance. Richard Franke reports declining productivity in the banking industry, which historically has been one of the industries most experienced in using high-tech information systems. And Dennis Hayes, who analyzes the layoffs and injuries associated with using technology in the workplace, concludes that the costs of litigating, treating, retraining, and replacing the computer-injured often remain unaccounted for in standard productivity measures (176). According to William Bowen, "So far productivity [in the United States] has grown more slowly in the computer age than it did before computers came into wide use" (267). For the moment, at least, the payoffs associated with technology seem to accrue more indirectly, as organizations exploit the symbolic dimensions of computers to help them create positive impressions that can produce an economic return on investments (Marakas and Robey).

Technology myths, however, are not the only obstacles to more fruitful literacy practices in a digital age. There are, in addition to these discursive forces, a whole host of pedagogical and institutional impediments that must be dealt with. For example, although the National Council of Teachers of English and the Modern Language Association both have position statements articulating the need to value computer-related work in English departments, such work still remains invisible within far too many tenure and promotion reviews (Rickly; Unsworth). Teachers of writing and communication are often not consulted during the process of designing computer-supported writing environments, and thus these environments frequently fail to align with the pedagogical and programmatic directions of academic programs (Batson; Handa; T. Howard, "Designing"). And teacher education courses, which bear the enormous burden of preparing the next generation of writing and communication instructors, must be expanded in central ways to address the multiple and vexing problems associated with putting computers in classroom settings (Bernhardt and Vickrey; Selber, Johnson-Eilola, and Selfe; Selfe, "Preparing"). Indeed, a recent survey by Sally Barr Ebest indicates that only 25 percent of the graduate teaching assistants in rhetoric and composition programs have an opportunity to teach writing in a computer-based classroom (68). Moreover, academic-industrial partnerships require considerable attention nowadays, as these partnerships have the potential to commercialize online spaces in ways that are incompatible with the goals of a liberal education. For example, my institution (Penn State) has entered into a large-scale agreement with Microsoft that has had the effect of discouraging important critique of the ongoing commodification of higher education (more on that agreement later).

But this book is not about identifying impediments to better ways of working. Although the obstacles that I have listed should be met head-on and with new approaches, critique alone will not prepare students to involve themselves fully, actively, and successfully in technological contexts. Critique is certainly one crucial aspect of any computer literacy program, for it encourages a cultural awareness of power structures. But students must also be able to use computers effectively as well as participate in the construction and reconstruction of technological systems. What is needed, then, is an approach to computer literacy that is both useful and professionally responsible, a somewhat unusual undertaking considering the binary oppositions so easily found in debates over the appropriate role of educational institutions in society. Some feel that the primary role of schools is to socialize students into the existing ideological order, while others believe that schools should teach various forms of resistance to power and authority. In Burkean terms, educators remain divided over whether education should be a function of society or whether society should be a function of education. However, neither an overemphasis on accommodation practices nor on resistance theories will result in a computer literacy program that is comprehensive, innovative, and relevant. For such a program to come about, a postcritical stance is needed.

*Toward a Postcritical Stance*

This book adopts a "postcritical" stance toward technology. My use of the term *postcritical* is straightforward and unambiguous and comes from two sources: the scholarship of Stanley Aronowitz on the impact of computers on the lives of working professionals, teachers included; and the scholarship of Patricia Sullivan and James Porter on critical research practices. From Aronowitz I take the pragmatic realization that, for a number of reasons that are culturally and historically determined (e.g., productivity myths, academic-corporate alliances, market demands, significant investments in educational technologies), computers in varying forms are here to stay in instructional contexts, and that the time and energy of teachers is therefore best spent not deploring computers but learning how to use them in ways that align with, and productively challenge, the values of the profession. From Sullivan and Porter I take the notion that any approach to computer literacy should have a "critical consciousness of its position (at least insofar as that is possible)" (42). Which is to say that teachers and students should be mindful of the ways in which they can unwittingly promote inequitable and counterproductive technological practices. Importantly, my use of the term *postcritical* does not consider technology to be a self-determining agent. In rejecting theories claiming that technology alone creates educational change, it locates the potential for such change in a nexus of social forces.

Rationales for a postcritical stance can be found in educational projects encouraging social change, especially in projects reasserting the importance of liberal arts instruction in a digital age, rearticulating the responsibilities of writing and communication teachers, and revealing the inequities perpetuated in officially sanctioned approaches to expanding the technological literacy of American citizens. To begin with, David Orr suggests why it might be important to locate computer literacy within the domain of liberal arts instruction. According to Orr and others concerned about the downsides of living in a technocratic world (e.g., endemic poverty, violence, and environmental decay; dehumanizing workplace practices; the dizzying pace of everyday life in a technoculture), conventional approaches in scientific and technical disciplines often fail to illuminate the key issues of our time for a number of reasons. Chief among them are the way such approaches tend to decontextualize technological subjects and objects in the classroom, therefore risking "no confrontation with the facts of life in the twenty-first century" (207). Alan Kay, a pioneer of the personal computer, points out a related problem as he critiques various misconceptions about education in technology instruction today, including theories assuming that students are empty vessels waiting to be filled and that school subjects are bitter pills that can be made palatable only by sugar-coating them with multimedia eye-candy ("Computers"). Kay contends that sound pedagogical assumptions need to replace these and the other misconceptions he elucidates before computer technologies can be of real service in classroom situations.

Needless to say, there are consequences associated with such conventional instructional approaches and misconceptions. In the context of computer literacy, for example, computers will be understood primarily in instrumental terms—as systems for supporting status quo, relatively hierarchical student-teacher relationships, or for automating repetitive and routine tasks, or for making difficult texts and concepts ostensibly more interesting to study. Relying on these articulations of technology, students will learn how to download lecture notes from the World Wide Web, register for courses using administrative software applications, run multimedia tutorials, exchange files with classmates over wide-area networks, employ graphics programs to create visual representations for reports and papers, and use personal digital assistants (small hand-held devices) to store—and share, through infrared beams—important e-mail and Website addresses. But although students will develop some extremely useful skills under an instrumental approach, they will have a much more difficult time thinking critically, contextually, and historically about the ways computer technologies are developed and used within our culture and how such use, in turn, intersects with writing and communication practices in the classroom. However, encouraging students to situate technology in broad terms is the job of humanities teachers, not only because the mission of liberal arts instruction is to develop whole persons capable of making balanced judgments in a technocratic world (Orr) but also because this crucial task is so rarely undertaken explicitly and concretely by the units most often charged with computer literacy initiatives in higher education: academic computing centers; departments of engineering, information science, and technology; and professional development services.

If situating technology broadly is one rationale for a postcritical stance, another is participating in the development and reconfiguration of literacy technologies, to the extent that is possible and desirable. Over the past several years, teachers have begun to question increasingly the perspectives informing the human-computer interface designs that support writing and communication activities. Dennis Hayes, for example, has discussed the Newtonian quests for speed and raw computing power that are driving hardware and software developments and leading to computer designs instantiating the objectives of generating capital and controlling networks and hierarchies of work. Johndan Johnson-Eilola has traced the cultural models influencing interface development practices in online research spaces, arguing that certain cultural tendencies toward valuing information can have the negative effects of technical decontextualization and social fragmentation ("Accumulation"). Cynthia Selfe and Richard Selfe have contended that human-computer interfaces, in certain popular instances, can be read as maps that value "monoculturalism, capitalism, and phallologic thinking" (486). And Sherry Turkle, in discussing the design of computer operating systems, has distinguished the values of simulation from those of calculation organizing visual approaches to interacting with computers (*Life*). But even though teachers have begun to question the perspectives informing human-computer interface designs—perspectives that are "far from immutable" and, in fact, "utterly negotiable" (Hayes 178) on some level—teachers have not always seen the development and reconfiguration of literacy technologies as their job or as the instructional domain of students in writing and communication courses.

Christina Haas and Christine Neuwirth attribute such myopia to the instrumental view of technology so often pervading departments of English. This view, which has been fully articulated and critiqued by Andrew Feenberg and other critical theorists, produces two diametrically opposed perspectives that, ironically, both position technology design as an out-of-bounds activity. In the first perspective, computers are not embraced at all, because what teachers should be focusing on, in a traditional sense, are text-based analyses of written artifacts. Associated with this belief, according to Haas and Neuwirth, is an antitechnology stance, the logic of which often goes something like this: Computers are evil, tools of the devil really, and English professors, as a last bastion of liberal humanism, must resist their encroachment on purer pursuits (326). The second perspective celebrates technology, but only insofar as it can support the more traditional goals of textual studies. So, in this case, for example, English professors use e-mail to exchange manuscripts with colleagues, subscribe to Internet discussion lists to engage in professional conversations about canonized authors, and search scholarly databases to retrieve archived materials. In neither perspective, however, is technology design considered to be the purview of English departments. Instead, an instrumental view allows for only two possible responses to technology: Users either accept or reject it, for technology is simply a neutral tool employed to understand experience and solve problems.

The implications of an instrumental view are entirely unambiguous. As Haas and Neuwirth explain, "other people are redefining reading and writing, while humanists maintain the speculative high ground, remaining above the fray and remote from those actually involved in the process of shaping technology" (326). But to allow others to determine the design of human-computer interfaces is to risk naturalizing a set of literacy perspectives that fails to support the pedagogical practices teachers of writing and communication find most effective and informative (Hansen; Schwartz; Kemp, "Computer-Mediated"). It also endangers the status of writing and communication teachers, which is often already disempoweringly low, especially in colleges and universities organized around technological imperatives or disciplines. Thus, rearticulating the responsibilities of teachers to include the design of literacy technologies is an essential task if the profession hopes to remain relevant pedagogically and to influence the computer interfaces shaping how students think about, and engage in, discourse-related activities online.

But the effects of technology design are not limited to redefinitions of writing and reading. Indeed, these effects, when considered in the context of race, class, and gender, can have a much deeper implication, one that indicates just how important adopting a post-critical stance can be. As the instrumental view suggests, computers can contribute not only to projects encouraging social change but also to those merely reproducing the dominant cultural values. In this way, computers are malleable in that they unevenly develop along particular axes of interest, depending on the tendential forces molding their shape and use. As Feenberg notes, computers can "evolve into very different technologies in the framework of strategies of domination or democratization" (91). Too often, however, computer technologies are aligned with competitive and oppressive formations that tend to shore up rather than address existing social inequities, despite what computer industry marketing hype would lead students and teachers to believe.

In an important case study of the Technology Literacy Challenge begun in 1996 by the Clinton administration, Cynthia Selfe analyzes how federally sponsored literacy programs—if teachers fail to pay attention to them—can actually contribute to the ongoing problems of racism, sexism, poverty, and illiteracy in the United States, notwithstanding the fact that such programs are often explicitly founded to expand the economic and educational opportunities of all citizens *(Technology)*. In her analysis, Selfe reveals how a narrow definition of literacy, one that fails to encourage a situated view of technology, has been motivated, at least in part, by an interrelated set of "cultural forces that serve both political and economic ends" (xx), which are often antithetical to the social goals of providing equal access to technology or using technology to encourage democratic activities and enrich instructional experiences. Among the conserving forces discouraging change, Selfe includes government initiatives safeguarding the success of American industrial and political efforts on both a national and international scale, private sector businesses creating an ongoing demand for their own computer products, and parents hoping to prepare their children functionally for an increasingly technological world by purchasing these products for the home.

In this list of conserving forces, however, Selfe also counts teachers of writing and communication, who tend to construct belief systems about technology that relegate its concerns to the background of professional life. Like Haas and Neuwirth, Selfe identifies a disturbing conflict in values between liberal humanism and technology. Such a conflict, she notes, allows teachers to deal with computers on their own terms, that is, when computers serve obvious or self-interested purposes. But this conflict also allows teachers to ignore computers when they become a source of discomfort or annoyance, for example, when computers seem threatening to what Catherine Belsey (*Critical*) would call our "common-sense" practices—those taken-for-granted ways of operating as teacher-researchers in educational environments (e.g., publishing in print-based forums, authoring and owning texts in a romantic sense, positioning ourselves as the sole source of expertise and authority in the classroom). Yet taking such an indecisive position is actually highly irresponsible, as Selfe so persuasively argues, for it is precisely when teachers ignore technology and its contexts that the real pedagogical and social damage is likely to be done.

In sum, if teachers fail to adopt a postcritical stance, thus leaving technology design and education to those outside of the field, it is entirely probable that students will have a much more difficult time understanding computers in critical, contextual, and historical ways; that technology designs, informed by pedagogical and cultural values not our own, will define and redefine literacy practices in ways that are less than desirable; and that computer literacy initiatives will simply serve to perpetuate rather than alleviate existing social inequities. This is not to say that humanists alone can radically alter or change the status quo or, for that matter, that all technologists necessarily eschew social issues. Rather, the point is that a wide variety of perspectives is needed in educational settings if students are going to be prepared both usefully and responsibly for writing and communication activities in a digital age. As Selfe so aptly puts it, "Literacy alone is no longer our business. Literacy and technology are. Or so they must become" (*Technology* 3).

## Clarifying the Problems and Challenges Ahead

To this point, I have discussed in fairly broad terms some of the problems and challenges existing in technology education, including obstacles to more productive literacy practices and the consequences of failing to adopt a postcritical stance toward technology. This discussion has used words like one-dimensional, instrumental, and decontextual to characterize approaches to computer literacy that teachers of writing and communication would find impoverished. Such broad characterizations, however, can lack a real sense of clarity for most of us unless they are illustrated in a very concrete manner. Thus, in this segment, let me offer an analysis of the type of reductiveness that I am talking about, one that is too typical of the way computer literacy issues have been addressed by colleges and universities. The example comes from Florida State University, but many other universities could have provided similar illustrations. This example helps to clarify problems and challenges, and it points to the directions in which teachers of writing and communication should be headed in the area of computer literacy.

Colleges and universities are beginning to embrace requirements for computer literacy, as employers and academic accrediting agencies strongly urge upper-level administrators to do so. Although there are no comprehensive statistics on the number of institutions with computer literacy requirements, a rapidly growing number of schools have adopted computer requirements of one form or another. The Southern Association of Colleges and Schools, for example, encourages institutions of higher education in the south to require all students to become computer literate before graduation. Responding to this encouragement, at least two schools

in the association have adopted specific computer literacy requirements. Houston Baptist University requires all students to become
familiar with the Windows operating system and Microsoft Office,
which includes standard word-processing, spreadsheet, and database programs. And at Georgetown College in Kentucky, incoming
students take an assessment test to determine their level of computer expertise. Depending on the results of this test, students are
advised to review specific technology areas using online instructional materials or take an introductory course in computer science.
Computer literacy requirements have also been instituted at the
University of Texas at Arlington, Old Dominion University, the University of the Virgin Islands, Marshall University, Utah State University, the University of Louisville, Westminster College, and many
other places.

Florida State University is typical in the way it defines computer literacy: Since 1998, Florida State has had a clearly articulated
policy requiring all undergraduate students to demonstrate basic familiarity with computer hardware, operating systems, and file concepts; a working knowledge of a word processor, spreadsheet, and
database program; and an ability to use the Web and e-mail (see
<http://lit.cs.fsu.edu>). These requirements are matched by similar
requirements at other schools. One way students at Florida State
can demonstrate competency is by passing an approved course. Students typically enroll in either Computer General Studies 2060 or
CGS 2100, which are offered in the computer science department
and described on its Website:

> CGS 2060: Computer Literacy. An introduction to infor-
> mation processing and computer applications. Hands-on
> experience with microcomputer applications such as word
> processors, spreadsheets, and database managers.

> CGS 2100: Microcomputer Applications for Business and
> Economics. Course enables students in business and eco-
> nomics to become proficient with microcomputer hard-
> ware and software applications that are typically used in

the workplace. The following topics are covered: hardware concepts, operating systems, word processing, spreadsheets, databases, networks, Internet, World Wide Web, multimedia presentations and information systems.

Besides passing one of these courses, students can demonstrate computer competency by passing a university-sponsored test. This test is offered on a regular basis and takes approximately 2.5 hours to complete. There are four parts to the test, three of which are hands-on and one of which is multiple choice. To prepare for the test, students are encouraged to bone up on basic computer concepts and Microsoft Office. In addition, they are encouraged to make use of a university-provided study guide, which outlines very specifically what students are expected to know and do. To illustrate the nature of the test, I reproduce the first three parts of the study guide below; the part not reproduced models Part 3 on Microsoft Word but focuses on Microsoft Excel and Microsoft Access.

Part 1, Multiple choice exam (on-line): Computer Concepts [50 points]. Students should have a text-book understanding of the following concepts and terms (as discussed in the latest edition of *New Perspectives on Computer Concepts* by June Parsons and Dan Oja).

Chapter 1: Computer, Central Processing Unit (CPU), Memory, Storage, Personal Digital Assistant (PDA), Server, Peripheral Device, Data & Information, Bit & Byte, Platform, Internet, Chat Groups, Instant Messaging, P2P, Dial-Up Connection, Cable Modem, DSL, DSS, ISP, Password Do's and Don'ts, Hypertext, URL, HTML, Browser, Search Engine, Netiquette, POP, IMAP, Web-Based E-mail, The Boot Process.

Chapter 2: Digital Device, Analog Device, Binary Number System, Kilobyte, Megabyte, Gigabyte, Motherboard, Microprocessor, ALU, Control Unit, Registers, Megahertz,

Gigahertz, Cache, RAM, ROM, Magnetic Storage, Optical Storage, Capacity (Floppy Disk, Zip Disk, CD, DVD), CD-ROM, CD-RW, PC Card, LCD, Resolution.

Chapter 3: Computer Program, Computer Language, Application Software, System Software, Operating System, Document Production Software, Spreadsheet Software, What-If Analyses, Data Management Software, Presentation Software, MP3, Groupware, System Requirements, Zipped, Software License, Shrink-Wrap License, Shareware.

Chapter 4: Filename Extension, File Specification, Defragmentation Utility, Computer Virus, Macro Virus, Worm, Denial of Service Attacks, Antivirus Software, Virus Hoaxes, CD-R, Zip Disk, Floppy Disk, Removable Hard Disk, MP3 Filename Extension.

Chapter 5: Communications Network, Twisted Pair, Coaxial, Fiber Optic, Bandwidth, Packet, Protocol, Intranet, Local Area Network, Wireless Network, Peer-to-Peer Network, Client/Server Network, TCP/IP, IP Address, Top-Level Domain, Modem, Cable Modem, DSL, Personal Firewall Software.

Chapter 6: HTML Tags, HTTP, Cookie, XML, Java Applets, Digital Certificate, E-Commerce, B2B, B2C, Electronic Wallet, Encryption.

Part 2, Hands-on Exam: Operating System/File Management and The Web [50 points]. Using the Windows 2000 user interface the student shall be able to: View drive and directory (folder) contents; Create directories (folders); Start applications; Create and save files to specific drive and directory locations; Run multiple applications; Minimize and maximize windows; Close applications; Delete and rename files; Move and copy files between hard drives and floppy drives.

Using Internet Explorer or Netscape the student shall be able to: Find a Web site from a given URL; Use WebLUIS to search the FSU databases on a given keyword; Use an Internet search engine to research a given topic; See if a given book title can be found in the FSU library; Check a class schedule on the Web; Save a webpage to disk.

Part 3, Hands-on Exam: Microsoft Word [100 points]. Our Microsoft Word 2002 Skills Exam is taken using Skills Assessment Manager (SAM). SAMxp tests a student's applications skills within the application itself. On this particular exam the students will be asked to carry out the following tasks in Word 2002: Insert text; Cut and paste text; Copy and paste text; Use Paste Special; Move text; Find and replace text; Use AutoCorrect; Insert symbols; Applying character formats; Modifying character formats; Check spelling; Use the Thesaurus; Check grammar; Apply the superscript font effect; Apply the subscript font effect; Apply an animation text effect; Highlight text; Use Format Painter; Insert a date; Modify a date field; Insert a date field; Apply a character style; Change paragraph line spacing; Apply a paragraph border; Apply shading to paragraphs; Indent paragraphs; Set Center tabs; Modify tabs; Add bullets; Add numbering; Create an outline; Apply paragraph styles; Create a document header; Modify a document header; Create a document footer; Modify a document footer; Apply columns; Modify text alignment in columns; Revise column layout; Insert page breaks; Insert page numbers; Modify page margins; Change the page orientation; Create tables; Modify tables; Apply AutoFormats to tables; Modify table borders; Shade table cells; Insert rows in a table; Delete table rows; Insert columns in a table; Delete table columns; Modify cell formats; Use print preview;

Print documents; Print envelopes; Print labels; Create folders for document storage; Create a document from a tem-
plate; Save a document; Use Save As; Add images to a
document.

Students scoring at least 210 points (or 70%) on this 300-point test
are "declared Computer Competent." But what does such a declara-
tion really mean? After fulfilling the requirement, what will students know about computers and, just as importantly, what will
remain a mystery to them, especially when it comes to using computers for writing and communication purposes?

On a practical level, the answer is that students will undoubtedly know a great deal. They will know, for example, how to manage files and certain aspects of computer interfaces (e.g., how to
organize and backup work in a variety of ways; toggle between multiple application spaces; make the most efficient use of screen real-
estate); they will know how to participate in online course activities
(e.g., how to exchange asynchronous messages; circulate drafts over
wide-area networks; search scholarly databases); they will know
how to control document structures (e.g., how to create and manipulate layout elements; integrate verbal and visual texts; generate
graphics from data sets). For what it is worth, they will also understand the ways in which certain generic components of a computer
work, knowledge that could aid them in troubleshooting technical
problems. In many instances, students will actually know more
than their teachers about operating computers, a conclusion supported by a University of California, Los Angeles survey. According
to this survey, which was conducted by the Higher Education Research Institute at UCLA's Graduate School of Education and Information Studies, staying up-to-date with technology affects more
professors than traditional stresses such as publishing demands and
teaching loads. Of the 33,785 faculty members surveyed at 378 colleges and universities, 67 percent fear the task of keeping current
with technology, even though 87 percent agree that computers enhance student learning (*The American College Teacher*). In a similar
study done by the Campus Computing Project, nearly 40 percent of

academic-computing officials at 557 colleges and universities cited helping faculty bring technology to the classroom as their number one challenge, despite vexing Y2K and e-commerce issues (*The 1999 National Survey of Information Technology in Higher Education*). According to Kenneth Green, founder and director of the Campus Computing Project, "It's fair to say that many faculty members have ceded to their students the whole issue of technology skills" (qtd. in Olsen).

But if, on the one hand, the computer competency requirement at Florida State promotes skills for working productively in practical terms, on the other hand, it fails to offer the perspectives needed for making rhetorical judgments. And although teachers may tend to lag behind students in the whole area of computer skills, when it comes to rhetoric the expertise of teachers is undeniably crucial. The requirement neglects important topics such as developing file-naming schemes that can be searched meaningfully; writing effective e-mail messages; participating appropriately in asynchronous discussions; analyzing the currency, authority, and reliability of Website content; and generating visual images that represent data relationships accurately and convincingly—among other things. The requirement not only bypasses such writing and communication concerns, however; it also fails to situate technology in social, political, and economic contexts, thus ignoring the implications of technology as well as the tendential forces helping to shape it. In this way, the requirement perpetuates the false assumption that the relationship between a technology and its construction and implementation is natural and not conventional.

In its practical orientation, the computer competency requirement at Florida State is not unusual. Indeed, at Old Dominion University, for example, the Student Technical Skill Requirement emphasizes using e-mail, the Web, and a word-processing program, but not critically analyzing these uses and their contexts. At my own institution, instrumental perspectives inflect the curriculum in a new School of Information Science and Technology. This school, which began matriculating students during the 1999–2000 academic year, has a laudable goal: to teach the use and application of information technologies and the social, cultural, and ethical implications that surround them. But on some level, the course requirements belie this goal, as students can largely avoid taking classes that contextualize computer technologies. In my estimation, this school should invert its approach in a way that brings social and technical learning together. That is, as opposed to consolidating the classes focusing on society and social policy in an optional track, these classes should constitute the required core, as opposed to courses in the organization of data, networking, telecommunications, logic and discrete mathematics, and programming. After building a social foundation, students could pursue technical interests or focus further on the implications of information technologies. Paradoxically, such a socially based curriculum would not only foreground humanistic concerns, but also provide the perspectives needed for successful technical practice: Case studies have shown repeatedly that useful computer products accommodate the contexts in which they are used (see Barrett; Wiklund; Winograd, *Bringing*).

That computer requirements and initiatives are often primarily skills-based should not be surprising, for behind them are employers and academic accrediting agencies influenced by corporate interests. For example, the new School of Information Science and Technology at Penn State was explicitly founded to address a shortage of high-tech professionals in the Pennsylvania private sector: Input and support in the development of the school have come from over twenty-five corporate sponsors, including AT&T, IBM, Lockheed Martin, Lucent, and Microsoft. In the same way, the computer competency requirement at Florida State has been rationalized along corporate lines. In an interview on National Public Radio, Ken Baldauf, the computer literacy czar at Florida State, declared that the goal of this requirement is to develop in students "the application skills that businesses are looking for." Although students could, in theory, take an approved course in the English department that complicates and expands on such a goal, the department does not offer one. In fact, when I contacted Wendy Bishop, a professor of rhetoric and composition at Florida State, about her university's computer literacy requirement, she was unaware of it. For this lack of awareness, the English department and Bishop should not be condemned. Rather, this situation merely illustrates the fact that faculty in English departments are rarely (if ever) consulted in institutional matters of computer literacy.

The examples analyzed in this section were not arbitrary or convenient choices. Both implicitly and explicitly they collectively lay bare many of the problems and challenges existing in technology education and in doing so make it evident that teachers of writing and communication need to cultivate approaches to computer literacy that are more useful and professionally responsible. It is clear from the examples, for instance, that computer literacy programs can take a rather monolithic and one-dimensional approach, ignoring the fact that computer technologies are embedded in a wide range of constitutive contexts, as well as entangled in value systems. And while computer literacy programs cannot and should not avoid practical issues, they can take a rather shortsighted approach that narrowly ties instruction to specific software features that will undoubtedly change with time. This state of affairs is even more disturbing when one considers the revolutionary rhetoric accompanying it, for the examples also call attention to the fact that technology is so often used uncreatively and conservatively. Although there is nothing inherently wrong with institutionally driven programs, computer literacy is an area that will remain impoverished as long as its parameters are defined and understood primarily in technical terms or in terms that are dictated by the private sector.

## A Portrait of the Ideal Multiliterate Student

Despite numerous attempts to standardize computer literacy in educational settings, there is no one perfect approach. As with any form of literacy, computer practices do not travel seamlessly or unproblematically across contexts, cultures, and communities. In light of this reality, the key is for teachers to develop a disciplinary approach that is not too prescriptive, one that is generative and directive while acknowledging the fact that every specific instructional situation may very well call for a unique solution, or at least one that accounts for local social forces and material conditions. For teachers of writing and communication who work in departments of English, the primary audience for this book, such a challenge can be a source of considerable confusion and apprehension. But it does not have to be so.

This book provides the framework for such an approach. That framework should not be construed as definitive or exhaustive, but rather as part of a larger, ongoing conversation about the special responsibilities of humanities teachers in a digital age. The specific contribution I make here, however, is not always in strict agreement with the current consensus within this conversation, and in fact has been motivated by at least two tendencies that have inhibited the progress of positive change. The first is a tendency to rely too heavily on one-way literacy models as a foundation for computer initiatives. That is, many teachers of writing and communication simply transfer wholesale to the screen their existing assumptions, goals, and practices. Although it is sensible and helpful to begin with current ways of knowing and working, such a model is ultimately limiting because it is non-dialogic: Not only does the model assume that technology is neutral, but it fails to recognize that technology can encourage teachers to reconsider taken-for-granted assumptions, goals, and practices.

The second thing that worries me is theory reductiveness, which has to do with how the profession tends to treat successive theories of computer literacy. It is not inaccurate to say that newer approaches have commonly driven out older ones. This is neither always nor automatically a problem, and in a sense one hallmark of a vibrant discipline is discernible shifts in the intellectual paradigms that animate its knowledge. More than occasionally, however, the theories that get expelled are useful, if imperfect. For example, many teachers have eschewed functional literacy for more critical approaches, a move that serves as a much-needed corrective to programs that focus on isolated features of software programs. But such a move does not change the fact that students must still learn effective ways to interact with computers and with those who are online. A better approach, then, would be more additive than substitutive: Students need both functional and critical literacies (although to be sure functional literacy as it has been traditionally mapped out is impoverished and dangerous and, for that reason, must be reimagined).

This all leads me to the framing concept for this book: multiliteracies. My view is that teachers should emphasize different kinds of computer literacies and help students become skilled at moving among them in strategic ways. The three literacy categories that organize my discussion—functional, critical, and rhetorical—are meant to be suggestive rather than restrictive, and more complimentary than in competition with each other. In other words, I do not provide a taxonomy that prioritizes theory over practice or vice-versa, or that must be rigidly adhered to in some abstract fashion. Instead, the macro-level framework of functional literacy, critical literacy, and rhetorical literacy, along with the many micro-level frameworks that can be found in individual chapters, function as heuristics that can help students assess the perspectives and practices that might be needed in any particular situation. If my approach is necessarily contextual in character, however, there is one sweeping statement I am prepared to make: Students who are not adequately exposed to all three literacy categories will find it difficult to participate fully and meaningfully in technological activities.

Table 1.1 conceptualizes the literacy landscape that students should be able to navigate. Each category has a metaphor, subject position, and objective, all of which help to characterize the nature and scope of a computer literacy program that focuses on multiple literacies. For example, the functional category is organized by a tool metaphor that stresses effective computer use, the critical category is organized by an artifactual metaphor that stresses informed critique, and the rhetorical category is organized by a hypertextual metaphor that stresses reflective praxis. No one metaphor could be complete and sufficient by itself, but collectively they offer a diversity of perspectives that have become associated with computer technologies. The goal is to help students both understand the ways in which all three metaphors filter experience and become adept at

## Table 1.1
The Conceptual Landscape of a Computer
Multiliteracies Program

| Category | Metaphor | Subject Position | Objective |
|---|---|---|---|
| Functional Literacy | computers as tools | students as users of technology | effective employment |
| Critical Literacy | computers as cultural artifacts | students as questioners of technology | informed critique |
| Rhetorical Literacy | computers as hypertextual media | students as producers of technology | reflective praxis |

using them at various times and in various combinations. Likewise, there are three subject positions connected to the literacy landscape: students as users of technology, students as questioners of technology, and students as producers of technology. Again, the goal is not to endorse one over another, but to help students learn to exploit the different subjectivities that have become associated with computer technologies. Although the rhetorical category mediates the binary division between functional and critical literacies to some extent—rhetorical activities like Web design demand both effective computer use and informed critique—I do not necessarily place a higher value on it: There will be times when an attention to functional or critical concerns should be paramount. A curricular implication of this relationship, however, is that rhetorical literacy might prove to be a particularly challenging place to start. In fact, one of the larger questions for teachers will be how to scaffold instructional activities that illuminate the relationships and interdependencies between these multiple literacies.

The objective of this book is not to focus primarily on what is wrong with computer literacy programs today. My feeling is that the profession has already done an excellent and careful job of pointing out problems: Most programs overemphasize technology in one way or another, fail to acknowledge its design biases, which are unavoidable, and fail to acknowledge the tendential forces shaping both technology development and use. To put it another way, the approaches to most computer literacy programs are far too decontextualized. Although technology critique should be an important and ongoing contribution of scholars and teachers practicing in the humanities, the profession also has an obligation to formulate better alternatives, to offer approaches and practices that are more responsible, broad-based, and productive.

Toward that end, this book offers more than a single assignment or syllabus. The framework I provide is illustrated with numerous examples and activities, but it signifies a larger-scale attempt to conceptualize computer literacy. Moreover, the framework represents a totality without being totalizing. This is a crucial point to keep in mind, because the main problem with so many formalized programs is that they put forward a universal approach to computer literacy that disregards the continuous and contingent interplay between context and technology. The other point that should be made is that the framework is not neutral: The very notion that it is workable relies on the idea that inclusiveness is good and that theory and practice should inform each other. It is likely that some in the profession would reject these premises.

The heart of the book lays out and develops a conceptual apparatus that can help teachers imagine the contours of a computer multiliteracies program. There are some patterns that can be found throughout chapters 2, 3, and 4. For example, each chapter discusses the elements listed in table 1.1 as well as includes heuristics to suggest ways of putting into practice the concepts and approaches that have been suggested. If there are discernible patterns throughout the core chapters, however, they are not exactly parallel. For example, I review the literature when it comes to functional and critical literacies because these areas have well-established disciplinary narratives that cannot be ignored. But, in the context of technology education, the narrative for rhetorical literacy is more nascent than the others. While I have no doubt that many teachers take a rhetorical approach, there is still much to be done to conceptualize the praxis required to help students become reflective producers of technology. For this reason, the discussion of rhetorical literacy looks ahead more than it looks back. Another variation can be found in the level of concreteness across arguments. I have done my best to provide examples that clearly illustrate key points, but sometimes being too specific can be counterproductive, especially if an example limits the imagination or the development of a concept. So I do not flesh out every single heuristic into a fully realized, complex assignment. Nevertheless, I have tried to use heuristics and examples that provide more than enough explanatory power to be useful.

Each chapter in the heart of the book has a distinct purpose. Chapter 2 tries to recover the concept of functional literacy in a way that speaks to scholars and teachers in the humanities. I am quite sensitive to the fact that the vast majority of functional approaches are not only overly simplistic but also downright harmful. Critics are right to condemn perspectives that understand literacy as a set of value-free skills that can be defined, learned, and measured in absolute terms and whose main purpose is to serve economic development. Such perspectives ignore the inextricable ties among literacy, power, culture, and context and as a result promote approaches to computer literacy based on mastery of technique. But there is no reason why functional literacy, which offers certain kinds of important access to a culture, cannot be reconceived in a more positive way as well as articulated with other types of literacies. Which is to say that functional literacy need not be disempowering and that functional and critical literacies need not be mutually exclusive.

The purposes of the next two chapters are less polemical and more conventional. The purpose of chapter 3 is to provide a specific and coherent framework for a critical literacy of computers. One valid concern raised in the literature on critical literacy is that its theory is often vague or difficult to apply. What does it really mean for a student to become critically literate in a digital age? There is no one right answer to this question, nor should there be, but the profession must provide responses that are concrete, comprehensive, and capable of being implemented. Chapter 3 offers such a response, one that gives students a metadiscourse they can use in order to identify and respond to the politics of technologies. The purpose of chapter 4 is similar in that it provides a specific and coherent framework for a rhetorical literacy of computers, which focuses on interface design and its intersections with certain broad areas of interest to the profession. Interface design is often considered to be a technical rather than rhetorical endeavor, but I contend in this chapter that interface design problems are more like writing than programming problems and that although all projects have technical aspects, mathematical and scientific formalisms are inadequate in design situations that involve social concerns and interactions. My hope is that chapter 4 will give teachers the background and confidence they need to begin exploring the design of twenty-first-century texts that defy the established purview of English departments.

Chapter 5 attempts to help teachers develop a full-scale program that integrates functional literacy, critical literacy, and rhetorical literacy in ways that are useful and professionally responsible. Change does not magically take care of itself, nor is the path to meaningful change ever straightforward or unfettered, especially in educational settings. Indeed, the whole area of technology will require attention, but this is not the only area. From there, the requirements spiral outward to encompass pedagogical, curricular, departmental, and institutional contexts. This assemblage of nested contexts implicates an increasingly broad set of forces and encourages a systemic perspective on change, because no single context can be understood in isolation from the others. An important conceptual point in chapter 5 is that the tripartite framework of functional literacy, critical literacy, and rhetorical literacy is fractal-like in that it can be applied in ever smaller scales to the curricular components of academic programs. This extensibility should help teachers envision and establish tightly integrated initiatives.

There will never be a final word on computer literacy: Technology and its constitutive contexts are dynamic, contingent, and negotiable by nature. But that does not mean teachers must work in an ad hoc fashion with little to no direction or structure. My goal is to provide at least some direction and structure for teachers of writing and communication who work in departments of English.

# 2 / Functional Literacy
## Computers as Tools, Students as Effective Users of Technology

> Some fear that teaching functional literacy will trivialize the curriculum, with images of reading lessons built around bus schedules, pie charts, and medicine labels. Others see a more complex cognitive base to the skills required for functional literacy and an unrealized opportunity to build literacy around problem solving, a general skill that many feel receives inadequate attention in the schools.
>
> —Richard Venezky,
> "Gathering Up, Looking Ahead"

In "How Undergraduates Learn Computer Skills: Results of a Survey and Focus Group," Philip Davis establishes empirically what I have long suspected anecdotally: In academic settings, students tend to learn about computers on their own, with the help of their peers, and by relying on various sorts of support resources. In the survey portion of his study, 1,176 Cornell undergraduates rated the effectiveness of eight methods of learning computer skills. Trial and error, credit classes, and peer support were clearly ranked as more effective than faculty support, online help, printed manuals, non-credit workshops, and drop-in clinics. In the focus group following up the survey, there was unanimous agreement among ten student leaders that teachers often assume that students already have specific computer skills and thus fail to provide any support or training. Such a situation, these leaders reported, is a source of considerable frustration and stress for many students.

Another take on this situation is that students often insist on being provided with individual, one-on-one instruction rather than learning the software for themselves. But without the ability to work independently, some teachers argue, students will never learn to scaffold their learning and skills, to expand on their knowledge of a piece of software in either functional or rhetorical ways. So some teachers require their students to learn (or teach each other) software skills and only rarely provide full-class, direct instruction. This interpretation does not refute what Davis reports but provides a different slant on it.

The main implication of his study, according to Davis, is that universities should increase their support of peer tutoring and other informal methods of computer instruction, which are both effective and cost efficient. Putting students in teacherly roles has obvious benefits for everyone, and so teachers should indeed do this regularly in a judicious manner. But I also believe that students can profit enormously from systematic instruction in computer use if that instruction avoids the pitfalls of certain functionalist approaches to literacy. However, in addition to assuming students are already computer literate or should be teaching themselves and each other, there are additional reasons teachers avoid taking up computer skills. For teachers of writing and communication, these reasons include the difficulties of figuring out an appropriate curricular place for the study of computers and devising a pedagogical approach that is not too abstract, not obsolete, and not antithetical to the social goals of the discipline.

This chapter addresses functional literacy in a way that diverges both philosophically and structurally from the established approaches teachers of writing and communication have come to distrust. While acknowledging the often reprehensible effects of official literacy agendas, I argue, first, that there are, in fact, some good reasons for helping students confront the complexities associated with computer use. Next, I offer a conceptual view of functional literacy by examining the tool metaphor, the dominant trope in discussions of computer literacy. An examination of this metaphor reveals what can be positive and not so positive about functional approaches. The remainder of the chapter outlines five parameters that animate a more productive functional approach to computer literacy: educational goals, social conventions, specialized discourses, management activities, and technological impasses. I illustrate these parameters with examples of students working in a classroom that requires online writing, research, and interaction. In a brief conclusion, I stress the limitations of functional approaches and the need for students to develop critical perspectives.

## Competing Visions of Functional Literacy

Teachers of writing and communication are not used to thinking about functional literacy in positive ways. Functional literacy has been reduced to a simple nuts-and-bolts matter, to a fairly basic skill based on mastery of technique. As Glynda Hull explains, functional approaches that equate literacy with basic skills "suggest literate abilities that are 'basic' in the sense of being simple and fundamental, involving the decoding or encoding of brief texts within a structured task or carrying out elementary addition and subtraction calculations" (663). This view understands functional literacy in much the same manner that current-traditional rhetoric understood written texts: not as socially or rhetorically embedded, but as expressions of grammar, style, and form, all of which could be learned in prescriptive and decontextualized ways. Moreover, functional literacy has been equated with a multitude of flawed practices and perspectives that undermine responsible educational objectives: Critics have argued that limited approaches to teaching functional skills overlook cultural contexts (B. Street), focus on vocational requirements (Knoblauch), and reinforce social norms and values (Giroux, *Teachers*). In considering the purposes and settings of literacy, critics have denounced functionalist approaches (oftentimes with justice) for supporting and maintaining the economic, cultural, and political status quo and for domesticating and dehumanizing students.

Such criticisms should certainly not be dismissed, particularly in a digital age where competency is so frequently understood and measured in mechanical terms. Although programming is no longer the central task of computer users, recent attempts at defining computer literacy have often been decidedly uninspired, if not harmful. Most such attempts straightforwardly cover the technical aspects of software applications, hardware components, and operating systems (see Baker; Barger; Brecher; Capron; Dougherty; Reiss; McGowan and Cornwell). Under this rubric, discrete, short-term goals can be met, but the drawbacks keep technical approaches from becoming a viable instructional strategy. "Literacy," as Sylvia Scribner reminds us, "has neither a static nor a universal essence" (72), yet the hallmark of functional literacy as it has been traditionally mapped out in technology settings is a focus on highly specific, stabilized skill sets detached from particular social contexts. Critics rightly reject this particular focus as myopic and irresponsible, even damaging.

Critics of the shortcomings of functional literacy are, all too often, accurate in their assessments, at least as far as those assessments go. For functional literacy often becomes a blunt tool with which ruling classes create minimally skilled workers. However, to paint functional literacy with the broad brush of repression misses the fact that functional literacy is a necessary if not sufficient condition of all other forms of literacy. But the potential exists for an alternative perspective. In fact, visions of functional literacy have not always been so disturbing.

For example, Kenneth Levine traces the linkages that have been established between "literacy" and "functional" since World War II, when these two terms first became routinely conjoined; and although he focuses primarily on numerous defects, his brief history reveals some unexpected positives. According to the history, the first authoritative publication on functional literacy to reach an international audience was William Scott Gray's 1956 survey of writing and reading conducted for UNESCO, the principal organization for international literacy efforts after World War II. In Gray's survey, functional literacy was not associated with work or any particular setting. As Levine explains, the survey "emphasized that the content of [functional literacy] training should reflect the needs and motivations of the groups served, and should aim for a self-sustaining standard—one which permits pupils to make independent use of what they have learned without further help from an instructor" (253). Thus, functional literacy, in this early articulation, was conceived as the ability not only to write and read on a minimal, survival-oriented level but also to construct new meaning through literate practices. This "original humanist strategy" (254), it should be noted, "was intentionally relativistic, allowing for different thresholds of literacy in various societies" (253). Gray's pluralistic formulation granted access to a culture, but in the "noblest and widest sense" (255).

But in political and diplomatic contexts, the abstract nature of Gray's definition was exploited, as various literacy campaigns appropriated the idea of functional literacy to justify the expense of adult training programs. People inevitably linked functional literacy with literacy for work, especially with concrete training in technological skills, because such a commonsense linkage capitalized on the economic benefits that could be derived from investments in literacy initiatives. Once this linkage was established, the social dimensions of literacy began to fade from sanctioned discussions, and it was only a matter of time before functional literacy became synonymous with a narrowly conceived, job-related literacy. The inevitable next step in this regression was for people to devise various schemes for assessing literacy, to satisfy sponsoring agencies. As Levine notes, however, in order to use the indicators so important to economic analysis, literacy needed to be treated as an entirely objective matter in which skills are gained through a developmental process that is universal. Such a psychometric testing paradigm assumed that if skills were clearly defined, they could be accurately measured (Cook-Gumperz). This assumption, in turn, transformed literacy into a cognitive skill considered to be socially neutral. And because functional literacy involved, by definition, the ability to do small, measurable things, it often stood in for more complex forms of literacy.

Although it has been increasingly tied to issues in labor productivity, functional literacy as Gray initially defined it was not pedagogically or ethically suspect, nor did it have prescriptive overtones. Moreover, others have attempted to conceptualize functional literacy constructively and to measure the positive benefits it offers to a culture. For instance, Colin Lankshear has explained that, in Greek thought, the concept of goodness was typically affiliated with the notion of function, which was extended to the ideal of living the good life: "On this view, for literacy to be functional is for it to enhance the uniquely human potential of every person to create the world of men and women, which is the world of culture and history" (16). Indeed, for teachers of writing and communication, constructing a workable functional literacy is crucial for several reasons. First, in order to achieve educational goals in academic settings, students must be able to control technological resources, a task that requires certain knowledge, skills, and attitudes. Second, in order to evaluate the efficacy of computers, students (as well as teachers and administrators) must be able to understand the ways in which writing and communication activities are organized in online environments. Third, in order to compete for rewarding work in a digital age, students must be able to demonstrate technological proficiency, because computer literacy requirements in recent years have increased dramatically for all job levels; this is especially important for people in the many sectors of the U.S. population who are systematically discouraged from using computers in K–12 schooling. Fourth, in order to enact change, students must have access to the language of the powerful, including the discourse of technology. Although these reasons justify a functional approach as one component of a computer multiliteracies program, the approach should not be universalizing or totalizing in design.

## Computers as Tools

The first step toward imagining a more fruitful approach to functional literacy is to consider its metaphorical dimensions, which at least partially illuminate the danger as well as potential of this mode of engagement. In a functional mode, a tool metaphor invariably influences how users think about and work with computers. On the negative side, this trope masks the political dimensions of technology as well as the ways in which it helps to structure a wide range of human activities. On the positive side, however, the notion of people as exploiters of tools encourages users to keep their task objectives and professional responsibilities in mind. Thus, the tool metaphor is Janus-faced in that it can be appropriated for both social and functional purposes.

The tool metaphor has been widely employed because of its strong commonsense appeal and because it is generative for novice users. In fact, on some level "tool" has simply become equated with technology, especially among such influential analysts as Joy Mountford, John Seely Brown, Howard Rheingold, Donald Norman, Saul Greenberg (*Computer-Supported*), and Alan Kay ("User Interface"), all of whom have helped to shape popular notions of computer literacy. The computer applications these analysts have characterized as tools include interface elements, collaborative writing and communication environments; and prototyping, thinking, and learning programs. Input devices and peripherals are also readily considered to be tools. Related metaphors occasionally found in the literature on computer literacy construct computers as instruments or vehicles, but, as philosopher Max Black might put it, tool is the "subsidiary subject" that most frequently filters functional discussions and understandings of computers.

The tool metaphor is potent in that it readily evokes a set of connections that at least partially demystify computers. As a tool, the computer is merely the latest culturally constructed apparatus for expanding the functional capacities of users. Like other apparatuses, the computer is a kind of prosthetic device that increases efficiency, enhances cognition, and spans temporal and spatial boundaries. From a functionalist design perspective, good tools become invisible once users understand their basic operations. A computer application that is well constructed allows users to focus on the assignment at hand or to explore activities and ideas appropriate to the application. In these ways, computers are just a means to an end, tools with practical utility that users manipulate for their own, often immediate, purposes.

Interface designer Elsebeth Sorensen explains the rationale behind this popular viewpoint. She argues that a tool perspective should guide the creation of computer conferencing systems because it forces software developers to focus on the communication goals of users and not on the technology itself. As she puts it,

> The philosophy behind the tool perspective is that the interface should support the user in forgetting the symbolic nature of the system; this perspective produces an interface design which does not aim to attract attention. In other words, it is designed not to cause breakdowns in the user's understanding and as a consequence forcing him [or her] to reflect and concentrate his [or her] attention on the system (the tool) itself. The user is supported in keeping his [or her] attention directed toward the goal of his [or her] actions: the dynamic linguistic interaction with other people. (199)

This design philosophy encourages interface designers to develop online environments that approximate physical realities—for example, the writer's desktop, the brick-and-mortar library, the hotel conference center—and therefore create the illusion of an environmental space that supports the "natural" orientation and organization of user work.

The tool metaphor can also be illustrated by looking at design advice aimed at a broader audience. In *Shared Minds: The New Technologies of Collaboration,* journalist Michael Schrage contends that appropriate tools are simply the ones that work the best in a given situation: "You don't cut your steak with scissors. Tools must fit the task" (65). Like Sorensen, Schrage is interested in computer conferencing systems, but he broods over the design ethic of standard office tools: The desk, Schrage points out,

> is designed for individual use. So is the phone. The personal computer is just that: personal. The dictating machine records individual thoughts. The photocopier supports high-speed duplication of all those individually generated memos and reports. . . . On the surface, there's nothing wrong with

that: individuals need tools to support their work. There is
nothing in the office, however, explicitly designed to support collaboration. (71)

To solve this problem, Schrage encourages users first to truly understand the dynamics of collaborative interaction—he spends an entire chapter defining collaboration and another distinguishing it
from communication—and then to demand computer technologies
that model in rich and powerful ways the contemporary signifying
practices of people working together. Such technologies, Schrage
claims, will make users more efficient and effective, plus add value
to their work.

I could further illustrate the tool metaphor, but the general outlook it encourages should be clear enough. Computers are created
by technical experts who attempt to design applications that will be
transparent to users, so they can conduct their business as quickly
and as easily as possible. Constructed as consumers, users consider
their available options and select the tool that seems to meet the
technical and functional requirements of the task at hand, which
are outlined in advance. Determining which tool is right always involves a series of trade-offs—no tool will be perfect for every situation. Users, in the subject position of consumer, either accept or
reject technology; trends in user choices presumably help technical
experts zero in on technology designs that need improvement. On
an ideological level, however, tools are accommodating in that they
get integrated into a culture in ways that do not challenge its dominant belief systems.

Said another way, the tool metaphor tends to mask the political
dimensions of computers. This fact has been pointed out by various
theorists offering an alternative to the most widely accepted philosophy of technology: instrumentalism. Andrew Feenberg argues
that an instrumental view sees technology as subservient to social
values established in the spheres of politics and culture. In standing
ready to serve human purposes, technology is considered to be
neutral, "without valuative content of its own" (5). The concept of
neutrality, according to Feenberg, usually has several implications:

technology is indifferent to the various ends it can be employed to achieve (the Internet can be constructed as an educational space or highly profitable entertainment system); technology is also indifferent to politics, as it can be transferred to any social context (a computer is a computer is a computer); as a rule, the neutrality of technology is attributed to its rational character (although a computer can represent data in a variety of ways, its underlying logic is binary in nature); the neutrality of technology also means that the same standards of measurement can be applied in different situations (across the board, computers automatically increase the productivity of users) (5–6). Given these points, Feenberg argues that, from an instrumental perspective, the only sensible stance toward technology is an "unreserved commitment to its employment" (6).

Albert Borgmann has also commented on the instrumentalist viewpoint in a way which on the surface seems to be unassailable: "Any concretely delimited piece of technology can be put forward as a value-neutral tool" (10). But, in his philosophical inquiry, he goes on to reveal a political alliance that the tool metaphor helps instigate: "The notion of technology as a value-neutral tool or instrument is congenial to that liberal democratic tradition which holds that it is the task of the state to provide means for the good life but wants to leave to private efforts the establishment and pursuit of ultimate values" (10). Here Borgmann is pointing out a social implication of instrumentalism: If technology is indifferent to its own ends, and if public policy encourages the marketplace to determine those ends, then it follows that technical experts and other elites will continue to control the shape of technology and to benefit from the effects of the tool metaphor.

Social implications have also been traced by Langdon Winner, who critiques conventional ideas of what technology is and what it means, ideas perpetuated in western culture by familiar terms used in everyday language (e.g., tool, instrument, vehicle). In his philosophical discussion, he depicts the "promiscuous utility" of technological objects and processes, which are "taken to be fundamentally neutral" in moral terms (6). Because Winner is particularly interested in how technologies influence the texture of modern life, from his angle the crucial weakness of an instrumental approach is that "it disregards the many ways in which technologies provide structure for human activity" (6). As he explains, "Individual habits, perceptions, concepts of self, ideas of space and time, social relationships, and moral and political boundaries have all been powerfully restructured in the course of modern technological development" (9). But the tool metaphor discourages users from contemplating the mediating role of computers and their multifarious impact on everyday life. As a result, it diminishes teacher understandings of the nexus of pedagogy and technology.

There are, however, facets of the tool metaphor that can provide a basis for constructing a more productive approach to functional literacy. In one way of thinking, the tool metaphor is useful for discussions of agency because it can help instill a sense of control in a world increasingly permeated by technology. In fact, other metaphors can be less than reassuring. For example, consider these contrasting representations of technology revisited by Sherry Turkle:

> The computer is Janus-like—it has two faces. Marx spoke of a distinction between tools and machines. Tools are extensions of their users; machines impose their own rhythm, their rules, on the people who work with them, to the point where it is no longer clear who or what is being used. (*Second Self* 170)

As a human extension, the computer is not self-determining in design or operation. The computer, as a tool, depends upon a user, who if skilled enough can use and manipulate its (non-neutral) affordances to help reshape the world in potentially positive ways.

If users employ computers for their own purposes, then the tool metaphor raises issues of responsibility silenced in such philosophies of technology as autonomous technology and technological determinism. Because notions of the latter are so highly variegated, as a relatively straightforward example consider the theory of autonomous technology described by John Street. According to

Street, this theory claims that "technology acquires an independent momentum, which not only puts it beyond human control but which also allows it to order all human activity, including politics" (23). "If technology is autonomous," Street continues, "choice and judgment play little part in the direction in which society is moved; one technical advance calls into existence another, and so on. It is a process that seems to have its own logic and its own driving force" (23). For example, the Internet time line at the PBS Website gives computer technology the appearance of autonomy ("Life on the Internet"). In the course of charting a series of events between 1962 and 1996 that led to today's staggering Internet growth statistics, PBS, in part, privileges several technological inventions: the engineering of communication networks at the RAND Corporation in 1962; the commissioning of ARPANET by the U.S. Department of Defense in 1965; the creation of the first USENET newsgroups by graduate students at Duke University and the University of North Carolina in 1979; the establishment of TCP/IP as the universal language of the Internet in 1983; the release of Gopher at the University of Minnesota in 1991; and the release of the World Wide Web at CERN in 1991. Although irrefutable in chronological terms, such a time line falls short of representing accurately or powerfully the decision-making contexts within which Internet development first occurred—the Cold War—and within which it continues to occur —the postindustrial workplace. So in attributing change to technological evolution alone, proponents of an autonomous theory of technology implicitly absolve those in power from their social responsibilities. On a sinister level, "The idea of autonomous technology can be used as a disguise for culpability" (J. Street 30). However, the tool metaphor implicates users in the process of creating societal change by implying a human-computer dyad and a self-conscious relationship that is task-oriented.

Another desirable effect of the tool metaphor is that it can help foreground disciplinary values. In suggesting a model for the role technology can play in curricular change, James Kalmbach remembers how important the tool metaphor was to initial efforts in computers and composition instruction:

> Viewing the computer as a tool has been a critical first step because writing teachers often came to the process of creating and administering computer-supported classrooms knowing little about computers but a lot about writing and the teaching of writing. Starting with what teachers knew about writing enabled programs to build on their strengths. The value of this instrumental view should not be underestimated. (263)

Nor should it be eschewed entirely now that the field is developing a better sense of the dialogic nature of teaching with technology. On one end of the spectrum, the increasing number of teachers employing computers for the first time can profit considerably from the standard instructional-design practice of articulating pedagogical goals and mapping out the ways in which an array of classroom technologies might support those goals. Kalmbach mentions that such a practice capitalizes on the strengths of a program, but it also provides a measure of comfort for anxious teachers. On the other end of the spectrum, the tool metaphor can help remind experienced teachers of a fundamental reason they mobilized computers in the first place. As Gail Hawisher, Paul LeBlanc, Charles Moran, and Cynthia Selfe note in their history of computers and the teaching of writing in American higher education:

> The community has had an agenda: the need to develop a view of how computers could help writing teachers move toward better, more just, and more equitable writing classrooms and, by extension, to a better, more just, and more equitable system of education—and, insofar as education incubates culture—toward a better society. (2)

Although a progressive side of working with computers is that they can challenge a wide range of educational assumptions that have become taken for granted, recalling preexisting goals leverages professional knowledge and reminds writing and communication teachers of their humanist charge.

A final conceptual point about the tool metaphor is that it is compatible with certain ways of knowing. Researchers have identified different types of schemata that vary considerably in nature. In a variety of disciplines, a distinction is typically made between declarative and procedural knowledge structures used in problem solving (Anderson; Dijkstra; Schmitt and Newby). Declarative knowledge is the "what" of learning, a knowing *that* or *about*. It consists of facts and concepts usually garnered from a textbook or lecture (e.g., what a computer is). In contrast, procedural knowledge underlies skilled action. A knowing *how*, it refers to an ability to do things in the world (e.g., how to use a computer). Although the exact relationship between these knowledge types remains fuzzy (see Ummelen), the declarative-procedural distinction prevails in studies of memory, expertise, and skill acquisition.

I raise this classification system not because I am interested in debates over the makeup of cognition but because it helps to delineate what it means "to know" as a user of technology. On a practical level, it is just not possible for students and teachers to be aware of all there is to know about computers. In fact, trying to comprehend everything can result in the very real phenomenon of information anxiety discussed by Richard Wurman, which is "produced by the ever-widening gap between what we understand and what we think we should understand" in a technological culture (34). But as the label implies, proceduralists insist that what users know about an object is coextensive with its operating procedures (Winograd, "Frame"). That is, user knowledge is determined at least partially by the ways in which an object is employed. It makes sense to read the manual packaged with a new computer, but a proceduralist would assert that learning to use the computer productively also requires trying and testing it repeatedly in the framework of meaningful activity. In turn, the computer becomes defined by the chosen field of user actions. Leaving aside the criticisms of this epistemological perspective, it constricts what must be learned and situates technology in a context where it can be immediately understood, used, and practiced.

In their book on informed engagement with technology, Bonnie

Nardi and Vicki O'Day argue that the tool metaphor "is useful for questions and discussions about utility, usability, skill, and learning" (30). Although the tool metaphor deemphasizes the political and constitutive aspects of technology, it encourages an attention to task objectives, task contexts, and the values and perspectives of the discipline. Moreover, the level of agency it ascribes to users can help inculcate in them a sense of control over technology as well as a sense of the professional responsibilities that might go along with using technological environments. With these metaphorical emphases as a conceptual backdrop, teachers can more easily imagine the parameters that might contribute to a more productive view of functional literacy.

## The Parameters of a Functional Approach

In the broadest sense, functional literacy includes those online activities considered to be customary in English courses at the postsecondary level, particularly in the areas of writing and communication. This scope obviously rules out such matters as mathematical modeling, advanced numerical analysis, and computer-aided design, as well as software installation and many other technical support tasks. But what does it include? A cursory response is that functional computer literacy includes the skills associated with writing and communication processes as teachers have come to understand them in a digital age. However, there is no exhaustive list of requirements that will satisfy all students and all teachers in every conceivable situation. Given this reality, it is useful to think about parameters that might help a program begin to develop its own emphases. Because performance is at issue here, I propose five parameters—educational goals, social conventions, specialized discourses, management activities, and technological impasses—as distinguishing qualities of a functionally literate student (see table 2.1).

### Educational Goals
A functionally literate student uses computers effectively to achieve educational goals. He or she learns to situate mechanical skills in a

## Table 2.1
Parameters of a Functional Approach to Computer Literacy

| Parameters | Qualities of a Functionally Literate Student |
|---|---|
| Educational Goals | A functionally literate student uses computers effectively in achieving educational goals. |
| Social Conventions | A functionally literate student understands the social conventions that help determine computer use. |
| Specialized Discourses | A functionally literate student makes use of the specialized discourses associated with computers. |
| Management Activities | A functionally literate student effectively manages his or her online world. |
| Technological Impasses | A functionally literate student resolves technological impasses confidently and strategically. |

pedagogical context, one that is consistent with a needs-driven approach to literacy according to which users invariably focus on what is important to them (R. Kay). In other words, teachers of writing and communication "attend to the categories of meaning that students bring to the classroom" (Aronowitz and Giroux 52). They create curricular spaces in which the interests of students are considered to be a legitimate focus of academic study. In being mindful of what is important to students, however, I do not cast off the expertise that teachers have to offer. Indeed, the parameter tends to accommodate the values of the discipline.

But what requires elaboration is not disciplinary preferences. Instead, the adverb *effectively* is key because it qualifies computer use in ways that are central to a functional approach. To start, teachers should bear in mind the categories that Thomas Barker uses to sort out the shifts in learning that software can demand. Relying on the pioneering research of Shoshana Zuboff, Barker derives contrasting characteristics of computer-mediated users and empowered users. Unable to manage change, computer-mediated users suffer the detrimental effects of technology. For these individuals, computers have become an alienating force that introduces a number of debilitating personal challenges. Computer-mediated users, for example, find themselves increasingly isolated and engulfed in information and perform poorly in remotely supervised situations (e.g., distance learning). Moreover, they are puzzled by the levels of abstraction associated with operating computers and thus are likely to be deskilled or disempowered in technological contexts. In contrast, empowered users have an altogether different relationship with technology. Although continuously challenged, they integrate computers more productively and cope reasonably well in dynamic environments. Unlike computer-mediated users, functionally literate users confront skill demands, collaborate online, and explore instructional opportunities. In other words, they employ computers as a tool in order to further their educational goals.

A variety of factors encourage empowerment, but controlling a computer enables effective use. Controlling a computer means that a student has the ability to harness the power of technology in an increasingly systematic way. Such an ability can be acquired by students if pedagogical activities stress three areas: understanding what computers are generally good at, using advanced software features that are often ignored, and customizing interfaces. These areas can be scaffolded to interrelate technology with specific educational goals.

Although the practical limitations of computers have been

discussed across the curriculum (Burns; Weizenbaum; Bolter, *Turing's Man;* Kemp, "Who Programmed"), what teachers have learned from research rarely trickles down to the level of literacy instruction. It should not be surprising, then, that students often believe computers can solve ill-defined problems that require interpretation, anticipation, judgment, intuition, creativity, novelty, or improvisation or that are steeped in ambiguity. But technology is not clever enough to do so, despite the claims in certain camps of the artificial intelligence community. Computers are driven by formal systems of rules and procedures and thus are particularly good at information-processing tasks that benefit from speed, accuracy, reliability, efficiency, repetition, and control (Walker; Johnson, Anderson, Hansen, and Klassen). They are less good, for example, at providing advice about writing, guiding research activities, and evaluating student texts. Although certain fields lend themselves to computer treatment (e.g., mathematics), online writing and communication activities demand rhetorical interventions. A functionally literate student is alert to the limitations of technology and the circumstances in which human awareness is required.

One way to make this point clear is to have students consider the textual analyses produced by grammar checkers, a technology that has been closely scrutinized by the computers and writing community since at least the early 1980s. Alex Vernon recounts the disciplinary debate over grammar checkers and extends it by providing a thoughtful discussion of the expanded functionalities that have become embedded in the word-processing programs students use today. After pointing out the possibilities and limitations of these functionalities, Vernon offers two reasons why teachers should incorporate grammar checkers into writing instruction: the checkers can catalyze interesting discussions about language conventions and usage authority; and they can help students improve their revising and editing skills (344). Another reason, however, is that the analyses of grammar checkers can help illustrate the things computers are not particularly good at. For example, in my classes I ask students to run a grammar checker on a professional document that is peppered with passive constructions. The program flags numerous instances of passive voice and invariably suggests to students that they turn the passive constructions into active constructions. Although computers can offer this type of rule-driven, nonrhetorical advice in a steady fashion, it is not helpful to students unless they first understand the situations in which passive constructions might be appropriate or effective. Which is to point out that machines cannot make rhetorical and ethical decisions about the location of action and agency in sentence structures.

If computers favor certain types of tasks, the really powerful software features applicable to the educational goals of students should be identified and exploited. Yet too often this happens infrequently or haphazardly if at all. I am reminded of a trade book published in 1992 by Robin Williams, a graphic designer. In *The PC Is Not a Typewriter,* she offered a pragmatic style manual for creating professional-looking documents on a personal computer. Desktop publishing was the focus, and a series of straightforward concepts allowed users to produce relatively sophisticated visual designs on a printed page. But Williams did more than just help users improve typographic quality. Her discussion emerged from an evolutionary perspective that challenged users to abandon typewriter rules and to consider the effects of computer technologies on document design and production. So why do so many students today still operate the computer like a glorified typewriter? In part because teachers often implicitly or explicitly dismiss student experiments with genres and formats, and in part because certain documentation styles remain quite traditional (the MLA style, for example, still uses underlining to indicate italicized text, and it puts angled brackets around Website addresses as opposed to permitting actual hyperlink designations). In addition, however, teachers have not paid enough attention to the so-called advanced features of software programs (e.g., style sheets, master pages, version controls, macros), which are typically explained in the associated help resources. Such features are not hard to grasp but require a pedagogical commitment deeper than cut, copy, and paste. The payoff, though, is a command over software features that manipulate text elements in ways that are significant and sometimes elegant.

For instance, in most courses students are expected to collaborate effectively with their peers in a community of writers who provide feedback and occasionally write together. The educational goal of effective collaboration is one that can be supported by the more advanced features of certain software programs. Needless to say, determining which features might be helpful depends, at least in part, on the model of collaboration being employed. My technical writing classes tend to employ a divide-and-conquer strategy because in nonacademic settings reports are often researched and written by multiple authors. One challenge for students, therefore, is to pull the discrete sections of a report together for both peer reviews and final production activities: Although reports are often written by (and for) multiple audiences, their structural elements must be unified. Uncoached about the technological features that might help multiple writers merge their texts in productive ways, students tend to set off on their own and create individual structures that seem to be workable. This situation not only wastes time down the road when students show up with a variety of files and formats that must be merged but also discourages valuable discussions of audience, purpose, context, and structure at the invention stage. So I combine my overview of collaboration models with demonstrations of the various software features that can support them. In the case of divide-and-conquer models, for example, I explain how a style sheet works and ask students to develop one for their collaborative reports. This style sheet makes it easy for students to create and merge consistent files because each text element has been identified and defined in advance. On a rhetorical level, however, the design of the style sheet requires students to understand how and why readers rely on the various structural elements of reports.

Teachers should also emphasize the fact that online environments can be customized to suit individual needs. Default configurations accelerate setup and use, especially for novice users, but they also assume a generic operator. However, working and learning styles in academic settings can be highly idiosyncratic. Although public-access machines tend to be locked down to some degree, students can redesign interface representations in both operating systems and applications. In my courses, for example, I encourage students to modify the properties of windows, toolbars, menus, icons, keyboard commands, shortcuts, startup documents, directory views, and desktop styles, items, and images. We also investigate the accessibility options for those who have trouble typing or hearing or seeing. Because an interface arrangement can be saved as a set of preferences, I ask students to design multiple arrangements that reflect different perspectives and educational goals. In addition, we also consider the ways in which computers can be directed to deliver individualized content, so that the Internet can be mined in a creative and convenient manner. An example would be the function in online newspapers that creates customized pages of headlines and stories based on the search terms and topics that students provide. One convenient aspect of this function is that students can easily redefine the search terms and topics as their research interests change. Although the desktop has become a more flexible communication environment, default settings cannot possibly accommodate all of the interests and viewpoints of users. Thus, students must be encouraged to understand the options and settings one can manipulate in order to organize a writing space that is intelligible and, as I will discuss later, manageable.

MyBookmarks.com is a Website I have used to introduce students to the notion that computer interfaces can be customized. This site provides a good example because its limited number of customization options are relatively powerful. MyBookmarks is a free Internet service that people can use to access their personal Web bookmarks from any networked computer. After students sign up for this service, the first thing I do is give them a bookmarks file to import, so that they have some content to customize. We then work through the first three options for customization. The first option allows students to manipulate fonts and colors. On the surface this option seems to be rather superficial, so I make sure to talk about the ways in which typography and color can assist users who do a great deal of reading online. The second option allows students to manipulate tool bars, page widths, and display modes (graphics versus text). It also lets students decide if the bookmarks will open in a new window or not. The third option allows students to decide if the bookmarks will be private or public. Because the point of the exercise is to introduce issues of personal customization, at this point I tell students to make their bookmarks private. The final activity is to edit the bookmarks file I asked students to import. Many users do not realize that they can edit bookmark names, which are simply stored in HTML files, yet this is one easy way to customize a heavily accessed menu. The bookmarks students import are for various Websites that provide resources for writers and researchers. Students first visit these sites to come up with descriptors that are meaningful to them and then edit the bookmark names; they also create folders in which to organize the bookmarks. The result of this exercise is a highly personalized menu structure that students can build on as they continue to write and research throughout the course.

At this point, teachers who want to introduce the next parameter (the social) can ask students to edit their user preferences so that the bookmarks become public via the Internet. The public nature of the bookmarks opens a pedagogical space for discussions of social conventions online. Are the descriptors you selected recognizable in a broader context? Does your menu structure employ familiar language? How might you revise the menu for other students in your major? These kinds of problem-posing questions can introduce the notion that social conventions also influence discourse activities in technological settings.

*Social Conventions*
A functionally literate student understands the social conventions that help determine computer use. Notwithstanding the popular claim that online activities can be more egalitarian because computers reduce contextualization cues (Selfe and Meyer; Sproull and Kiesler; Kiesler, Siegel, and McGuire), technology does not create a social vacuum. Although controlling a computer is essential, so too is decoding the expectations that have been adopted in socialized network spaces.

Consider the results of an empirical study of asynchronous

communication. Brenda Sims compared e-mail use at Southwestern Bell Telephone and Convex Computer. She learned not only that the computer programs that writers employ shape the linguistic features and formats of their messages but also that differences in organizational culture can influence the rhetoric of e-mail. For example, at Southwestern Bell, an established telecommunications business, e-mail tended to circulate among employees at the same hierarchical level, and messages exhibited the characteristics of paper-based genres. Sims attributed such controlled behavior to a rigidly structured work environment in which employees felt pressured to conform to the norms of traditional communication. The setting at Convex, however, was unconventional, as is often the case in new or small computer companies. Here, e-mail use cut across the entire organization, and discourse habits reflected a more relaxed and creative atmosphere. These findings indicate that settings of work can shape user expectations and understandings of emergent technologies.

But the work settings of users is not the only factor that shapes social conventions online. For example, in her longitudinal study of one Usenet newsgroup, Nancy Baym discovered that external contexts, group purposes, and participant characteristics can influence the dynamics of online conversations. All discourse is multiply situated, and computer-mediated communication (CMC) is no exception. As Baym puts it, "CMC use is nested in the national and international cultures of which its participants are members. From this they draw a common language, usually but not always English, common ways of speaking, and a good deal of shared understanding" (141). Hence, the styles and patterns of communication exhibited in Usenet newsgroups often echo preexisting practices in a discipline. In addition, group purposes can influence discussion topics and the extent to which participants invest in the topics. Baym linked markers of online conversations to either professional or recreational goals, although in his research on e-mail use, Irvin Peckham describes playful activities that confound this distinction. Finally, participant characteristics can affect CMC outcomes. According to Baym, one characteristic that is particularly potent is perception of the medium. Among the individuals she studied, for example, the perception of an online space "was a major determinant of whether or not people used it socially" (148).

In classrooms involving computer-mediated communication, the types of factors discussed by Sims and Baym—work settings, external contexts, group purposes, and participant characteristics—seem to be no less forceful. Indeed, when Robert Yagelski and Jeffrey Grabill studied two undergraduate writing classes, they found that the nature and rate of participation in the online discourse was influenced by a number of social forces—among them, the nature of the course and the ways in which students understood its purposes and structures, the nature of the in-class face-to-face discourse, the ways in which the teachers assigned and managed online conversations, student perceptions of computers as communication media, and student understandings of the roles of participants in online discourse. In the discussion of their results, Yagelski and Grabill note that "online discourse might exhibit very different characteristics in different classroom contexts" (36). Given the evidence that studies of asynchronous communication provide, this situation probably has at least as much to do with shifting conventions as it does with shifting technologies.

So participation online revolves around normative behaviors determined, at least in part, by a wide range of social conventions. No great surprise there. But by what method might such conventions be illuminated in the classroom? To date, a common approach has been to cover the rules of etiquette that have been developed for interaction on computer networks. University policies on acceptable technology deployment routinely list these rules, as do textbooks for courses in writing and communication. Often, the discussions in textbooks focus on manners in cyberspace. For example, Jan Rune Holmevik and Cynthia Haynes suggest to students that MOO users should "be nice and friendly" and avoid "offensive language or actions" (41). In addition, rules of etiquette can take into account the nature of communication in an online medium. For example, Janice Walker and John Ruszkiewicz advise that when it comes to e-mail messages, students should use a subject line that accurately "describes the topic" and avoid "the use of all-capital letters," which represents the "electronic equivalent of shouting" (55). Guidelines such as these remind students that there are boundaries and expectations online and that the Internet connects individuals and cultures as well as computers. In this way, rules of etiquette are a valuable starting place.

However, as Carl Herndl argues, textbooks tend to dilute ethnographic research because the political and material conditions of authorship encourage overly practical advice. Thus, to move classroom discussions beyond rules of etiquette, I ask students to study and produce thick descriptions of the social conventions in actual computer-mediated communications. Margaret McLaughlin, Kerry Osborne, and Christine Smith have constructed a taxonomy of reproachable conduct on Usenet that can frame this type of instructional activity. These researchers collected articles posted to five popular newsgroups for a three-week period and coded numerous instances of unacceptable behavior. The taxonomy they constructed organizes these behaviors into seven categories: incorrect or novice uses of technology, bandwidth waste, violation of network conventions, violation of newsgroup-specific conventions, ethical violations, inappropriate language, and factual errors. This classification scheme organizes and extends online rules of etiquette in important ways. Thus, I ask students to use the scheme to help them analyze the social conventions of a newsgroup in which they are interested.

I should mention a pitfall in this assignment: the inclination to generalize findings from one or two sites to the entire landscape of networked computers. Studying and producing thick descriptions cultivates an informed perspective, but it would be foolhardy to assume that the aforementioned taxonomy accurately represents or exhausts reproachable conduct in all cases. In her work on computer networks as social spaces, Linda Harasim reminds teachers: "Each particular networld has its own culture and norms for acceptable and appropriate communication. Standards vary as to what is considered legal, tasteful, and manageable communication" (31). Furthermore, conventions for online discourse are still in a somewhat embryonic state (Hawisher and Moran) and consequently can be difficult to predict or pin down. Nevertheless, functionally literate students not only recognize that social conventions limit and shape communication online but are capable of analyzing the discourse forums in which they are interested and discerning productive modes of engagement. Thus, teachers should be sure to cover primary research methods and the methodological complications that arise when one tries to investigate social processes in electronic environments (see Jones).

*Specialized Discourses*

A functionally literate student makes use of the specialized discourses associated with computers. Historically, a focal point of courses in computer literacy has been the components of a computer. Students studied the development of computational devices and then memorized the different parts of a modern machine. A final exam asked students to label internal and external sketches of a typical system. I suspect such an exercise was invaluable to future scientists and engineers, for it helped them to understand and express what goes on inside a computer. But there are other discourses that must be emphasized if students hope to converse productively about their technological projects.

Cultural privileges accrue through effective discourse practices. That is, one must effectively appropriate the language of a community in order to have a voice within it (Bazerman; Bizzell; Bruffee). Greg Myers substantiates this claim: he traced the tensions within two biologists who were attempting to argue that controversial new research or research falling between two specialized fields can be entirely congruent with the established directions of a field. The proposal writers he studied used personae, citations, significant vocabularies, and other linguistic devices to assert the importance of potential contributions that were situated on the margins of their specialty areas. If Michel Foucault had observed the rhetorical moves these biologists made, he might say that they acknowledged the controls over discourse production that a discipline can exert. As Myers puts it, biologists "learn the rhetoric of their discipline in their training as graduate students and post-docs, but they relearn it every time they get the referees' reports of an article or the pink sheets on a proposal" (240).

Closer to home, in a widely cited essay, David Bartholomae described requirements for the type of student English teachers tend to hear: "He [or she] has to learn to speak our language, to speak as we do, to try on the peculiar ways of knowing, selecting, evaluating, reporting, concluding, and arguing that define the discourse of our community" (273). However, in his critical look at how the profession has imagined the effects of such social forces, Joseph Harris provides a perspective that is useful to computer users. He appreciates the fact that communities "instigate and constrain" (98) the things that can be said but also points out that "the borders of most discourses are hazily marked and often traveled" and that "the communities they define are thus often indistinct and overlapping" (103). Harris complicates the idea of a coherent disciplinary discourse and maintains that the job of teachers is to help students negotiate the multiple and contradictory discourses in which they will be implicated as writers and communicators. In a digital age, these discourses invariably include the various rhetorics that inform the design of literacy technologies.

To date, the language of computer networks has captured a great deal of attention because teachers have confronted it repeatedly under urgent circumstances. In computer-supported writing facilities, students and teachers need to know immediately about file servers and synchronous conferencing systems, list commands and domain names, Ethernet and e-mail. The ability to talk on some level about the infrastructure of an online classroom is critical to just about any responsible measure of instructional success. And when problems crop up in these facilities—and they always do— the troubleshooters will need a precise description of the conditions of the situation. The facts of existence in academic institutions have also encouraged teachers to become better versed in the argot of computer connectivity, which, as Tharon Howard notes in his overview and glossary of wide-area networks, is not only technical but exclusionary. Howard admonishes teachers to embrace the language of an appropriate technology that historically has been monopolized by an elite few. In his words, teachers "must have this language if they are both to understand how network technologies can support or defeat our pedagogical goals and to wrest computing resources away from economy-oriented university computing centers" ("WANS" 42).

But students also need access to the discourses that constitute online environments. For while certain everyday computer terms must be mastered, interfaces are informed by a variety of disciplinary specialties. In the late 1970s, the Media Lab at the Massachusetts Institute of Technology anticipated the convergence of the computer industry, the print and publishing industry, and the broadcast and motion picture industry (Brand). By 1987, the Lab housed eleven interdisciplinary work groups with many alliances among them: Electronic Publishing; Speech; The Advanced Television Research Program; Movies of the Future; The Visible Language Workshop; Spatial Imaging; Computers and Entertainment; Animation and Computer Graphics; Computer Music; The School of the Future; and Human-Machine Interface (Brand 12–13). Nicholas Negroponte and former MIT President Jerome Weisner assumed that graduates of the Media Lab would "be required to pursue studies in epistemology, experimental psychology, filmmaking, holography, and signal processing, as well as in computer science" (Brand 11). The Venn diagram that illustrated the merger of the computer industry, the print and publishing industry, and the broadcast and motion picture industry prophesied an interdisciplinary relationship that has come to steer the multimedia directions of twenty-first-century computer technologies. Although interfaces have been reconfigured in dramatic ways, one implication for users is that they readily encounter the lingo—and territory—of several different industries and the numerous perspectives that inform them.

I am sanguine about the chances students have to appropriate the discourse of the computer industry because it permeates nearly every aspect of university settings today. However, in too many instances, the discourses of the print and publishing industry and the broadcast and motion picture industry get shortchanged, especially in departments of English. The reasons for this have to do with the relatively glacial pace of curricular change and the fact that teacher training in computer use typically adopts an instrumental rather than a pedagogical approach. Nevertheless, the categories and distinctions within these neglected industries anchor the new media landscape and help frame the software suites that have come to dominate college campuses. For example, the principles of the print and publishing industry are central to document production efforts, yet these principles remain a mystery to numerous students, who if pressed would struggle to articulate an informed rationale for their typographic or document or graphic designs. They also remain a mystery to many English teachers. In fact, given how computers tend to get treated in English classes, students are often actively discouraged from seeing, for example, the discourses of typography or graphic design as important. The broadcast and motion picture industry represents a special challenge in that its discourse is farther afield. Nonetheless, multimedia texts depend upon this discourse, which pervades the software programs used to create them. For example, the theatrical interface metaphor in MacroMedia Director emphasizes unfolding actions rather than static displays of information: Multimedia designers select their cast (various media objects), arrange them on stage (in a visual display area), and write a script (via manipulations of the timeline). In short, students must be able to understand a unique combination of symbolic representations that are woven together nowadays in some of the most common platforms for writing and communication activities.

But how does one encourage students to appropriate the various discourses of literacy technologies? There is no simple answer here. A certain amount of immersion and uninterrupted time in technological contexts helps, but I do not find osmosis to be a particularly reliable or responsible approach. So I have developed a few pedagogical strategies that are a bit more direct. One way to quickly introduce the parameter of specialized discourses is to invite students to use advanced engines for their Internet searches, which rely on the discourses of the library and the computer industry. For example, in order for students to take advantage of the advanced functions in HotBot, a popular search engine, they must be familiar with Boolean operators and word stemming and the different elements on the Internet that can be searched. Some of these elements are fairly obvious (e.g., images, MP3 files, video clips), but some searches demand more domain knowledge of the computer industry, such as searches for file extensions, JavaScripts, and sites that employ Shockwave, VRML, and ActiveX technologies, technologies that are used to enhance the Web. In this fashion, advanced search engines make it clear to students that a comprehension of at least two specialized discourses can help them become better researchers.

A more ambitious approach would be to create an actual assignment that requires students to more deeply engage the specialized discourses of the software programs that are central to a course. An assignment I employ draws on the techniques of task analysis, a methodology used to help people design software and its documentation from a user-centered perspective. In general, a task analysis is a systematic process by which designers attempt to understand better the tasks and work contexts of computer users. There are several recursive stages in task analyses, which should occur toward the very beginning of the software development process. Designers study user contexts and represent the activities in those contexts (often) in workflow diagrams, create descriptive scenarios in order to understand the workflow processes on a finer-grained level, convert the workflow representations into concrete sets of user tasks, break those tasks down into discrete steps, reorganize the discrete steps in ways that closely model the real activities of users, create user scenarios to test the logic of the reorganized tasks, prototype an interface based on this explicit model of user behavior, and validate the prototype with the help of users. Task analyses can be problematic if they serve as a substitute for serious user engagement or if designers assume a strictly causal relationship between workflows and user actions (Mirel). Still, they encourage an attention to operational problems instead of the implementation problems associated with software development that have tended to fascinate computer programmers.

My use of this methodology sidesteps such concerns because I employ it in the postproduction context of end-user education. That is, task analyses can provide a means by which to help students locate and map out the specialized discourses that have been incorporated into software programs. For this more limited activity, the part of the methodology that is important is the stage in which user tasks are decomposed into discrete steps. To start the assignment, I select a software program that will be important to the course and show students how to conduct a task analysis, which in this case is basically just a list of the user steps and options that are associated with a menu item. For example, in DeskScann, a program students can use at Penn State to digitize images, a task analysis for the Image Type option under the Custom menu would include the following steps: (1) Select Image Type from the Custom menu; (2) Select the color content of the image (color or black and white); (3) Select the style of the image (drawing, halftone, or photo); (4) Click Okay. The one option users have is to sharpen the image by varying degrees of intensity when it is scanned. I use this example here because it is brief—task analyses can become quite involved, especially for menu items that have layers of options. But what this brief example does show is a pretty typical instance of a specialized discourse that often puzzles students. What is a halftone? How is it different from other types of images? And under what conditions might I want to use one? These are the kinds of questions students often ask, and not just about image types. For example, the discourse of color in DeskScann (hue, saturation, intensity) also seems to mystify students on a regular basis.

Once students have completed their task analyses, the rest of the assignment is relatively straightforward. Because the analyses provide an exhaustive map of the various specialized discourses that constitute the software program, we select out a subset of discourses associated with the features that are particularly relevant to class activities (this aspect of the assignment makes a connection between the functional parameter of educational goals and the functional parameter of specialized discourses). I then assign the different discourses in the subset to different groups of students and ask them to research and report back to the class on the contexts from which these discourses were appropriated, including any off-line contexts, and what might be learned from them about productive computer use. Students who have researched the contexts for the theatrical discourse in MacroMedia Director, for example, have learned that a background in certain aspects of film and theatre can illuminate the workings of Director. Likewise, students who have researched the contexts for the publications management discourse in Adobe PageMaker have learned that a background in the history of printing and type can illuminate the workings of this program. On one level, then, a focus on specialized discourses can help students develop conceptual schemata for the ways in which software programs operate. On another—and no less important—level, they can remind students that the knowledges represented in online environments originate from numerous sources and communities, not just the computer industry. So a concentration on the discourses and practices of this particular industry would be incomplete, at best. At worst, such a one-dimensional focus would produce the harmful and distorted approaches to computer literacy that I criticized in chapter 1.

### Management Activities

A functionally literate student effectively manages his or her online world. This unremarkable assertion seems self-evident, and in certain ways of thinking it is. For example, no proof or explanation should be required when it comes to the maintenance computer-based activities routinely call for, such as changing passwords, backing up files, and deleting old versions of documents. But because computers help students organize their ideas on a meaningful level, housekeeping cannot be the only management issue given due consideration. To some extent, how students handle work influences the elements that comprise the mosaic of thoughts associated with a writing or communication project.

Computer users create and collect an astounding amount of information. A culture of accumulation has been encouraged by the ease with which vast materials in multiple media can be digitized, circulated, and stored. As David Shenk writes: "With virtually no effort and for relatively little cost, we can capture as much information as we want. The capturing requires very little planning or forethought, and in fact is built right into the design of our machines" (29). Undeterred by the positive prospects of this state of affairs, Shenk subsequently raises a red flag: "Only as an afterthought," however, "do we confront the consequences of such a low transaction cost" (30). To put the consequences in perspective, they seem to be so profound that print-based protocols of reading have been modified and multiplied to help computer users attend to the prodigious volumes of information with which they are continuously deluged. In other words, readers of online texts have begun to develop alternative reading strategies (Sosnoski). Not only that, but what has been collected by a computer user often stands in for the totality of the reading experience, even though it is only one aspect of that experience. For example, a MOO transcript is often used to stand in as the official, total representation of the MOO session (MOO sessions take place in online spaces that support various kinds of real-time interaction). However, by leaving out temporality, the transcript does not provide a sense of the important, often crucial lags between one post and the next. The same thing happens, on a different level, when students assume that the Internet holds everything; it can be difficult to get certain students to think that they should go to the library rather than just use Google or Yahoo for their research.

The question of resource management has been attacked from a number of different angles. Some have criticized the conventional file and directory structures that underlie the ubiquitous desktop metaphor currently governing the management of information on almost every computer. For example, Scott Fertig, Eric Freeman, and David Gelernter propose a time-ordered versus location-based architecture that organizes electronic objects in a manner that more closely parallels the ways in which people tend to imagine the complexion of their discursive work. Others have addressed the matter of resource management as an application issue. For example, Starr Roxanne Hiltz and Murray Turoff offer concrete features that enable users to more easily manage massive sets of communications in a computer conferencing program. In addition, researchers have developed meta-level search engines that cut across systems and hierarchies and filter huge dataspheres. For example, Daniel Dreilinger and Adele Howe focus on algorithms that strive to enhance and refine the results of large-scale queries on the Internet. Looking toward the future, some researchers anticipate a day when computers will completely take over the task of information retrieval and management. In fact, Hal Berghel reviews the literature on intelligent agents and concludes that some of the major hurdles in making autonomous software robots work effectively on behalf of computer users have already been cleared.

Technical solutions to the problem of how to deal with electronic information are undoubtedly indispensable, and a functionally literate student takes advantage of software attributes that automate management activities in ways that are helpful. Some of the features ready for use already are detailed filters for screening and organizing e-mail messages; list commands for altering listserv subscription options (e.g., Digest, NoMail); resources for personalizing home pages that index favorite sites and search engines and that provide content that is automatically updated; utilities for remotely accessing and capturing research bookmarks for the Web; and shareware programs for carrying out the important jobs of maintenance, repair, data recovery, and data backup. Although I have no direct evidence, I suspect many teachers overlook these solutions because they appear to be the responsibility of campus computer support.

Although computer skills and writing skills cannot be so easily separated, a barrage of technical fixes will not always provide a complete or satisfactory solution to the problems associated with resource management, in large part because such problems always seem to have social dimensions of one sort or another. To illustrate this point in a more general way, let me take a brief detour through the case of teledemocracy, the process of political participation that has appeared online. Proponents vehemently argue that technology improves the political process because it amplifies discourse and increases the avenues available for public participation. "Optimists see the Internet as the seedbed for a new politics," Graeme Browning proselytizes, "one free from the distorting influence of mass media and closer to the democratic ideas at the core of our Republic" (xi). Leaving aside the fact that large news organizations like CNN have some of the most popular sites on the Web, an underlying assumption of online activism is that students are apathetic because they do not have objective knowledge about political issues or easy access to politicians; the all-inclusive resources on the Internet, so the logic goes, will rescue representative government because in cyberspace students can endlessly access, search, and study the legislative record. However, the counterargument—one that students quickly pick up on—is that neither more data nor better-managed data warehouses will necessarily produce an enlightened body politic. As Theodore Roszak explains, "we must [also] insist upon a new standard of political discourse" (165). His contention, in a sentence, is that "it is the vitality of issues that saves democracy" (167), not technological fixes all on their own. In fact, the end result of teledemocracy initiatives that are driven by a more-is-better logic is likely to be an overabundance of unmanageable information that not only defies navigation and use but also obscures rather than clarifies debates about the public good.

Resource management activities in writing and communication courses call for a similar approach, one that draws on hybrid solutions with both technical and social aspects. Given this reality, an important step for students is to be able to size up the management activities that can be successfully turned over to a machine (this step harkens back to the functional parameter of educational goals and reminds students that, to some degree, the different parameters are interrelated). Student questions will necessarily reflect local systems and policies and thus include institutional as well as technical dimensions. For example, can shareware programs be downloaded and installed in a public laboratory? What are the constraints in personal networked spaces? Are software utilities available to help manage online work? Although often invisible, elaborate apparatuses usually exist to manipulate and protect materials on communal computers or on private computers connected to university networks.

But the activities that cannot or should not be entirely mechanized are harder for students to visualize. Consider the distinction between file-related tasks and communication strategies: The former has to do with productivity and the latter with people and projects. Although both of these management activities are essential, they can be contrasted in the framework of graphical e-mail programs, if one contemplates an attachments folder over against the inbox. As most people know, an attachments folder collects files e-mailed to a user. Assuming an environment that automatically decompresses and decodes the files (a MIME-compliant environment), the main chore for students is to organize their attachments so that they can be searched and used in an effective manner. At a minimum, this involves manipulating file formats, file names, and directories. On the other hand, the inbox presents more of a social challenge. Here, students must manage not only large amounts of information but also priorities, relationships, and collaborative activities. So in spite of the fact that management activities will probably vary from student to student, they almost always unite technology and literacy in ways that require social judgments, as this rather mundane example of e-mail management demonstrates.

In the classroom, the ubiquity of e-mail provides an easy way to illustrate the importance of management activities. To highlight their sociotechnical aspects, I introduce a useful feature of e-mail that very few of my students actually use: filters (at present, popular Web-based e-mail clients like Hotmail do not provide adequate filtering capabilities, so my approach works best with POP mail clients such as Eudora or Outlook Express, clients that tend to provide a richer array of options for managing e-mail). Filters allow computer users to take more control over their e-mail by creating scripts that automate the ways certain (inbound or outbound) messages get treated. For example, one could create a filter that automatically places the attachments from project collaborators into a unique folder. However, this script would go unexecuted if collaborators supply the wrong subject line or send attachments from e-mail accounts they do not normally use. That is, social as well as technical conventions must be established and followed in order for some e-mail filters to take effect. This is one reason why very few students tend to use filters: setting them up is a commitment to supporting long-term managerial structures over the short-term ease of just pressing the delete key or individually sorting messages manually as they come in.

To introduce the workings of filters in a pedagogically oriented fashion, I have students create several filters at the start of each semester that reflect course structures at a broad level. From there, students can create additional filters to manage finer-grained activities. For example, I ask students to create filters for course assignments, course announcements, and personal messages from me. As might be expected, each of these filters calls for a different set of parameters. The purpose of the filters for course assignments is to organize all of the messages related to a single assignment into one space. So if the course has five assignments, we create five filters. However, because the parameters for these filters are variations on the same theme (course assignments), the requirements for students are not that hard to remember: the subject line for messages related to the first assignment must start with "Assignment One," the subject line for messages related to the second assignment must start with "Assignment Two," and so on. The purpose of the filter for course announcements, which anyone can send, is to call attention to e-mail messages that are time-sensitive, such as changes in due dates, updates to the class Website, or last-minute notices about guest speakers on campus: It is easy for students to overlook such messages in a full inbox. Thus, the parameters for this filter change the status of announcement messages to the highest priority and alert students to their arrival by playing a simple beep. The purpose of the filter for personal messages from me is to create an archive of the review comments I have made on student projects. Over the past few years, I have increasingly read and responded to student work online, primarily using the annotation tools in Microsoft Word to embed comments in student files, HTML files included.

But I have found that students do not always keep track of the numerous files I return to them over the course of an entire semester, even though I have created a management scheme for file names. So the parameters for this filter place my comments into a single folder and automatically return an e-mail message to me to confirm that the files were received by the student. Not surprisingly, one of the biggest challenges associated with the use of e-mail filters is social in nature: Students must not only act in accordance with the parameters that have been defined, but retrain themselves so that the inbox is no longer the sole focal point of their asynchronous communication.

*Technological Impasses*

A functionally literate student resolves technological impasses confidently and strategically. Students reach technological impasses when they lack the computer-based expertise needed to solve a writing or communication problem. A basic example would be when students do not have the expertise to turn off the grammar checker that by default analyzes all of their writing in real time, including brainstorming and note-taking sessions. There are several indicators of technological impasses that are relatively easy to recognize, such as stalled progress on a project or asymmetrical contributions during the phases of a collaborative project that require technical expertise. Thomas Duffy, James Palmer, and Brad Mehlenbacher identify two types of technological impasses: performance-oriented and learning-oriented. Teachers should be particularly interested in performance-oriented impasses because these take place amid the various tasks of writing and communication. Learning-oriented impasses are generally less compelling on the grounds that English courses should not be a place where students are simply trained to operate computers and their programs in decontextualized ways.

Unproductive reactions to technological impasses are a function of numerous determinants. Analysts often allude to a digital generation gap that seems to include anyone who was not raised on a computer (Papert, *Connected*). But studies of apprehension paint a much more complicated picture of computer anxiety, phobia, and

trouble. Self-efficacy beliefs such as low expectations and debilita-
tive thoughts can impinge upon user responses to computer pre-
dicaments (Martocchio), as can other psychological, behavioral,
and affective factors. For example, statistical research has obtained
significant correlations between computer anxiety and math anxiety
and moderate correlations between computer anxiety and both computer experience and mechanical curiosity (Heinssen, Glass, and
Knight). Furthermore, race and gender have been known to influence user attitudes toward computers in significant ways (Brecher;
Parasuraman and Igbaria). In fact, Faith Gilroy and Harsha Desai
argue that women and minorities have been unusually susceptible
to computer anxiety because in historical terms their technological
opportunities and experiences have been so severely limited. Why
has this been the case? Some indict the exclusionary values that
pervade technological contexts, values that champion epistemologies aligning with the power, authority, and politics of the dominant
cultural formations (Markussen). On a cultural level, these values
tell women and minorities that they will not be computer experts,
a conclusion that can become a self-fulfilling myth, especially when
admitting that one needs help is viewed as confirmation of an un-
suitability toward technology. Thus, apprehension should not be
conflated with negative attitudes. One can be open to change and
yet paralyzed when it comes to technological impasses.

Systematic responses to user breakdowns have varied, but some
of the major ones are discussed in the intervention process proposed by Raymond King and Michael McNeese: assessment, treatment, adaptive computing systems, and collaborative support systems. Although there are certain aspects of these approaches that
could be helpful, for the most part they are either unworkable in the
context of English departments or contrary to a socially informed
perspective on computer literacy. Moreover, the clinical discourse
of intervention and treatment found throughout the literature on
computer anxiety and phobia, which constructs technological impasses as instances of psychological trauma, can be less than appealing to humanist scholars and teachers. Still, let me briefly

explain the interrelated parts of the intervention process and point out aspects that could be useful in classroom settings.

The first part of the process is assessment, and King and McNeese recommend "an easy-to-administer assessment instrument to predict who is likely to harbor manifestations of apprehension when confronted with computing tasks" (207). Although I agree that some sort of assessment vehicle could be useful, I am unconvinced that psychological anxiety inventories hold the key. Therefore, chapter 5 offers diagnostic activities teachers can use to learn more about student attitudes toward computers. The second part of the process, treatment by means of "Systematic Desensitization" (207), is more problematic. King and McNeese suggest therapeutic sessions that try to alleviate the provoking constituents identified during the assessment stage by linking them to techniques for progressive muscle relaxation. I am not sure what to make of this suggestion, but I do know that it is unworkable in the context of English courses. So too is the third part of the process: adaptive computing. Adaptive computing systems should be somewhat familiar to teachers because many computers today have features that assist students with disabilities. However, the state-of-the-art systems discussed by King and McNeese, those that adjust their interfaces based on the emotional and psychological states of users, are too expensive and experimental to be considered realistic solutions at this point. The fourth part of the process, instituting collaborative support systems, holds the most promise. Collaborative support systems supply a structure that enables users to share their fears and difficulties when it comes to computers. On a basic level, one can imagine the utility of an e-mail list where a community of engaged and generous students answer questions related to technological impasses. To sum up, then, certain types of assessment activities and collaborative support systems could be useful in writing and communication classrooms.

If major parts of the standardized process proposed by King and McNeese are not viable, micropolitical practices provide alternative approaches that students can internalize. Unfortunately, teachers have been in the habit of either brushing off or working around technological impasses in the classroom, often because they are embarrassed to admit that they might not have all of the answers. Indirect attempts to provide support schemes are invaluable and should be carried on. That is, teachers should continue to take advantage of campuswide resources, invest in documentation, prepare students as technical consultants, set up help notebooks in which students record problems and solutions, and provide electronic environments that foster useful interchanges about technological impasses. However, teachers should also embed more formal discussions that help students reason systematically about breakdowns.

On the order of rhetorical exigencies, the key is to situate technological impasses in a broader context so that their characteristics can be organized and understood. Ben Shneiderman developed an early syntactic-semantic model of user knowledge that helps to clarify a central shift in thinking students need to make. As the model indicates, syntactic knowledge about computers is motley and device dependent; it is acquired by rote memorization and thus forgotten rather quickly (43). An example would be the exact sequence of steps needed to transfer HTML files to a university server from a Macintosh computer running Fetch 4.0.3 as an FTP client. In contrast, semantic knowledge is structured and therefore more easily remembered. It is device independent and amassed in purposeful circumstances (43). As Shneiderman notes, semantic knowledge can be conveyed by showing examples, offering general theories or patterns, relating concepts to previous knowledge, describing concrete or abstract models, and indicating examples of incorrect use (49). For example, in the classroom, semantic knowledge about the transfer processes used for HTML documents could be anchored by analogy to the concept of copying files or downloading content from the Internet. Other pedagogical tactics could explain client/server technology and situate FTP as a species of TCP/IP, the suite of Internet protocols that includes the familiar Hypertext Transfer Protocol (HTTP). Although syntactic knowledge is important, semantic knowledge assists users in imagining problems and understanding computer systems.

However, against the backdrop of specific scenarios, the syntactic-semantic model thins on an applied level. Suppose students reach an impasse for which they do not have either syntactic or semantic knowledge. What should they do in such an ordinary situation? I would say that functionally literate students should be able to call up heuristics that help them represent the impasse in a meaning-ful way and solve it in a systematic way. Toward this end, one rela-tively simple heuristic I have invented has three parts. The first part asks students to phrase an impasse as a qualitative question. This part encourages them to focus on process and meaning rather than cause and effect. For example, instead of fixating on the fact that the grammar checker is triggered by "ungrammatical" sentences (cause/effect), a more fruitful approach would be to ask this ques-tion: How can I turn off the grammar checker? This seems utterly obvious, and it should be, yet believe it or not, I often have students who think that the only way to turn the grammar checker off is to stop writing "ungrammatical" sentences. In other words, some stu-dents have bought so deeply into the logic of the machine that they almost always see themselves as the causal root of technological im-passes.

The second part of the heuristic asks students to locate the qualitative question in a classification matrix derived from empiri-cal research on user-aided design. According to usability specialist Kevin Knabe, five categories exhaust the majority of computer-user concerns: goal questions (What can I do with this?), descriptive questions (What is this? What does it do?), procedural questions (How do I do this?), interpretive questions (Why did this happen? What does this mean?), and navigational questions (Where am I?) (286). For example, "How can I turn off the grammar checker?" is clearly a procedural question, although the impasse could have also been phrased as an interpretive question: Why is the grammar checker triggered as I write? The third part of the heuristic matches these five categories with appropriate forms of assistance. Parasitic facilities such as tracking systems and visual organizers can answer navigational questions, for example, whereas interpretive questions should be directed at more comprehensive resources (e.g., reference documents, campus help desks). The procedural question about the grammar checker would lead students to a user manual or on-line help system, two forms of assistance that characteristically include elaborated procedural instructions. Although heuristics complement a syntactic-semantic model of user knowledge, they also help students become more resourceful and discover effective ways to work through performance-oriented impasses.

## Conclusion

These five parameters—educational goals, social conventions, specialized discourses, management activities, and technological impasses —provide a framework within which teachers of writing and communication can conceive a productive approach to functional literacy that encompasses computers. On the whole, they serve as an alternative to the prescriptive lists of software skills churned out in academic settings by technologists and administrators who fail to problematize modern literacy practices that seem to be given and natural but in fact are subject to social forces. Although the parameters provide a structure, they should be seen as suggestive and conceptual rather than rigid and monolithic.

As I argue in this chapter, the promise of certain types of functional literacy should not be underestimated. The perspectives of functional literacy can not only encourage productive and efficient computer use, but the tool metaphor adumbrates issues of responsibility and foregrounds disciplinary values. Moreover, the knowledge, skills, and attitudes that students need cannot be derived from ad hoc approaches or approaches that disregard the fact that computer literacy is dynamic and varies with context. Carolynn Van Dyke argues that teachers need not follow the lead of bureaucrats in defining computer literacy. She advocates an instructional outlook that prizes exploration and communication over strict vocational preparation, which is often shortsighted and reductive. Along these lines, the functional approach I offer helps students succeed in technological contexts and develop a fluency needed to critique those contexts.

But because the tool metaphor tends to conceal the political aspects of computers, the peril of functional literacy is serious and real and should not be discounted. The instrumental lenses associated with the tool metaphor do not prod students to focus on biases and implications nor on what is happening with them and to them in technological environments. So although functionally literate students may be equipped for effective computer-based work, such work will remain obsequious and underdeveloped without the richly textured insights that critical perspectives can provide. Thus, the next chapter discusses critical literacy as a humanistic overlay that is crucial to students of writing and communication in a digital age.

# 3 / Critical Literacy
## Computers as Cultural Artifacts, Students as Informed Questioners of Technology

> The design of the cyberspace environment in the twenty-first century will not only be crucial to our quality of life in general, it will be fundamental to the distribution of wealth and power. From the software to the hardware, from the interface to the infrastructure, decisions are now routinely being made which will affect the future; and they are decisions which serve the interests and values of some social groups far more than others.
>
> —Dale Spender,
> *Nattering on the Net: Women, Power and Cyberspace*

**H**istorically speaking, courses in computer literacy have not concentrated on critical literacy as teachers of writing and communication think of it. I have already mentioned that nonrhetorical skill sets have constituted the core of most such courses and that their background and theory have focused primarily on data representations, numbering systems, operating systems, file formats, and hardware and software components. That is why the previous chapter reconceived of functional literacy in ways that foreground contexts of production and use in academic settings. To be fair, a few educators have articulated curricular blueprints that appeal in part to the social turn the discipline has taken (Arnow; Leister; Kiper and Bishop-Clark). Yet all too often these blueprints are either sketchy in terms of English studies or restricted in their view of what counts as a critical issue. Moreover, when critical issues are covered in computer literacy courses, they are usually compartmentalized in a unit that subordinates rather than integrates humanistic concerns.

Unfortunately, the more things change, the more they remain the same. I recently reviewed a proposal to revise a course in computer applications for students in the liberal arts at Penn State. The rationale for the revision cited Internet and software developments, and the course description claimed that a major emphasis would be placed on the social effects of information technologies. But, in its direction and orientation, the syllabus broke with this important emphasis in a striking manner. Not only was it organized in a modelike way around different types of computer applications, but only a single class session—the penultimate one—was explicitly devoted to social effects. And even these effects were limited to the predictable (if important) stock areas of censorship, privacy, and copyright. As I reviewed the proposal, I was reminded of what Douglas Noble said in the mid 1980s about computer literacy courses that fixate on technical content: "The technical focus shifts attention away from social questions and portrays computers as something to learn rather than something to think about" (610). Indeed, students in this course would not be encouraged to multiply situate computers or question their designs or challenge the grand narratives in which computers are implicated. Thus, the proposed course trains students but does not really educate them as citizens and empowered knowledge workers.

This chapter is about critical literacy, about the ways students might be encouraged to recognize and question the politics of computers. I start with an overview and interrogation of the assumptions of constructivism, a popular perspective in the literature on computer literacy, but one that does not adequately emphasize political aspects. I therefore turn to critical literacy as a conceptual foundation upon which teachers can build a program of political critique. Next I explore computers as cultural artifacts, a generative metaphor of identity that foregrounds critically both contexts of production and use. The last section of the chapter defines and illustrates four parameters of a critical approach to computer literacy: design cultures, use contexts, institutional forces, and popular representations. In this section, I contend that metadiscourse heuristics are a key to helping students become critically literate in a digital age.

## The Contributions and Limitations of Constructivism

Constructivism is a prominent and useful framework in discussions of computer literacy, even if it fails to adequately consider the politics of technologies. In oversimplified terms, constructivism is a philosophy of learning based on the premise that learning is an active process in which students construct new knowledge based upon their current/previous knowledge. As an epistemology, constructivism embodies a contested theoretical terrain that invariably challenges the objectivist paradigm. But its discourse has not remained on a philosophical level. Teacher-researchers have developed a wide range of concrete frameworks that attempt to guide classroom activities in a learner-centered direction. Because constructivism incorporates certain viable educational perspectives, it has become a dominant viewpoint in the literature on computer literacy. However, as Stuart Greene and John Ackerman point out, "research in a constructivist tradition has focused primarily on two factors: prior knowledge and task representation" (385). For this reason, constructivism is unlikely to provide a sufficient foundation for critical literacy upon which teachers can build a program of political critique.

Because I will take a broad view in this section, I should first mention that there are several strains of constructivism. For example, George Bodner, Michael Klobuchar, and David Geelan differentiate personal constructivism, radical constructivism, and social constructivism. In technological contexts, forms of constructivism have been derived from cybernetic and information theories (Thompson). Richard Prawat consolidates six perspectives on constructivism as either modern or postmodern in their tendencies. In part, his distinction hinges on the extent to which knowledge is considered to be the property of individuals or social formations. Although there are various schools of constructivism with subtle and not so subtle variations in perspective, the roots of constructivism are typically traced back to the work of Giambattista Vico, Jean Piaget, Jerome Bruner, Lev Vygotsky, and John Dewey.

In a general sense, constructivism advances two propositions.

The first is that knowledge is constructed through active and not passive means (Ben-Ari; Kafai; Lester, Fitzgerald, and Stone). The second, in the words of Ernst von Glasersfeld, is that "the function of cognition is adaptive and serves the organization of the experiential world, not the discovery of an ontological reality" (162). Simply put, we learn and understand how things are in ways that reflect our lived histories. David Jonassen offers a definition that clarifies the intellectual stance toward knowledge production that constructivism often takes:

> Constructivism is the belief that knowledge is personally constructed from internal representations by individuals using their experiences as a foundation. Knowledge is based upon individual constructions that are not tied to any external reality, but rather to the knower's interactions with the external world. Reality is to a degree whatever the knower conceives it to be. ("Thinking" 32)

As a conceptual understructure for instructional pursuits, constructivism can be understood against the antithetical and objectivist theories of behaviorism and cognitivism.

Behaviorists contend that behavior is altogether observable and determined primarily by environmental factors. In order to predict and control human performance, behaviorism abandons introspection and focuses on the associations between stimuli and responses. Thus, learning concentrates on the formation of patterned reflexes. In the behaviorist classroom, teachers arrange situations and consequences and students react but do not contribute to the conditions of the pedagogical environment. Cognitivists claim the discarded territory of introspection. They stress mental structures and the processes that organize, store, and retrieve information, so the epistemology of cognitivism aligns closely with the rationalist tradition. But cognitivism and behaviorism often share a primary instructional goal: to transfer expert knowledge in an effective fashion (Ertmer and Newby). Teachers in a cognitivist classroom, however, attempt to organize and sequence material in psychological networks that facilitate optimal processing. Students are involved in that they draw on previously learned knowledge and help to control the pace of instruction. As Jonassen explains, constructivism rejects a key premise of both cognitivism and behaviorism: that meaning exists apart from experience ("Thinking"). Instead of projecting the structure of an external world onto students, constructivists link epistemology and learning in ways that value multiplicity. The result is a more active classroom that privileges exploration and interpretation.

In "From Puppets to Problem Solvers: A Constructivistic Approach to Computer Literacy," Angie Parker provides an example of constructivism in action. Parker redesigned her computer literacy course in order to eliminate the large-screen demonstrations that had come to anchor her lessons in the use of integrated software packages. Instead of program functions, the centerpiece of her revision is a set of ill-defined problems that situate computer uses in real contexts, suggest course requirements, and promote authentic collaborations. In the database portion of the course, for instance, students conduct survey research on the Internet and then create a software architecture that productively organizes the data. The assignment also includes a written report (rather than a software examination) whose structures accommodate the variable nature of projects. This approach can be considered constructivistic because it invites students to pursue personal interests, shape pedagogical environments, and become self-directed in educational situations.

There are more elaborate examples that attest to the widespread influence of constructivism. Seymour Papert (*Mindstorms*) developed the Logo programming language in order to provide a hands-on environment in which the outlines of constructivism could be imagined and assessed. Likewise, Jonassen (*Computers*) authored a suite of electronic "mindtools" that attempt to cultivate critical thinking and foster interaction in schools. Amy Bruckman and Mitchel Resnick identified constructivism as the foundation for MediaMOO, a popular text-based virtual reality environment for educational and professional communities. Constructivism also inspired Paula Hooper, who devised African-centered instructional experiments that help students of color gain confidence in their abilities to solve difficult math problems. And constructivism has been instrumental in the hypertext learning spaces designed by Rand Spiro, Paul Feltovich, Michael Jacobson, and Richard Coulson. I could discuss other initiatives, but overall such researchers have relied on a cluster of major objectives formulated from the epistemology of constructivism. These include situating pedagogical activities in larger tasks or problems; respecting the goals of students; designing tasks that are authentic in their cognitive demands; supporting learning in complex environments; allowing students to drive the educational process; creating situations that both support and challenge students; encouraging students to consider alternative perspectives; and providing opportunities for reflection (Savery and Duffy 137–40). Needless to say, classrooms that mobilize these objectives represent a considerable improvement over classrooms that embrace objectivist models of education.

Constructivism as it has been envisioned in the discourse on computer literacy should be recognizable to teachers of writing and communication, although there is an important difference in emphasis that should be noted. Not only are English departments committed to the development and promotion of pedagogical advancements, but the profession has been motivated by similar philosophical perspectives. For example, the social constructionist approach in rhetoric and composition undermines the epistemologies of rationalism and empiricism, insists upon the fact that there can be multiple realities, and locates personal experience in an epistemic realm (Bruffee). The theoretical orientation in rhetoric and composition has centered on the role language plays in the knowledge production process, which is characterized in every respect as social in nature. In the typology that Prawat presents, this orientation falls within the domain of postmodernism because knowledge is considered to be an outgrowth of discursive interactions. On the other hand, constructivism is also indebted to modernist beliefs that view knowledge as the handiwork and property of individuals. Such a "Piagetian" or "schema-driven" (Prawat 215) brand of constructivism is quite prevalent in discussions of computer literacy.

As a case in point, consider the method D. Scott Brandt uses to teach information retrieval skills for the Internet. On an abstract level, Brandt visualizes constructivism as a pedagogical offshoot of cognitive theory. As he puts it, "Cognitivists seek to explain what goes on during learning, and constructivists seek to apply it to the classroom" (113). From this position it follows that Brandt would rely heavily on cognitive models of knowledge construction: "Both constructivism and cognitive theory assert that learners use internal, mental models to help them interpret and incorporate experiences, and then construct knowledge" (113). Although most constructivists employ cognitive theories to some extent, Brandt has chosen to make them the cornerstone of his instruction, and that is what diminishes the method he employs. His decision to privilege mental models belies the supposition that knowledge is developed through language and that meaning is constructed in social processes of interpretation. The upshot is a pedagogy that frequently casts teachers and students into traditional subject positions. If the key to learning is effective mental models, as Brandt would lead teachers to believe, then the job of teachers is to assess and leverage student experiences: "Given that learners tend to have disparate or incomplete mental models of information retrieval, teachers have to start by connecting to those models already in place, such as an understanding of the organization of information in a phonebook" (115). Unfortunately, Brandt does not continue in a more enabling fashion. His focus remains on ways to match the mental models of students with an array of predetermined goals for knowledge construction in a "target" system.

Brandt is not alone in his account of constructivism. In fact, there is no shortage of pedagogical projects that claim to be grounded in its philosophy but that in truth overaccentuate the perspectives of cognitivism (see Hadjerrouit; Simons; Zucchermaglio; Allen and Hoffman; Norman and Spohrer; Sargent, Resnick, Martin, and Silverman; Soloway, Norris, Blumenfeld, Fishman, Krajcik, and Marx). The concern I have is that these projects establish a pattern of influential work in which the contexts of computer literacy are not considered to be essentially social. Nevertheless, constructivism represents a step in the right direction because even its more limited articulations tend to contemplate knowledge as a construction of assumptions rather than an accurate reflection of the intrinsic and verifiable properties of technological systems.

## The Aims of Critical Literacy

Set against constructivism, critical literacy is a neglected framework in computer literacy programs that have been institutionalized in educational settings. Whereas teachers of writing and communication have increasingly called for reflective approaches, conventional programs rarely dwell on social, political, and economic contexts. As a rule, then, students are not encouraged to ask important questions when it comes to technology development and use: What is lost as well as gained? Who profits? Who is left behind and for what reasons? What is privileged in terms of literacy and learning and cultural capital? What political and cultural values and assumptions are embedded in hardware and software? This situation becomes all the more disturbing when one realizes that computers often exacerbate the very inequities that technology is so frequently supposed to ameliorate.

As such an uncomfortable line of questions implies, a critical approach to literacy first recognizes and then challenges the values of the status quo. Instead of reproducing the existing social and political order, which functional modes tend to do, it strives to both expose biases and provide an assemblage of cultural practices that, in a democratic spirit, might lead to the production of positive social change. Paulo Freire and Donaldo Macedo argue that "a person is literate to the extent that he or she is able to use language for social and political reconstruction" (159). This assertion operates as a useful point of departure because functional approaches to computer literacy characteristically construct literacy as a neutral enterprise that serves the utilitarian requirements of a technological society.

Like constructivism, critical approaches make use of the sociology and pedagogy of Bruner, Vygotsky, and Dewey, but they also

variously take up the rich traditions of Continental social and political theory as well as perspectives that politicize the educational
process. For instance, Wendy Morgan tells teachers that "Critical
theories of literacy derive from critical social theory and its interest in matters of class, gender, and ethnicity" (1). In her study of
literacy as social exchange, Maureen Hourigan covers these matters
and also issues of race and multiculturalism in the writing classroom. Peter McLaren casts a broad theoretical net in his discussion of critical literacy research and the postmodern turn: "Critical
literacy draws on the disciplines of Freirian/neo-Marxist, poststructuralist, social semiotic, reception theory, neopragmatic, de-
construction, critical hermeneutics, and other postmodernist perspectives" (319). To consolidate generally and simplistically, I think
it is fair to say that critical literacy researchers exploit the lenses
and methods that help illuminate the production and distribution
of ideology as it works to naturalize the interests of certain groups
and not others.

Although the frames of reference cut across a vast range of social concerns, according to Freire and Macedo there are shared values in studies of critical literacy. These include "solidarity, social
responsibility, creativity, discipline in the service of the common
good, vigilance, and critical spirit" (156). On a pedagogical level,
such values are mirrored in the tenets that guide the critical projects that have begun to appear more routinely in writing and communication classrooms. To paraphrase Wendy Morgan, the key tenets are as follows: that knowledge and truth are determined by
sociohistorical forces; that the subjectivities of individuals are multiply shaped within the ideological practices of a culture; that the
inequities constituted in cultural configurations are the result of
systematic efforts; and that social inequities can be surmounted if
their causes are pinpointed and understood (6–7). As the last tenet
suggests, critical literacy is predicated on hopeful expectations, not
the themes of nihilism and quietism so often associated with postmodern theory.

One provocation for critical literacy is traditional educational
theory, which propagates wider societal arrangements (Apple).

Joseph Kretovics cogently maintains that since the beginning of the twentieth century a technocratic rationality has governed educational discourses in ways that impede transformations in the interest of social justice. Within this framework, the knowledge and research that are considered to be legitimate must be portrayed in clear functional terms. The effect is a curriculum that not only fails to develop higher-order skills but also perpetuates the immoral conditions of social inequality. Yet, as Henry Giroux notes, "the purpose and meaning of schooling extend beyond the function of a museum safeguarding the treasures of cultural tradition or the needs of the corporate state for more literate workers" ("Literacy" 372). So one ambition of teachers interested in critical approaches is to inculcate an emancipatory tenor into conventional educational practices.

But critical literacy is also a response to the apolitical texture of social construction. In fact, as Ira Shor points out, "Specifying the political forces in any rhetorical setting is a key distinction of critical literacy, separating it from other writing-to-learn proponents and epistemic rhetoricians" (18). If Kenneth Bruffee and his supporters ushered social constructionism into the profession, which encouraged the profession to see the constitutive capacities of language and knowledge claims as social understandings arbitrated in specific historical and cultural contexts, their work was not really interested in gestures of control that regulate belief systems (Trimbur). Rather, they concentrated on consensus and the interpretive acts of negotiation that lead to normative values in communal situations. This focus, however, has been particularly problematic for proponents of critical literacy because they aspire to reveal shifting parameters of authority and authorized forms of repression. Social construction is certainly an important perspective, yet as Charlotte Thralls and Nancy Blyler warn, consensus can be "not so much an index of agreement as an exercise of power" (17).

Of course, as with any viewpoint, there are criticisms of critical literacy that should also be acknowledged. These criticisms call attention to a modernist reliance on rational argument to enact social change, language acts that ironically serve to solidify the categories and binaries that have contributed to the oppression of subordinated groups, and an inclination on the part of some to see critical literacy itself as immune to critique (W. Morgan; Jay and Graff). Furthermore, in "Why Doesn't This Feel Empowering? Working Through the Repressive Myths of Critical Pedagogy," Elizabeth Ellsworth has taken scholars to task for being too vague in their discussions of critical literacy. In this often-cited article, she reports on her review of the literature and concludes that it "consistently strip[s] discussions of classroom practices of historical context and political position" (92). It is judicious to question the abstract use of such code words as "critical," for (as Ellsworth contends) they can fail to both name ideological agendas and suggest concrete pedagogical programs. She therefore admonishes teachers to be more explicit about the politics and applications of critical literacy.

Given these criticisms, one responsible path is to define and illustrate a specific set of parameters that suggests the qualities of a critically literate student, a task I take up in the last section of the chapter. But this set of parameters can be introduced here with an example that begins to clarify the scope of a critical literacy of computers. Chapter 2 cited a qualitative study by McLaughlin, Osborne, and Smith that offered a taxonomy of reproachable conduct on Usenet, an enormous computer network that supports asynchronous conversations. This study catalogued standards that reflect broad expectations about effective participation in online communities. The conventions represented in the taxonomy are valuable because they help students avoid the types of offenses that could alienate them from professional interactions on the Internet. In this way, McLaughlin, Osborne, and Smith identified ritualized impulses that reinforce the status quo.

But such guidelines ignore crucial questions of power distribution and control, as Johndan Johnson-Eilola and I demonstrated in our study of an online forum conventionally defined as open, the listserv discussion list TECHWR-L (Johnson-Eilola and Selber). Many of the students, teachers, and practitioners on this list asserted that the forum was a free and open one devoted to all technical writing issues. We were not surprised to hear their egalitarian

claim, for researchers have long felt that technology somehow lib-
erates students to speak freely, outside age, ethnicity, gender, and
race constraints, as well as other status and physical appearance
markers that can keep individual voices from being heard (Faigley,
"Subverting"; Flores; Hiltz; Lanham; Cooper and Selfe). However,
as one can imagine, problems arose when the group tried to define what counts as an appropriate or inappropriate topic, especially in a field as fragmented as technical writing. In sum, what we
discovered was that silence, power moves related to ethos and professional rank, and other language-related mechanisms restricted
topics that transgressed conventional boundaries. That is, in most
instances, only those ideas aligning with the dominant perspectives were listened to, tolerated, or encouraged. Thus, in this particular asynchronous discussion space, it was acceptable to talk
about software, grammar and usage, and collaboration, for example,
yet threads on racism, sexism, affirmative action, drug testing, and
other weighty matters were thwarted because they questioned fundamental worldviews. We concluded that if the Internet is to do
more than replicate current structures, teachers and students must
look critically at not merely what we talk about and how we talk
about it but also at how it was that we reached these decisions in the
first place and if we might change them.

This study of asynchronous communication begins to delineate
the purview of a critical literacy that counterbalances functional approaches. It highlights the fact that there are power relations associated with the development and use of technology and that it can
be difficult to introduce positions that challenge utopian beliefs
in the liberating capacities of technology. So one area of critical literacy is alert to the mechanisms through which online activities are
standardized and controlled. As I will explain later, the other areas
have similar sorts of sociopolitical goals.

But the summary point I want to make now is that the framework for a critical literacy of computers comes from a multitude
of humanistic traditions. Paul Dombrowski has traced humanism
in both its classical and modern senses. "Broadly speaking," he
observes, "humanism is the emphasis of the human over the non-

human. It involves studies turned more toward humankind itself than toward the physical, non-human world, for example, toward literature or ethics" (4). When I invoke the term humanism, then, I am not referring to a liberal commitment to the individual as an autonomous agent or subject, one that, to quote Catherine Belsey, is a "free, unconstrained author of meaning and action, the origin of history" (*Subject* 8). Instead, I mean to marshal various humanistic traditions that have stressed such ideals as justice, equality, civic action, public service, and social responsibility. Although human-centered perspectives are not uncommon in certain branches of constructivism, their general objective is to help computer users become more comfortable and productive in functional terms. A critical literacy, in contrast, interrogates biases, power moves, and human implications.

## Computers as Cultural Artifacts

If a tool metaphor organizes the functional side of literacy, the trope students will encounter consistently in critical literacy projects is the artifact metaphor. How might this metaphor influence the ways students come to understand computer literacy? In what ways could it be generative? As this section indicates, the artifact metaphor encourages an attention to the non-neutral dimensions of computers and their non-neutral contexts. Although the Janus-faced tool metaphor has been appropriated for social as well as functional purposes, it does not emphasize the concerns of critical literacy. However, quite the opposite is true for the artifact metaphor, which sheds critical light on contexts of both production and use. In terms of production contexts, the artifact metaphor encourages an attention to the political, social, and even psychological assumptions embodied in computers as well as any unintended consequences of their designs. In terms of use contexts, it encourages an attention to the actions of computer users and the larger cultural forces that have an effect on them.

As cultural artifacts, computers are material products of human activity and agency. But they are more than just that. Computers instantiate the values of disciplines and institutions and individuals. Take hypertext, for example, which can assume a wide range of forms and be employed in support of radically different aims. In the online classroom, hypertext can automate the tasks of turning pages and accessing references—an approach that values traditional notions of textuality and intertextuality while providing students with quantitative improvements in terms of navigating efficiency and speed. But the same technology can also support a panoply of collaborative interactions, such as the negotiation of conflict that must often occur for students to avoid groupthink. In this case, hypertext provides a social space in which the processes of collaboration can be reexamined—an approach that values qualitative changes in social structures and interactions. What makes certain models of hypertext privileged, then, is not solely a function of technological possibility. Rather, as artifacts of a culture, hypertext applications are encouraged or discouraged by a variety of social forces. As John Street explains, "Technology is invested with meaning and expectations, and any account of its role in modern society must recognize the implications of this process. The effect of technology on the way we live is partly determined by the images, ideas, and practices which are incorporated in it" (16).

Historian of science Michael Mahoney has critiqued technology narratives that are blind to social forces. He indicates that computer programmers have viewed the subject of software creation as inherently mathematical, even though it is emblematic of disciplinary priorities and beliefs. A logical consequence is the sentiment that pedagogical problems can be solved entirely by quantification and computation—a belief that has its counterpart in literacy workers who devise software systems to teach students how to eliminate grammatical errors. In addition, a mathematized perspective is apt to view the computer as a neutral device, for its underlay of ones and zeros unambiguously yields rational results. However, as Mahoney argues, "Computers are artifacts, programs are artifacts, and models of the world created by programs are artifacts. Hence, any science about any of these must be a science of a world of our own making rather than of a world presented to us by nature." As I will argue, this constructed world includes not only computer-based environments but also the settings within which they are embedded in higher education.

Although the anthropological dimension of the artifact metaphor calls attention to the "ambivalent" character of technology (Feenberg), it also provides a basis for cultural critique. I am thinking specifically of a critical strategy discussed by George Marcus and Michael Fischer that ethnographers use to bring studies abroad to bear on domestic cultural issues: defamiliarization by epistemological critique. Marcus and Fischer argue that "The challenge of serious cultural criticism is to bring the insights gained on the periphery back to the center to raise havoc with our settled ways of thinking and conceptualization" (138). They narrate the work of four anthropologists—Clifford Geertz, David Schneider, Mary Douglas, and Marshall Sahlins—who shed light on biases in Western culture that contribute to utilitarian explanations of social life that are taken for granted. Douglas, for example, draws on observations in African societies and Great Britain to show that American conceptions of environmental risk are formulated in political contexts that highlight certain dangers and subordinate others. Marcus and Fischer discuss the methodological complications with projects of repatriation (e.g., the position of the researcher in self-critical studies), but they are also concerned about criticism that does not pose alternatives to the conditions being criticized.

For computer literacy, a critical strategy would be to seek oppositional discourses that defamiliarize commonsensical impressions of technology in educational settings. In chapter 1, I outlined several myths associated with computers that have become particularly powerful in the minds of teachers and university administrators. I indicated how computers have been envisioned as value-neutral devices that inevitably level the social and economic playing field, enhance instruction, and increase productivity. The master narrative of technological determinism binds progress with computers in such a compelling way that teachers are deterred from important questions of agency. Yet some teachers have objected to uncritical perspectives that define the computer as an autonomous agent advancing along a predetermined path. Peter Lyman, for instance, notes that "the computer chip and program are ultimately texts which may be criticized in the same manner as any other text, and which might be rewritten to reflect the values and social relations of other social groups" (7). Thus, computers can be interpreted as cultural artifacts ineluctably bound up in historical and social systems of production and use. Such an interpretation, however, depends upon an increasingly expanded sense of the scope of an artifact.

Before I unpack the artifact metaphor in more detail, I want to comment quickly (and incompletely) on the role of intention in the creation of technology. It is indeed a shameful fact that certain technologies have been designed in order to repress subaltern groups. Harley Shaiken reports on a machine shop that installed an override switch on an automatic turret punch press so that the company could send the symbolic message to workers that management was in control. Harry Braverman discusses automation practices in American manufacturing facilities that deskilled workers to the point where employer decisions could no longer be questioned. And Langdon Winner mentions a number of examples in which the designs of technologies have served purposes of domination: the design of college campuses to diffuse student demonstrations; the design of industrial plants to deter union activities; the design of overpasses to segregate people of color who ride city buses. These horrid examples—there are many others—remind teachers and students that on some level a suspicious posture is defensible, that all feelings of technological mistrust have not originated in conspiracy theories spun from mere paranoia.

Still, at least two other explanations (not excuses) for abusive designs are possible. First, a design can be socially inattentive. Prior to the 1970s, people with disabilities, for the most part, were not accommodated in the designs of such everyday technologies as buildings, buses, and plumbing fixtures, a reality that had the effect of excluding people with disabilities from active participation in public life, including educational activities. But, as Winner remarks, "It is safe to say that designs unsuited for the handicapped [*sic*] arose more from long-standing neglect than from anyone's active intention" (25). Second, a design can have unexpected consequences. Victoria Leto shows that, despite the efficiency and convenience of domestic technologies, home washers for clothes and dishes have had the unforeseen effect of severely regimenting the social spaces of women. Although the gendered nature of the division of labor actually gave women a common, supportive, social space away from men, the privatization of washing separated women from each other while continuing the gendered division of labor. A lesson for teachers and students, therefore, is that the efficacy of technological designs must be continuously evaluated, not just in the course of the development process but also in actual situations of use.

In what ways could the artifact metaphor assist the critical enterprise of defamiliarization, so that the interests that are always-already associated with computers can be detected? At the outset, it is useful to keep in mind that technologies can be deconstructed in psychological terms. That is, productive artifacts materialize certain intellectual assumptions about users and uses. John Carroll and Wendy Kellogg have spoken eloquently on this point. In their usability efforts in human-computer interaction (HCI), they observe that "HCI artifacts embody psychological claims in contexts of use: aspects of the interface engender psychological consequences and in this sense make claims about the user's behavior and experience" (8). To illustrate, Carroll and Kellogg analyze the assumptions embodied in an online tutorial for a text editor. As a reduced-function training environment, the tutorial allows students to make errors but blocks the technological consequences of those errors. At issue here are the claims of this instructional technique for user education. On the one hand, it seems reasonable enough to disable advanced features or command sequences that are illogical, because trying to recover from a serious error could derail a lesson for novices. On the other hand, error blocking prevents the free exploration of software, an operation that appeals to certain kinds of learners and that locates pedagogical control in the domain of learners (Wiedenbeck and Zila). In "Reconceiving Hypertext," Catherine

Smith argues that "Missing in most hypertext theory is acknowledgment that thinking is to some extent socially, culturally, and historically constructed and that thinkers, as a result, may differ in how they form ideas" (225). The creators of this particular tutorial recognized its biases, but all too often a process of reification occurs in which computers are encoded with psychological perspectives that come to be seen as natural.

If computers can embody psychological claims, their designs are also influenced by social forces. The basic functions in popular computer games, which are often violent and misogynistic (Cassell and Jenkins), unequivocally prove this point. But the imprint of social forces can be less apparent, especially to an unsuspecting user. Students and teachers may not recognize, for instance, that the architecture of computer networks and systems can reflect tacit assumptions about appropriate behavior in an educational institution. For example, in my courses I have used an application for asynchronous exchanges developed at Penn State that echoes distinct educational suppositions. The option for threaded discussion organizes messages by topic, user, and date and allows students to search for keywords, but only the teacher can initiate a topic. Similarly, the fishbowl option allows teachers to isolate the conversations of certain students, while the rest of the class voyeuristically looks on. In their research on the computerization of worklife, Rob Kling and Tom Jewett state that "artifacts of many kinds may not function well when their (implicit or explicit) social designs do not foster workable social systems" (276). I abandoned the application because it was not amenable to the less hierarchical forms of education to which I am committed.

But uses of computers are not preordained by their social and psychological designs. For example, at Penn State I have also scrutinized an application that teachers across the curriculum can use to assemble online quizzes. In an era in which computers pervade university settings in ostensibly positive ways, it is no accident that programs have proliferated to mechanize assessment activities, especially those that can be tedious or time consuming. The application integrates five question formats: multiple choice, true/false, short answer, check-all-that apply, and equation (an equation question includes a math equation that is solved by using a set of defined variables). Teachers create editable question banks from which they build online quizzes that can contain hints and feedback mechanisms; teachers who know HTML can insert graphics, audio, and video. Quizzes are automatically graded, and the program either saves the scores to a secure data file or sends them to the teacher in an e-mail attachment. Although the technology is impressive, I cannot find a sound pedagogical use for its intended purposes. As Brian Huot points out, "many belief systems that inform traditional notions about computers and assessment conflict with the social and contextual notions of language that support current practices in the teaching and study of writing" (232). However, I have exploited the technology in a way that subverts and expands its objectives: I use the question functions in order to assess my own instructional practices. For example, after a first assignment I typically prepare a questionnaire that queries students about the rhythms and expectations of the class. I have also taken spontaneous polls that help me gauge the interests of students. I "should" create quizzes with the program but instead produce formative course evaluations that are easily administered and automatically summarized.

That technologies can be so easily undermined suggests the limitations of an emphasis on tools. Artifacts as physical products must be studied, yet their social backdrop should not be overlooked. There is a cadre of researchers in computer-supported cooperative work that is interested in the arguments that surround interface design projects. Their thesis is that the fruits of such projects are not just "naked" artifacts, as Allan MacLean, Richard Young, and Thomas Moran have put it, but problem understandings that have been complexly reasoned out and explicitly represented. In recognition of the central role of discourse, "artifact-centered information spaces" (Reeves and Shipman) have emerged that unite design discussions and design tasks, two development processes that historically have evolved in a disjointed way. One of the more visible spaces was engineered by John Smith at the University of North Carolina at Chapel Hill. His Artifact-Based Collaboration

(ABC) system helps software developers merge their ideas and efforts to create a computer program. In software development, an artifact consists of concept papers, requirements, specifications, programs, diagrams, references, user manuals, and administrative reports (Smith and Smith). The ABC system manages the intertextual relations amid these documents and captures synchronous and asynchronous interactions as designers negotiate large structures of intricate ideas. Systems like ABC help collaborators capitalize on their collective intelligence, but they also dramatize the impact of group dynamics as well as a constraint of traditional institutional structures: Distributed hypermedia environments as open spaces for discussion and commentary can be antithetical to the logic of bureaucracies.

However, contexts of use deserve at least as much attention as contexts of design, for although some teachers have invented software to support the tasks of writers and communicators (see LeBlanc), the majority of teachers face the entanglements of curricular integration. Computers portray highly idealized versions of literate practice, not an account of how students actually experience or engage an artifact. In their meditation on the deficiencies of decontextualized approaches to human-computer interaction, Liam Bannon and Susanne Bodker ask the following question: "Can we put an artifact under the spotlight and discern its uses, never mind its design rationale? We think this is extremely problematic. For the artifact reveals itself to us fully only *in use*" (237). My micropolitical takeover of a computer program for assessment is proof of the sway pedagogical tactics can have over the manifestation of an artifact. But students can also contribute to the signification of technologies. In collaborative situations, for example, it is not unusual to find several students huddled around a "personal" computer, involved in interchanges that encourage them to share a mouse and keyboard. Such situated maneuvers confound standard utilization models to such an extent that some have started to rethink the view that computers should always be oriented toward single-person use. Hence, Saul Greenberg ("Designing") contends that, in schools, computers might be seen more productively as public artifacts because their treatment depends, at least in part, on how they fit within the ecology of an instructional space, which includes the preoccupations and practices of both students and teachers.

As Lucy Suchman argues, however rationally they are planned, purposeful actions are always carried out in the context of particular circumstances: "all activity, even the most analytic, is fundamentally concrete and embodied" (viii). That is why astute teachers carefully investigate—and participate in—computer-supported classrooms, in an effort to understand the materiality of online literacies. Yet I have a bone of contention even with certain contextual approaches. Classrooms as sites of situated action are nested in larger structures that rarely receive adequate consideration. But there are profound social, political, and economic factors within and without the academy that impinge upon instructional spaces in a direct way. I refer here to such factors as the privatization and commercialization of public universities, institutional retrenchment and reallocation, the rising cost of higher education, and shifts in student demographics and public expectations, not to mention power issues, race and gender matters, and merit and its rewards. Although broad challenges and trends in American higher education might appear to be the turf of university administrators, there are very real interdependencies and strains at the pedagogical level. For example, I recently created a distance education course that was steered heavily by circumstances extrinsic to the English department. Not only did a conservative university position on intellectual property influence the content I selected, but the instructional designer I worked with provided standardized templates that were difficult to resist because they leveraged a mature network of commercial and institutional resources. Mike Markel has commented eloquently on the fact that effective teachers of writing and communication are already prepared to be ideal distance educators. I certainly agree with this sentiment, but a wider collection of social forces must also be noticed and navigated.

Imagined in artifactual terms, computers can be defamiliarized as inherently cultural in both origin and consumption. Their affordances disclose psychological and social preferences crafted in interpretive communities in which competing perspectives eventually decompose to singularly approved designs. Yet, in practice, computers are seen and understood across dynamic settings in ways that reveal multiple and contradictory uses. So the artifact metaphor evokes a doubled set of situated involvements that mark out the literacy landscape of computer technologies. As Gayle Ormiston notes, "However it is construed, presented, or deliberated, technology today reflects the dreams, hopes, and fears and the fluctuating and variegated needs, objectives, and capabilities of those interested in it and those affected by it" (15–16). I would add that, in educational settings, those affected are not encouraged frequently enough to consider—in a systematic fashion—the conditions that construct perceptions of computers and their boundaries. Unlike the tool metaphor, the artifact metaphor projects students into the critical role of questioner. The challenge for teachers is to discover frameworks that cultivate that role.

## The Parameters of a Critical Approach

Thus far, I have cited a variety of researchers who have called for an educational system that prepares students to be social critics rather than indoctrinated consumers of material culture, with critique generally defined as the cultural study of power in situated uses of computers. Let me now turn to a set of parameters that suggests the qualities of a critically literate student (see table 3.1). My view is that students who are critically literate can work against the grain of conventional preoccupations and narratives, implicating design cultures, use contexts, institutional forces, and popular representations within the shape and direction of computer-based artifacts and activities.

One fruitful way in which to consider these parameters is through the familiar pedagogical apparatus of metadiscourse heuristics. Let me deal with heuristics first and metadiscourses second. From the Greek term *heuriskein,* meaning to discover or find, heuristics are problem-solving strategies that can guide students as they attempt to formulate possible responses to a writing or com-

## Table 3.1
Parameters of a Critical Approach to Computer Literacy

| Parameters | Qualities of a Critically Literate Student |
| --- | --- |
| Design Cultures | A critically literate student scrutinizes the dominant perspectives that shape computer design cultures and their artifacts. |
| Use Contexts | A critically literate student sees use contexts as an inseparable aspect of computers that helps to contextualize and constitute them. |
| Institutional Forces | A critically literate student understands the institutional forces that shape computer use. |
| Popular Representations | A critically literate student scrutinizes representations of computers in the public imagination. |

munication problem. As opposed to algorithmic approaches, which are precisely defined and structured, heuristic approaches provide a suggestive framework that can help students systematically probe the contingencies and dynamics of the author-to-readers intention structure, including the rhetorical situation. Whereas algorithmic approaches set down fixed rules for organizing an argument, for instance, heuristic approaches help students determine the most effective organizational pattern given the particulars and complexities of a specific communication situation. An example would be inventional schemes from classical rhetoric that involve common or special topics *(topoi)*. More contemporary examples of heuristics include the dramatistic pentad of act, scene, agent, agency, and purpose (Burke); the tagmemic perspectives of particle, wave, and field (Young, Becker, and Pike); and the more ideologically inflected schemes of social-process theorists whose approaches go beyond the textual and rhetorical level to the discursive level, encouraging students to interrogate more fully the character and function of institutions, subjectivities, cultural values, and social values (McComiskey). Heuristics like these have long been a staple of writing and communication instruction. In fact, Lester Faigley ("Competing") notes that some of the earliest researchers in composition studies, including Janet Emig, were motivated by an attention to heuristics in cognitive psychology. And while two of these early researchers, Janice Lauer and Ann Berthoff, engaged in a spirited debate over particular heuristic procedures, neither one questioned their overall efficacy as aids for student writers, only the disciplinary domains from which heuristics should be appropriated.

The types of heuristics I am especially interested in are those that provide a metadiscourse that can focus student attention in a decidedly politicized fashion. Such heuristics invite students to approach an artifact with inquiries about it that are different from the ones directly imagined by author-to-readers intention structures, making available an oppositional discourse that can be used to critique a dominant discourse, a factor that is crucial to any critical literacy program, as sociolinguist James Gee has indicated. Gee distinguishes between primary discourses, which are unconsciously acquired in familial settings, and secondary discourses, which are consciously learned in schools and other highly formalized institutions that regulate language use and behavior in ways that tend to maintain the social and political order. There is a distinct advantage for students whose primary discourses are well-matched to the secondary discourses they are being asked to develop and control. And when this situation goes unacknowledged—and it often does—harm can come to those who have acquired non-mainstream discourses.

But there is also a critical aspect to secondary discourses that can function more consciously as a form of power and liberation. Gee maintains that learned literacies can be liberating if they include metadiscourses that can be used to critique the ways in which other discourses "constitute us as persons and situate us in society (and thus liberating literacies can reconstitute and resituate us)" (153). For Gee, literacy is emancipatory when it encourages students to put multiple discourses in conversation with each other, that is, to critique one discourse with another, in order to develop critical analytical capacities. As he explains, "Meta-knowledge is power because it leads to the ability to manipulate, to analyze, to resist while advancing" (148). This metaknowledge consists of learned (versus acquired) insights into the ideology in dominant discourses. Such insights, according to Gee, can enable students to become more attuned to the "violent" aspects of literacy, as Elspeth Stuckey might put it, and as a consequence become more compassionate and sympathetic participants in the discourses that invariably shape the world around them.

There are various metadiscourse heuristics that can help students develop critical metaknowledge about a technological artifact and its social contexts. One can rather easily imagine investigative frameworks drawn from any number of useful theoretical locations, including feminist theory, critical race theory, cultural studies, science studies, postcolonial theory, postmodernism, disability studies, radical pedagogy, and the like. The heuristic I offer accommodates and illuminates the parameters for a critical approach to computer literacy that have been put forward here: design cultures, use contexts, institutional forces, and popular representations. It comes from the work of Bryan Pfaffenberger, who has theorized at least one way power can circulate in technological contexts. Although postmodernism is deeply suspicious of grand narratives that attempt to provide encompassing explanations, James Berlin makes the case for contingent metanarratives, for "heuristical" methods of proceeding that "provide connections while never determining in advance exactly what those connections will be" (*Rhetorics* 74). In this manner, Pfaffenberger offers a contingent metanarrative that can help students make some sense, however provisional and partial, of an enormously complex and complicated landscape: the politics of technology. His theory is not meant to be a universal or definitive explanation, only one plausible and informative account of the technological construction and reconstruction of political power.

Before explaining Pfaffenberger's theory and turning it toward the objective of preparing students to be critically literate, I should spell out more completely the pedagogical approach I am recommending. The computing infrastructure of a university affords ready access to the discourses that are connected to conventional technological practices in higher education, and these are the dominant discourses I ask students to interrogate via heuristics that provide oppositional metadiscourses. On the face of it, a computing infrastructure might not appear to be the most inspired choice. After all, it is a fairly obvious choice, as well as one that could seem less than imaginative if the scope of an infrastructure is defined primarily in technical terms. Although there is a good deal to consider when investigating the politics of hardware and software artifacts, this critical task can and should be taken to another level of sophistication and insight by broadening the investigatory scope to include the entire complex of artifacts, activities, and forces that constitute a technical system.

Theorists often encourage us to think of technologies as systems rather than things (Borgmann; Feenberg; Foucault; Winner). This encouragement stems from the realization that culture, politics, economics, and social institutions have all become inexorably intertwined with technology, producing an overdetermined milieu in which its directions, uses, and representations can potentially be shaped by a wide range of factors. Consider something as basic as a course Website. One could study its interface and undoubtedly produce an instructive political critique. However, in order to characterize the political dimensions in a more accurate and robust manner, additional questions would need to be posed and pursued: Is the site affiliated with any officially sanctioned initiatives? Are there institutional rules for site design? Are there systems in place to support site development, and if so, what is their influence over design tasks? What is the nature of the use context? Does work on the site count toward tenure and promotion, and if so, exactly how? Is there an institutional stance on the site as a piece of intellectual property? And so forth. The answers to these questions and others like them help to characterize technology as a systemic formation constituted by discourses embedded in social, political, historical, and material relations. This characterization departs in significant ways from mechanical and atomistic perspectives that depict technology as a discrete, self-directed, and highly neutral phenomenon.

Pfaffenberger presents a theoretical narrative that supplies one map of a political dynamic in technological systems composed of various discourses, actors, and contexts. There are three elements in this narrative: technological regularization, technological adjustment, and technological reconstitution. It begins on the production side of the equation with technological regularization, as designers invariably shape artifacts and activities in ways that affect the distribution of power in a social formation. But Pfaffenberger is quick to point out that the raw force of technical features is ultimately not enough to provoke the continued actions of users. In his words, "An artifact's political affordances are inherently susceptible to multiple interpretations. For this reason, an affordance cannot be sustained socially in the absence of symbolic discourse that regulates the interpretation" (284). Thus, the hegemonic key to compliance is not only an artifact embodied in political terms but also includes the myths and rituals that can naturalize—and reinforce—the concomitant ideologies. The narrative continues in the realm of computer users who if dissatisfied engage in various transformative activities that endeavor to alter the social contexts or features of technologies. Technological adjustment strategies attempt to make artifacts more tolerable to those whose identities have been adversely signified, while technological reconstitution strategies openly challenge established technical systems. Such strategies, if they are to be successful, must exploit the ambiguities inherent in technological regularization.

There are discernable power moves associated with each element in the narrative. These moves are characterized by an oppositional metadiscourse that is rather elaborate on the surface, but one that is well worth the intellectual investment for students because it holds much explanatory power. Let me briefly illustrate how the narrative works and introduce some of its critical metadiscourse. Pfaffenberger offers a typology of eleven regularization strategies that can be detected in, or clearly associated with, technological innovations (see table 3.2, which lists the strategies in his own words). These innovations, in the form of artifacts, activities, systems, or processes, fabricate sociotechnological contexts that are projected into everyday social worlds crucial to the achievement of constructed political aims. In other words, to achieve its intended purposes, a technology must be located in an environment that is sympathetic to its politics. The typology clarifies this reliance and provides a metadiscourse that students can use to identify biases, belief systems, and political blind spots.

Let me illustrate one of the regularization strategies listed in table 3.2. Polarization is a power move whereby "different versions of essentially the same artifact are created for no reason other than to reflect and to reinforce race, class, gender, or achievement categories" (Pfaffenberger 293). An example would be Girlhoo.com, a thematic search engine that arranges information in patterns that sustain social stereotypes. In structure and style it unabashedly imitates Yahoo, one of the more popular search services, but this apparent infringement of intellectual property is not an instance of polarization (I say apparent because it could be argued, weakly in my opinion, that Girlhoo is a critical commentary on the male-oriented structure of Yahoo). Rather, the issue is that the organized content tends to shore up essentialist notions of women. Feminist scholars warn about representations that totalize women as homogenous, unconflicted, or unified subjects (Flax). But the white, middle-class orientation of Girlhoo does just that, for its links sex-type social and intellectual activities in ways that cast women into largely traditional roles. Users of Girlhoo happen upon no shortage of pointers to sites about beauty, fashion, Prozac, relationships, breast implants, and the like. One of the more comprehensive site

### Table 3.2
The Power Moves Associated with Technological Regularization

| Stage | Power Moves |
|---|---|
| Technological Regularization | **Exclusion:** Access to the technology and its social context is denied to persons who fit into certain race, class, gender, or achievement categories. |
| | **Deflection:** The technology provides compensatory goods or services to people in an attempt to deflect attention away from what is really going on. |
| | **Differential Incorporation:** The technology is structured so that people of different social categories are incorporated into it in ways that reflect and attempt to reinforce their status. |
| | **Compartmentalization:** Access to the technology and its benefits is in principle open to all, but access is rigidly structured to keep some persons at arm's length. |
| | **Segregation:** Access to the technology and its benefits is in principle open to all, but it is so expensive or difficult to obtain that few can enjoy it. |
| | **Centralization:** Access to the technology and its benefits is in principle open to all, but the system is constructed so that users have little autonomy and so that significant decisions are reserved for central management. |

*Continued on the next page*

## Table 3.2 *Continued*

| Stage | Power Moves |
|---|---|
| Technological Regularization | **Standardization:** Access to the technology and its benefits is in principle open to all, but at the price of conformity to zealously maintained system standards and rules of procedure, which diminish local autonomy and marginalize local culture. |
| | **Polarization:** Different versions of essentially the same artifact are created for no reason other than to reflect and to reinforce race, class, gender, or achievement categories. |
| | **Marginalization:** Inferior versions of an artifact are expressly created for or distributed to persons within subordinate race, class, gender, or achievement categories. |
| | **Delegation:** A technical feature of an artifact is deliberately designed to make up for presumed moral deficiencies in its users and is actively projected into the social contexts of use. |
| | **Disavowal:** An artifact that is specifically developed for menial or poorly compensated occupations is actively avoided or rejected by those of higher status, thus reinforcing the status distinctions. |

areas focuses on the kitchen. It is true that more serious search engines can be found that cover different strands of feminism, careers in science, medical research, activist groups, and influential women in politics and history. However, regressive sites like Girlhoo, which are abundant, reflect and reinforce gendered perspectives that can be read as detrimental to women.

But computer users are not utterly defenseless in repressive situations. As Pfaffenberger explains, "it would be wrong to view even a highly successful regularization strategy as a total victory for its political promoters: Most regularization efforts fail to suppress redressive social processes" (297). "The nature of regularization," Pfaffenberger continues, "is that it creates areas of inconsistency, ambiguity, interpretive flexibility, and outright contradiction" (297). There are various redressive social processes that could be used to address the politics of Girlhoo. For example, a teacher might introduce this search engine as an artifact to be studied rather than as a tool to be used. Such a discursive maneuver resituates Girlhoo in metaphorical terms that open up valuable pedagogical spaces for critical reflection. Another tactic, this one more ambitious, would strive to equalize the stereotypes. Girlhoo includes a function that lets users recommend new items for its indices; thus, students could be encouraged to suggest, on a regular basis, sites that characterize women in more productive ways. The secret to the success of this operation would be the free-market trope that consumer preferences should drive the directions of the Internet.

Pfaffenberger organizes such potential user reactions into two categories: technological adjustment and technological reconstitution (see table 3.3, which lists the categories in his own words). Technological adjustment mobilizes either discursive or mechanical approaches in order to make artifacts more tolerable to those whose identities have been adversely signified. There are three possible moves in this area: countersignification, counterappropriation, and counterdelegation. These moves challenge technological regularization in that they attempt to neutralize the undesirable aspects of useful artifacts. Technological adjustment, however, is something of

## Table 3.3
The Power Moves Associated with Technological
Adjustment and Reconstitution

| Stage | Power Moves |
|---|---|
| Technological Adjustment | **Countersignification:** Computer users surreptitiously substitute cultural narratives that undermine or contradict the processes of technological regularization.<br><br>**Counterappropriation:** Computer users reinterpret dominant discourses in an attempt to alter patterns of technological access and control.<br><br>**Counterdelegation:** Computer users engage in micropolitical acts of modification that adapt technologies to users. |
| Technological Reconstitution | **Antisignification:** Computer users create counterartifacts that displace the politics of technological regularization.<br><br>**Reintegration:** Counterartifacts are co-opted and brought back into the controlled space of regularization. |

an indirect tactic because it does not openly challenge established technical systems. In contrast, technological reconstitution represents a more aggressive response, although one must be wary of re-integration efforts, conservative attempts to co-opt artifacts once they have been reconstituted. In a successful occurrence of technological reconstitution, computer users create counterartifacts that displace the politics of technological regularization. Technological reconstitution is produced by acts of antisignification, which either reverse or negate the dominant discourse. The categories of technological adjustment and technological reconstitution organize interpretive strategies of resistance and, in the process, provide a second metadiscourse, one that students can use to respond to the dominant discourses that have become associated with conventional technological practices.

Toward the end of his theory explication, Pfaffenberger is apprehensive about processes of "designification" in which technologies "become taken for granted, routine, and part of the natural attitude of everyday life" (309). Some argue persuasively that the present transition from print to computer-mediated communication provides a vantage point from which to reconsider commonsensical assumptions and practices (Joyce; Spender). That may be true, but for numberless students, computers have already become designified as neutral tools that are not subject to question except in the most obvious of circumstances, such as computer failure. For these students, metadiscourse heuristics can provide conceptual lenses with which to magnify and clarify the politics of technology. My approach is to use Pfaffenberger's theory as a metadiscourse heuristic, asking students to explore the ways in which power can circulate in the computing infrastructures on campus. The parameters for a critical approach to computer literacy guide this exploration down a rhetorically sensitive path. Which is to say that students are encouraged to see the computing infrastructures as constituted by at least four closely related—and often indistinguishable—contexts: design cultures, use contexts, institutional forces, and popular representations.

*Design Cultures*
The design cultures parameter refers to the practices and perspectives of the people who are responsible for designing and maintaining a computing infrastructure. These people include those who design hardware devices, local and wide-area networks, software programs, desktop configurations, physical spaces, policies and procedures, pedagogical activities, and more. Teachers of writing and

communication have been increasingly active designers and maintainers of many different aspects of computing infrastructures, and our own practices and perspectives should not be seen as immune to political critique. However, the dominant discourses do not come from English departments, not by any stretch of the most fertile imagination. They come from commercial software vendors, centers for academic computing, science and technology disciplines, and institutionalized computer literacy initiatives (like those critiqued in chapter 1) that concentrate on the workings of software programs and hardware devices. By and large, the dominant discourses can be characterized as well-intentioned but not particularly critical, especially when it comes to the effects and implications of design cultures.

Students have varying levels of access to these dominant discourses. The most immediate and direct way in is through the technological artifacts of a design culture, which reflect and instantiate its assumptions, attitudes, and values (this is not to say that design determines use, only that design encourages uses in certain directions that can be resisted by critically conscious individuals or altered by social forces). I realize that the most expedient path is not always the most instructive or interesting one. Indeed, analyzing an artifact apart from its design culture cannot illuminate that culture in the same way that a more triangulated approach can, one that, for example, also includes interviewing designers and studying the disciplinary discourses that influence their projects. Such approaches are certainly feasible in institutions that develop or modify software for student use or that are truly serious about participatory design practices that involve the university community. But the technological artifacts themselves can serve as a sufficient means of access because the other parameters of a critical approach to computer literacy cover use contexts, institutional forces, and popular representations, which also illuminate factors that can shape the political aspects of a computing infrastructure.

If students are asked to use Pfaffenberger's theory as a meta-discourse heuristic to explore the politics of design cultures, there are numerous and varied analyses of a computing infrastructure that could be produced. Although the analyses used throughout this section are my own, they model the kind of thinking teachers can expect from students who have been equipped with an education that enables them to work in critical ways. I have already presented one sample analysis that involves a gendered search engine (Girlhoo.com) and the regularization strategy of polarization. And there is no doubt that similar artifactual analyses could be done that focus on race, class, or achievement categories, all of which are visibly linked to issues of access.

In the United States, the gap between the haves and have-nots has widened significantly since the advent of personal computers; inevitably, access to computers still too often is limited among impoverished citizens. Consequently, studies of the digital divide consistently report that upper- and middle-class families tend to own up-to-date computers and subscribe to online services; wealthier school districts tend to have equipment and pedagogical support structures that are less available to poorer ones; schools in the suburbs tend to have more computers per student than their urban counterparts; and employees who are able to use computers tend to earn more than those in similar jobs who cannot (Ratan). On college campuses, there is a significant black-white technology gap that has been correlated with the economic conditions of academic institutions (Kreuzer), and women continue to be discouraged disproportionately by activities in computer-related disciplines that stress aggression, domination, and competition (Turkle and Papert). I am not suggesting that this troubling state of affairs has been brought about solely by the politics of design cultures, only that these politics are implicated with crucial issues of access, a fact that can help students focus their critical analyses of computing infrastructures.

But let me provide a second sample analysis. This one involves the regularization strategy of delegation and requires a teacher who is interested in the politics of pedagogy as a course subject matter. Delegation is a power move whereby a "technical feature of an artifact is deliberately designed to make up for presumed moral deficiencies in its users and is actively projected into the social contexts of use" (Pfaffenberger 293). To clear up the concept of delegation, Pfaffenberger discusses the feature on photocopy machines that resets the copy number to zero after a job has been run, so that subsequent users will not inadvertently make unwanted copies. The presumed moral deficiency is a lack of consideration for others. In the context of computers, a feature that attends to this flaw is the time-out mechanism for dial-in modem access, which disconnects users after a reasonable period of inactivity in order to allow others a chance to connect to the network. Additional safeguards that readily come to mind protect against intentional breaches of privacy and security. Examples of the unprincipled behavior I allude to here include disclosures of personal information to unauthorized individuals, network intrusions that corrupt intellectual work, and impersonations of one user by another, often with the intent to harass or distribute offensive materials. Users clearly value the design steps taken to ensure an adequate level of protection from such immoral, not to mention illegal, activities, even if the steps involve minor inconveniences. Nevertheless, there are examples of delegation that students and teachers may be less than sanguine about.

I personally struggle with surveillance tools in distance education that presume a lack of commitment to, and faith in, students. Plagiarism is a problem deeply rooted in higher education that should be contemplated, especially in view of the argument that plagiarism as it is conventionally understood relies on gendered metaphors of authorship that reinforce social prejudices (R. Howard). But the software environments involved in plagiarism cases can also encourage pedagogical styles based on control and fear. In popular platforms for the delivery of distance courses, teachers can monitor student actions in ways not possible in other contexts. The program I use, for example, tracks the number of times a lesson has been accessed and the average amount of time students spent on it. Moreover, for each individual student, it tracks access times, site hits, and the number of documents that have been opened and posted; the program then rank-orders the students based on this dubious data. I realize that, if contextualized, descriptive statistics such as these could be helpful to teachers, especially if the patterns suggest pedagogical improvements. Yet I also know that surveillance often substitutes for compassion, content knowledge, and engagement. In her ethnographies on the nature of computerized workplaces, Shoshana Zuboff studied the corrosive effects of modernization on employee behavior. One of the disturbing things she noticed is that, as computers monitor work activity in seemingly benign modes, human beings are measured in a real-time, non-stop fashion. That is, computers monitor not just the work, but the worker. Indeed, in the case of distance education, computers provide permanent time studies that not only collect data but also pace and discipline students.

What redressive social processes might be imagined in response to this situation? One example would be a counterdelegation move in support of actual adjustments, albeit modest ones, to the established technical system. These adjustments, as Pfaffenberger puts it, can "thwart a delegation strategy by disarming, muting, or otherwise suppressing the operation of a technical delegate" (303). "A technical delegate," Pfaffenberger explains, "is a technical feature that seeks to compensate for the moral deficiencies of users by technical means" (303). In other words, counterdelegation moves, which can involve a certain amount of technical expertise, are micropolitical acts of modification that adapt technologies to users. In my example, I questioned surveillance functions in distance education that presume a lack of commitment to, and faith in, students. Yet, in the application I use, students could easily thwart these functions. Indeed, my recommendation would be to use the course URL as a home page location, so that each time the Web browser is started, for whatever purpose—educational or personal—a site hit is automatically registered for the course; this default setting could be remapped weekly to register hits for individual lessons. On a discursive level, such a feat of counterdelegation finds support in the Orwellian narrative that users are dehumanized when they are programmed into conformity to the logic of computer systems.

Search engines and distance education environments are just two aspects of a computing infrastructure that can illuminate the politics of design cultures. Other aspects should be somewhat self-evident if one considers, for example, the design responsibilities that have been assigned to a center for academic computing. But the distance education sample analysis is an especially interesting one because it requires teachers to amplify the politics of pedagogy. Students do not typically have access to tracking functions and tracking data, which exist in most distance education environments in one form or another. As a matter of fact, many students do not even realize that their educational activities are being monitored by the system. So in order to critically analyze these surveillance measures students must be alerted to them as well as granted access to them, a process that requires teachers to share certain online privileges. This gesture of solidarity shows students that teachers themselves can and should be critical of the very artifacts they employ.

*Use Contexts*

The use context parameter refers to the more immediate environments that help to situate and constitute a computing infrastructure, such as courses, computer classroom spaces, and curricular requirements. Although a design culture and its non-neutral artifacts make up one influential context, this is hardly the only context that determines how computing infrastructures get developed and used on university campuses. In a very real sense, then, a computing infrastructure encompasses a much larger territory, one infrequently investigated by teachers of writing and communication. Patricia Sullivan and James Porter critique a set of essays in computers and composition that they consider to be driven too theoretically by decontexualized research practices. One of these essays is a prominent article on the politics of computer interfaces by Cynthia Selfe and Richard Selfe. Sullivan and Porter question their definition of the interface as only the "visual and physical features of the computer," arguing instead that "it's hard to make judgments about the hegemony of the technology itself (as formalized, abstracted system) without examining the situated interactions between technology and users" (135). In asserting that users must often adopt the values of interface designers who are overwhelmingly white, middle-class, and male, the worry here is that Selfe and Selfe have attributed too much agency to the computing infrastructure. That is, its politics tend to override all other forces and factors.

A similar kind of critique was launched by Clay Spinuzzi, who argues that inquiry into technological artifacts routinely "bleaches out the very things that make us human: culture, society, history, interpretation" (42). Spinuzzi conducted a study of four decades worth of writing and communication activities surrounding a traffic accident location and analysis system at the Iowa Department of Transportation. Drawing on constructivist and genre theory, he shows how uses of this particular system were governed not only by its built-in features but also by a dynamic activity network that included various actors, communities, noncomputer tools, and objectives. Particularly fascinating is his discussion of how users interacted with the system in ways that were unintended by its designers. Thus, Spinuzzi foregrounds a matrix of cultural-historical forces that influenced the direction and appropriation of a technological artifact in one nonacademic site.

But what about academic sites? How might use contexts be characterized in terms that are meaningful to writing and communication teachers? One example comes from a study I conducted of the forces that shape how hypertext gets treated in technical writing programs (Selber). Although hypertext has become a standard component of computing infrastructures, as might be expected, its purposes and instantiations diverge widely across specific settings. In the seven sites I studied, hypertext was variously influenced by instructional objectives, the roles teachers assumed in classroom settings, the perspectives that informed pedagogical practices, other classroom materials, the types of academic departments that housed the programs, and the curricular requirements of the programs and their methodological and theoretical perspectives. Although such influences have rarely been articulated as an aspect of computing infrastructures, they in fact help to mediate interactions between users and computers in ways that are significant.

Other characterizations could be offered, but the point is that traditional descriptions of computing infrastructures often fail to represent contexts of use. I suspect this has something to do with the prevailing impulse to define technology from an instrument-centered perspective, which encourages a focus on designing artifacts to solve educational problems, without attention to the social forces that affect (and are affected by) technological matters. However, as Carolyn Marvin reminds us in her historical study of electric communication in the late nineteenth century, technologies "are not fixed natural objects; they have no natural edges. They are constructed complexes of habits, beliefs, and procedures embedded in elaborate cultural codes of communication" (8). Thus, computing infrastructures comprise much more than design cultures and their necessarily political artifacts. Computing infrastructures are always-already part of a much larger ecology that involves a variety of socially constituted systems, all of which interact in dynamic and often unpredictable ways to construct an expanded infrastructure shaping possible instructional futures.

In use contexts, the dominant discourses associated with computer policies, computer classroom designs, and curricular requirements should be easily accessible to students. Although there are other discourses that could be examined, these areas should serve as productive sites for critical investigation because their discourses are public and affect student life on a daily basis. In fact, the three examples offered here represent actual situations in which contexts of use contributed to a heightened sense of marginalization among different constituencies in an academic community. The regularization strategy in operation is differential incorporation, whereby a "technology is structured so that people of different social categories are incorporated into it in ways that reflect and attempt to reinforce their status" (Pfaffenberger 292).

The first situation occurred several years ago and concerned the amount of server space allocated to students, staff, and faculty members. By default, all students and staff were given just two megabytes of space for their Websites, while faculty were supplied with three times as many megabytes. Although additional server space was available to students, they were charged for it unless a faculty member was prepared to underwrite a multimedia project that was educational in scope. But the twist is that student accounts remained active for six months after graduation; in contrast, the accounts of faculty and staff were closed upon termination of employment. Thus, the clear message was that computer users were extended professional courtesies only when those users were in a position to contribute to the institution. The second situation involved a paraplegic student in one of my courses whose needs were not accommodated by the computer classrooms in which English instructors taught. The university was committed to the assistance of persons with disabilities—a pledge required under federal nondiscrimination laws—and technical support and equipment were available but only in specialized labs that could not be reserved for regular class sessions. So each period this student was reminded of her second-class citizenship, as she contended with an already atypical instructional setup (a crowded computer classroom) without the benefit of a raised table for her wheelchair, an oversized monitor, or a document holder to position papers upright at a workable angle. The third situation occurred in the context of academic advising activities. For years I encouraged students to enroll in upper-division courses on the design of computer-based instructional systems, to help them prepare for jobs as practitioners of technical writing. Yet such courses often had math prerequisites that precluded the enrollment of English majors, even though the courses did not draw on math in a central way. The prerequisites, in essence, served as social filters that established an arbitrary relationship between calculus and the design of human-computer interfaces. Philip Davis and Reuben Hersh noticed a similar situation in MBA programs: Calculus is not used extensively by business persons, executives, or entrepreneurs, but business schools often have a calculus requirement because it boosts prestige and cuts down on the number of applicants. So in each of these examples—policies on server space, computer classroom designs, and prerequisites for computer-oriented classes—the resources of an institution gravitated in the direction of power and privilege.

As a responsive move, countersignification suggests redressive social processes that can be used to address the regularization strategy of differential incorporation. In this move, the focus for students and teachers is on the dominant discourses that help to engender the politics instantiated in computers by design cultures. Users, in acts of countersignification, surreptitiously substitute cultural narratives that undermine or contradict the processes of technological regularization. This discourse substitution resituates artifacts in networks of social relations that elevate the status of those individuals or practices that have been diminished. According to Pfaffenberger, "Countersignification gives people a way to live within the system without suffering unhealthy losses of self-esteem. In this sense, it is a form of accommodation to regularization" (301). To clarify, it is a form of accommodation in that users work in oppositional ways within an existing infrastructure as opposed to creating or seeking out an alternative infrastructure. In my illustration of differential incorporation, I used three examples to demonstrate that use contexts can structure technologies so that people of different social categories are incorporated into them in ways that reflect and attempt to reinforce their status. Yet, in each of these instances, interpretations could be generated through problem-posing approaches to rearticulate the stigmatized perspectives of users.

In the first example, the unequal distribution of server space might be construed not in the context of instructional design and policy, where students are often made to feel inferior, but in the coarse realities of capital campaigns in which universities must leverage technological resources in order to establish financial support. Such an intellectual exchange can be accomplished if students are encouraged to see educational institutions as demystified businesses, something that is not that much of a stretch for students for several different reasons, including the fact that education has been too often conceived of as a goal-oriented business transaction. How are computing infrastructures funded on a campus? Are there different levels of access to them that result, at least in part, from the economic models in place? In what ways does technology relate to fundraising efforts? (And just why do so many universities now provide students with free e-mail for life?) Such problem-posing questions take into account the economic contexts of education, asking how student subjectivity is constructed by the dominant discourses associated with technological regularization. In the second example, students with disabilities can be made to feel inadequate because their personal situations do not accommodate standardized technical designs, or, in contrast, an emphasis can be placed on attitudes toward disabled people and the injustices perpetuated through ignorance and insensitivity. In my course, this emphasis emerged from an atmosphere of courage fostered by a paraplegic student who not only challenged normative assumptions about computing infrastructures but also dispelled widespread misconceptions about the disabled. The problem-posing approach involved our enthusiasm as a class about hearing her stories of discrimination and using them as the basis for an unplanned project on the politics of adaptive computing on campus. In the third example, arbitrary prerequisites for computer classes could be parsed as yet another instance of institutional practices that stratify disciplines in terms of power, resources, and status. Despite persuasive arguments in English studies that posit the relevance of a liberal education in a digital age, students are perpetually subjected to negative stereotypes that construct the humanities as soft ("feminine") subjects and the sciences as hard ("masculine") ones. But these stereotypes, which demoralize students, could be denaturalized with discourses that foreground stratification systems and the social processes by which inequalities are produced, legitimated, and maintained in university settings. What contributes to the establishment and perpetuation of disciplinary pecking orders? Why might certain school subjects be considered to be gendered? How are curricula and their prerequisites established on a campus? Such problem-posing questions take into account the hierarchical character of educational sites, asking how student subjectivity is constructed by the dominant discourses associated with technological regularization. Although there are other strategies of technological adjustment, countersignification practices should bear fruit because they make the most of the constitutive powers of language.

Like design cultures, use contexts contain dominant discourses that influence the activities associated with using a computing infrastructure. But a difference is that teachers and students can have much more control over use contexts, even in university-operated facilities, because there is a greater range of possibilities for micro-political action. The challenge is to position the dominant discourses of use contexts as an important area of scrutiny in computer literacy projects. Computer policies, computer classroom designs, and cur-ricular requirements are just three areas that can bring these dis-courses to critical light. But such areas are particularly meaningful in that most students have had to deal with them over and over again. Although familiarity can make it difficult to see political as-pects, familiarity coupled with metadiscourse heuristics can allow students to more fully imagine the political realities of a use context and possible responses to them.

### Institutional Forces

If the parameter of use contexts refers to the more immediate envi-ronments that help to situate and constitute a computing infrastruc-ture, the parameter of institutional forces refers to the less immedi-ate factors that still have roots in university settings, such as those related to centralized resources, tenure and promotion policies, and academic-corporate alliances. This less-more distinction can be rather fuzzy at times, in large part because institutional forces often have a measurable impact on use contexts. Moreover, although I tend to concentrate on those things operating from "above" the de-partment level, there are plenty of examples that confound this di-vision. For instance, many faculty consider tenure and promotion to be institutionally driven processes, yet needless to say a department and its personnel are crucial to any specific case. But the point is that there are larger forces that impinge upon computing infrastruc-tures in a direct and immediate fashion, and critically literate stu-dents should be aware of them.

Although Pfaffenberger discusses centralization and standardi-zation as regularization strategies, they can provide insight into the nature of institutional forces, which do not always have nega-tive consequences but should be watched closely if people are to understand the issues. Let me deal with centralization first and standardization second. Will computers serve to centralize control or redistribute power in productive ways? This question is not new, yet it persists because there is so much at stake in the answer. And the answer depends on who you ask and on the circumstances under which computers are used. To be sure, ample evidence exists to substantiate either outlook, sometimes even in the same context. For example, Internet applications legitimize the need for academic computer centers that can manage individualistic resources for different kinds of departments with diverse goals and constituencies. Hypermedia programs encourage users to navigate delimited databases in an idiosyncratic fashion. And peer-reviewed journals provide online forums in which readers can publish unmoderated commentaries on officially sanctioned discourses. In each of these instances, there are elements of centralization and decentralization that are in tension with each other.

In 1980, Herbert Simon discussed the consequences of computers for centralization and decentralization in organizations. He noted the inclination to characterize centralization pejoratively and decentralization positively and cautioned against this binary opposition. Centralization, Simon argued, is commonly equated with bureaucracy or authoritarianism while decentralization is equated with autonomy, self-determination, or self-actualization. But the truth of the matter is that certain functions of centralization can be helpful. At Penn State, for example, the computer classrooms are maintained by central administrators who seek organized input from academic units on the pedagogical directions that should be taken. The challenge for the English department is to capitalize on the economies of scale in ways that enable us to protect our principal interests. This involves priorities and a series of calculated tradeoffs, such as working with a computing infrastructure that is not always perfectly tailored to meet the needs of writing and communication courses. However, I would prefer to cope with an imperfect situation if its resolution requires a faculty effort that is disproportionate to the payoff. To put it another way, on occasion it makes more sense to draw on institutionalized resources and structures than to expend the time and energy required to create better alternatives.

Still, centralization practices often consolidate control away from those who are supposed to be empowered by computers, and this consolidation becomes all the more problematic when such practices crisscross institutional levels. The classic struggle is with a computer center that attempts to hold sway over individual departments. I have witnessed situations in which teachers were not permitted to install registered shareware programs because autocratic procedures of operation defined the job of configuring computing infrastructures as the territory of computer technicians. But I have also watched in astonishment as teachers who claim to be radical educators made unilateral decisions about departmental software programs, controlled the distribution of student e-mail messages, and reined in character privileges in MOO spaces. Because the centralization of power can be furthered with computers, teachers and students should be on the lookout for conduct that is antithetical to the goal of equal access to technological infrastructures that have been designed and managed in a participatory manner.

Like centralization, the standardization of computing infrastructures can be advantageous to students and teachers (in fact, the Internet works precisely because of standardized protocols). Imagine an educational institution in which no standards exist for the exchange of digital information, or the more likely scenario of multiple standards that have not been reconciled. In either case, it could be laborious, if not impossible, simply to share a data file or pass a message or collaborate online in other ways; moreover, users would have to master divergent systems in order to be productive. In addition, having a wide variety of systems increases costs and requires nimble technical personnel who can solve an array of quirky interoperational puzzles. Although any one of these headaches might compel a user to plead for standardization, there can be downsides to this measure that should not go unnoticed. In fact, there are cogent reasons for writing and communication teachers to be involved in the process of standards creation.

Lin Brown outlined the difficulties of standardizing computing infrastructures for large-scale institutions like educational institutions. These difficulties include a shaky foundation of research upon which to base standards decisions, the politics of standards creation, and the potential for standards to stifle innovation. Brown addressed computer engineers, but her concerns are salient in the context of access. As to research upon which to base standards decisions, researchers have surely just started to understand computers as a location for literacy education, one that is difficult to describe because rapid technological change frustrates both longitudinal studies and generalized conclusions. For this reason, teachers should push for adaptable institutional standards until more durable observations have been amassed that account for the disparate literacy experiences of students. The politics of standards creation concerns the potential for conflicts of interest. Standards should typically be developed in interdisciplinary committees in which the intellectual commitments of English departments are openly represented, not by omnipotent technical faculty who have direct ties to private enterprises. Although this sounds utterly reasonable, institutional standards can evolve out of exclusive academic-corporate alliances, such as technology transfer projects that incubate specialized applications. Finally, the tension between standards and innovation should not be ignored. If software controls how computers operate, it also, as journalists Jim Nesbitt and Jim Barnett report, "channels the way people think, write and do work in ways that stifle creativity and groundbreaking thought" (par. 3). The argument these journalists offer is that a singular machine setup limits the imagination because alternative perspectives are not represented. That is why some teachers in standardized situations have developed redressive social processes to help students arrive at writing and communication practices that are genuinely meaningful. One of my own strategies is to standardize document specifications, particularly file formats (output), but not process approaches. As a result, students can conveniently share work that has been created in individual ways.

If students are asked to use Pfaffenberger's theory as a metadiscourse heuristic to explore the politics of institutional forces, they will undoubtedly discover dominant discourses that shape the computing infrastructures on campus. Indeed, my students have pointed out a clever regularization strategy (deflection) in which a campuswide technology program "provides compensatory goods and services to people in an attempt to deflect attention away from what is really going on" (Pfaffenberger 292). The Penn State–Microsoft Program, which in various configurations partners Microsoft with an enormous number of educational institutions, provides students and departments at Penn State with brand-new software that they can use freely for academic purposes. To participate, students can initiate contact with the Microcomputer Center on campus in order to obtain the software once the university establishes their eligibility (students are eligible if they are continuously enrolled Penn State students who own a computer and who have paid all tuition and other charges, plus an Information Technology Fee of $130 per semester for network use, lab use, and extensive technical support). Students either download the software from a secure server or borrow installable CDs from a lending library on campus. If a student has a Windows-based computer, for example, the software includes the latest version of the Windows operating system; the latest version of Office Pro, which contains Excel (spreadsheet), Word (word processor), PowerPoint (presentation), Publisher (desktop publishing), Access (database), Outlook (e-mail and information management), and Small Business Tools (business and customer management); the latest version of Visual Studio Professional, which contains a suite of development applications (e.g., Visual C++, Visual FoxPro, Visual InterDev); and the latest version of FrontPage, for HTML development. The upside of the Penn State–Microsoft Program is incontrovertible: at educational resale costs, the free software still amounts to a windfall of well over $500; teachers can make reasonably safe assumptions about software access on and off university grounds; and extensive tutorials and workshops have been built up with centralized resources to educate and support students.

However, campuswide enthusiasm has masked potentially dangerous dimensions of the program. From one point of view, it is nothing but an abundantly fertile seedbed that Microsoft has planted to grow its installed consumer base. But in fact, as Jonathan Sterne notes, teachers can unwittingly contribute to the success of deflection strategies. He argues that

> Instead of carrying a neutral valence or even a positive one, the very idea of computer literacy is conflicted at its core: while educators clearly intended computer literacy as the ability to control machines, the language of literacy can easily degenerate into the project of creating consumer populations for communication technologies. (192)

This train of thought might resonate with distance education students who are excluded from the program, I suspect, because they are typically profiled as already networked and unusually motivated. Furthermore, the program begins to erode the oversight teachers should have in instructional settings. If Microsoft systems are used to manage administrative data at Penn State, they have also become the default selection in pedagogical undertakings. But, as Stephen Doheny-Farina has argued, users—not employers or technicians—should define their own relationships to computing infrastructures. He is worried about privacy rights, yet other issues are also at stake. I admit that, if consulted, in all likelihood I would recommend Microsoft Office as a productive suite of applications for students in writing and communication courses, although FrontPage as a Web development environment can be astonishingly cryptic and unfriendly to non-Microsoft Web browsers. Nevertheless, the point is that teachers who have expertise useful to the critical evaluation of literacy technologies should not be expected to simply adapt to whatever political deals have been struck by the power structures of increasingly corporate universities. To some extent, the Penn State–Microsoft Program has been a real boon, but it abates reasonable critique of the ongoing commodification of higher education (as well as critical comparisons between Microsoft and non-Microsoft software programs created for similar purposes).

In response, counterappropriation provides students and teachers with redressive social processes that can be used to address the regularization strategy of deflection. If countersignification substitutes discursive contexts, counterappropriation reinterprets dominant discourses in an attempt to alter patterns of technological access and control. How might such an effort develop? Pfaffenberger offers an example by recalling the cultural history of aviation. Early popular images characterized flight as a fundamentally masculine endeavor in which chivalrous pilots took innumerable (and interesting) personal risks. Needless to say, such a perilous representation did not instill confidence when air transport became available to the general public, a fact exploited by female pilots who were eager to shed their gendered roles. In a move of counterappropriation, the airline industry welcomed traditional feminine stereotypes that could convince the masses that flying was neither difficult nor dangerous. However, as Pfaffenberger points out, counterappropriation often "rejects only some of the negative status implications of regularization. It accepts others to the extent that properly reinterpreted, they can legitimate access to artifacts" (302). That is, while feminine stereotypes enabled female pilots to have access to airplanes, such stereotypes paradoxically limited their professional opportunities.

Not surprisingly, the cultural history of computers exhibits parallel patterns of counterappropriation. As computers emerged out of specialized research sites, highly scientific and technical images were not amenable to the establishment of computers as mundane artifacts that could be centralized and standardized in institutional settings. Thus, the computer industry acknowledged and even encouraged representations that announced computers as usable machines that could be mastered by ordinary people. The tool metaphor helps teachers become involved because it constructs computers in ways that highlight instructional philosophies and activities. But this metaphor also restricts teachers because its neutral dimensions insist that teachers do not need to know about the design issues associated with computing infrastructures, which are considered to be the domain of impartial technologists. This situation presents many questions for students to reflect on: Who controls the computing infrastructures in an educational institution? In what ways do academic-corporate alliances contribute to patterns of centralization and standardization? And who really profits from these patterns? In the context of counterappropriation, such problem-posing questions invite students to consider dominant institutional discourses and how they might be reinterpreted in order to alter patterns of technological access and control. In the case of the Penn State–Microsoft Program, one option would be to reinterpret the design of computing infrastructures as a pedagogical rather than technical task, one that includes student perspectives. Although the early mythos of academic computing presented infrastructure design as an inherently technical activity, this construction has slowly begun to give way to institutional calls for teacher participation. The objective for teachers is to exploit these calls in ways that help to create a new mythos which expresses a connection between infrastructure designs, pedagogical actions, and institutional forces.

As both concepts and practices, centralization and standardization can lead students toward an increased awareness of the politics of institutional forces. Academic-corporate alliances are convenient sites within which students can explore such forces via critical metadiscourse heuristics, although centralization and standardization should be considered to be potential starting points and not the only choices. There are certainly other choices that can shed light on the institutional forces that affect computing infrastructures and user access to them. For example, with some success I have asked students to investigate the working conditions of part-time and non–tenure-track instructors who are often the recipients of outdated computer equipment and who are often prioritized toward the bottom of rank-ordered lists for maintenance and pedagogical support. Generally speaking, students are surprised to find out that there are huge differences in status among their teachers and that certain groups of teachers can have even less access to computers than students do. So status is another avenue into the realm of institutional politics. Still other avenues are suggested by the additional power moves associated with technological regularization.

*Popular Representations*

This parameter refers to representations in the public imagination that contribute on some level to the ways in which computing infrastructures get constructed and employed. By representations I of course mean those images, narratives, and tropes that have insinuated their way into our collective subconscious, usually through the mass media. Although attitudes toward computer technologies can be ambivalent and complex, the popular representations that have been woven into the fabric of Western culture play no small part in helping to establish and define the dominant discourses that prevail in university settings. This is hardly news to those teachers who ask their students to critically analyze the often unhealthy and unrealistic ideas fed to them through the diet of popular culture messages. Still, some of these messages can be rather subtle and do not always produce easily recognized impacts on computing infrastructures. So let me provide an example to clarify the content and scope of this parameter.

In the months both before and after the first copies of Windows 95, Windows 2000, and Windows XP were released, Microsoft and its major operating systems received an enormous amount of media attention. In fact, few events associated with the computer industry have been so ambitiously covered in evening news reports and weekly magazines, not to mention the energetic conversations on the Internet among educators and academic administrators relying in central ways on computer technologies to support their work. At least two dominant topics emerged from these different conversations. The first one related to technical issues and included the following kinds of concerns: Is the new operating system sufficiently stable? If so, should I adopt it? What are the benefits? Is the new operating system compatible with my current software programs, or will I need to purchase new programs to take advantage of its features? If I use the new operating system, can I still exchange files and collaborate easily with people running an older operating system? These concerns, of course, are extremely critical in any work environment: Even a minor upgrade in a single software application, let alone a major upgrade in operating systems reported to contain some millions of lines of computer code, can wreak havoc on well-established tasks and procedures, creating more problems than improvements for computer users. In addition, when Windows 95 was released it was important to consider the mechanics of an operating system claiming to support true 32-bit architecture, particularly for those teachers interested in multi-media development.

The second topic that emerged related to business ethics and the law. In this case, the questions revolved around antitrust issues: Is Microsoft too big? Does it have a monopoly on the operating system market for personal computers? Is Microsoft engaged in anti-competitive practices? If so, what should the government do about it? And, in terms of government actions, what is in the best interest of the public? These thorny questions deserve attention—protecting free market competition is one partial way to encourage technological innovation in the computer industry. Moreover, with the vast majority of computers today running Microsoft operating systems (some estimate that nine out of ten personal computers use a version of Windows), it is important to protect what little diversity exists in how human-computer interactions get represented in on-line environments. Indeed, because computer users are an increasingly diverse group in both intellectual and cultural terms, software should support different ways of knowing and learning.

These two areas—technical and ethical—were debated and discussed in great detail in the popular media, as they should have been. The people selling and supporting the updated operating systems touted their new features and the ways these features might make computer users more productive, while those taking more critical positions scrutinized the business practices of Microsoft, both in general and in terms of how Microsoft brought these particular products to the marketplace. From an educational perspective, however, noticeably absent from the conversations about how Windows operating systems would revolutionize teaching, learning, working, and knowing (no one ever accused Bill Gates of being unambitious) were considerations of the larger forces and factors that might make such a revolution possible. Even among most critical participants in the discussion, for example, there was little to no mention of the cultural and pedagogical assumptions informing the software, of the challenges in creating professional and institutional environments that encourage teachers to move their classes online, of the difficulties in devising computer-based course assignments that meet the instructional goals of educational programs, of the literacies that online environments tend to privilege, or of the results of actual online learning experiences. For all the talk of bits and bytes and unfair business tactics, a number of really tough questions were ignored, leaving the public and the profession with a distorted view of what is required in human terms if computers are going to productively support everyday teaching and learning activities.

The point of this example is that the discussions surrounding the release of major Windows operating systems rehearse almost exactly the same discourse, one that encourages users to think that computer technologies—all on their own—can bring about meaningful educational change. This common progress narrative typifies the sorts of popular representations that have been consistently interpreted in Western societies as the gospel truth. There is no shortage of popular representations that attribute to computers an impressive array of essential causal powers, nor is there much of a sustained effort in educational settings to paint a more complicated picture for students. However, what is particularly noteworthy about this example is the subtle way it works. The focus on anti-trust law is meant to bring a critical perspective to the situation, serving as a corrective to functional discussions that concentrate on technical arguments and explanations. This is not a problem in and of itself, but such a focus can serve a kind of metonymic function by which the whole complex of critical issues comes to be represented exclusively by certain narrow aspects of it. Which is to say that the dominant discourse effectively defines away the more intractable issues, building the meaning of the whole from the perception of a particular part. This is a dangerous (if prevalent) ideological condition because it occludes the social and pedagogical dimensions of computing infrastructures.

To get to the heart of the matter, students should be asked to reflect on the popular representations that are implicated with technological regularization. Issues of access can provide an effective gateway because so many representations construct computing infrastructures as intrinsically democratic spaces that will most assuredly bring about positive social change, especially for those segments of the population that have been historically disenfranchised. Although access narratives have foregrounded the initial obstacles to capital equipment acquisition and, to a lesser extent, the open-ended costs of periodic upgrades and repairs, certain regularization strategies remind students that technological access can be successfully restricted in a number of less obvious ways. The regularization strategy considered here is segregation, whereby "access to the technology and its benefits is in principle open to all, but it is so expensive or difficult to obtain in social terms that few can enjoy it" (Pfaffenberger 292).

Decades ago, Intel chairman Gordon Moore accurately predicted the exponential growth in computer power that users prize today. According to Moore's Law, the computational power of a chip doubles every eighteen to twenty-four months, which is to say that the standard university computer now contains a microprocessor that can undoubtedly handle the usual work of students and teachers in writing and communication courses. This multiplication of capacity has been accompanied by a steady decrease in the cost of hardware and software, a rhythm that signals an end to prohibitive computer prices. Media commentators and others point to these parallel trends as evidence that universal access will soon be achieved, that it is only a matter of time before the public as a whole can profit equally from computers. But the flaw in this narrative is that the social requirements for access have not been factored in, and these can be costly or hard to secure or both. Indeed, it is both expensive and difficult, for example, to provide access to meaningful educational opportunities and to people who understand how to use computers effectively.

This fact can be driven home if teachers ask their students to consider the dominant approach to systems analysis and possible responses to it. On university campuses, one important responsibility of a systems analyst is to recommend technological infrastructures that are suitable for students and teachers. As Rob Kling notes in his research on computerization, the dominant approach is inspired by "discrete-entity" narratives (369) in which an emphasis is placed on the development of technical relationships. In these narratives—examples of which I ask students to identify in popular culture messages, a task that is surprisingly easy to complete—computer resources are represented as individual pieces of equipment, applications, or techniques that can be seamlessly integrated into the ways we live and work. The unstated assumption is that computers, which are considered to be value-neutral devices, can be understood independently of larger social structures and forces. When Speaker of the House Newt Gingrich quipped that a tax credit for laptop computers should be given to the poorest of Americans, his proposal did not include support for peripherals, phone lines, or Internet services, let alone educational opportunities that might untangle the knotty features of computing infrastructures. According to Gingrich's paradigmatic example of a discrete-entity narrative, the one-time purchase of computers should be enough to rescue the digital underclass.

Discrete-entity narratives and the systems analysis processes they encourage can be addressed with the responsive move of technological reconstitution. As I have mentioned already, this move typically represents a more aggressive reaction than technological adjustment and its strategies of countersignification, counterappropriation, and counterdelegation—three strategies that offer effective ways to minimize the detrimental aspects of computer technologies and contexts. In successful acts of technological reconstitution, computer users create actual counterartifacts that displace the politics of technological regularization. Technological reconstitution represents a more aggressive reaction, and as a result, teachers and students should be wary of potential reintegration efforts, which are conservative attempts to co-opt artifacts once they have been reconstituted.

Pfaffenberger discusses the development of online bibliographic databases as a clear-cut instance of technological reconstitution. He explains that in the 1950s and 1960s, rebellious librarians created online databases in response to "what they saw as the unscientific, unsystematic, and technically conservative ethos of librarianship" (306). What is more, these librarians called themselves "documentation specialists" or "information scientists" and, besides that, collaborated across educational institutions and with the private sector. The first thing to note in this example is that the insurgent nature of technological reconstitution is produced by acts of antisignification, which either reverse or negate the dominant discourse. If traditional library practices were unscientific, unsystematic, and conservative, online databases would be the exact opposite: scientific, systematic, and flexible. However, strategies of reconstitution hinge on the creation of countercontexts and even counterregularization strategies to enable them. For this reason, in addition to the online databases, the rebellious librarians also created new job titles, partnerships, and narratives that touted databases as enormously progressive educational technologies.

In the context of processes that determine suitable computing infrastructures for students and teachers, hypertext-like or web narratives suggest possible responses that recognize the need for social resources. In fact, hypertext itself could be regarded as an example of technological reconstitution. The hallmark of essays on hypertext is an argument that mobilizes the logic of antisignification: Books are static, linear, hierarchical, author-centered, and dialogic, while hypertexts are dynamic, nonlinear, nonhierarchical, reader-centered, and polylogic. This oppositional discourse has cultivated ideological rhetorics of liberation, which in turn have prompted a flurry of hypertext programs, courses, claims, and theories. Web models of systems analysis mobilize the logic of antisignification in similar ways. Kling notes that "web models view computer-based systems as complex social objects whose architecture and use are shaped by the social relations between influential participants, the infrastructure that supports them, and the history of commitments" (373). So if discrete-entity models focus on technical relationships, web models focus on human relationships and the ways computer uses are constrained by the availability of social resources, which are neither unlimited nor inexpensive, especially in academic settings.

At the assignment level, this contrast can become the basis for a critical literacy project. Because technological reconstitution produces counterartifacts that displace the politics of technological regularization, I ask students to design a social process that can be used to determine suitable computing infrastructures for students and teachers in writing and communication courses. For example, students might design a process that requires them to interview teachers in order to learn about their pedagogical support structures (or lack thereof). This assignment not only stresses that technologies are more than physical artifacts but also defines systems analysis as a humanistic activity that requires a considerable measure of disciplinary knowledge. Although most universities have well-established processes for determining the efficacy of computing infrastructures, as might be expected these often echo discrete-entity narratives in that they focus on technical relationships. However, such processes, whether they be codified or in some way understood, provide the contrast needed to call to mind the logic of antisignifaction. What types of social versus technical resources do students need in order to be successful? What about teachers? And are there popular representations that might be exploited to support more socially based models of computerization? Students use these problem-posing questions as a guide to design a social process for systems analysis. Class projects have indicated that students need access to tenure-line faculty members who specialize in the study of literacy and computers, articulated English courses that take up the cultural complications of computer technologies, and computer labs that support collaborative work with a technical staff that can assist writers in development. In addition, class projects have indicated that teachers need access to released time for research, professional development activities that target English content areas, and student assistants who are competent enough to help jump-start and maintain electronic projects. On the whole, students tend to discover that if computers have diminished in price, the social resources required to ensure equitable access can be steep, not only fiscally but also politically (especially in terms of the cultural capital required to establish computer literacy as an accepted intellectual currency in English departments).

A final point is that counterartifacts can be co-opted in reactionary moves of reintegration, a conserving dynamic in technological reconstitution that should be emphasized to students. The intent of reintegration, as Pfaffenberger makes clear, is to "gain control over these artifacts by bringing them back into the controlled and ordered space of regularization and then performing technical modifications that blunt their revolutionary potential" (307). In the earlier example of online bibliographic databases, the response of the traditional librarians was to exercise their control over institutional resources, so that the database design process could not proceed without them. Once involved in the design process, the librarians, who were worried that the online databases would either deskill or replace them, negotiated technical features that preserved their primary expertise in subject classification systems. The end result was a human-computer interface that could not be employed systematically without the skills of traditional librarians.

Likewise, one can imagine reactionary moves of reintegration in the context of systems analysis processes. A successful move can be found in processes that give primary attention to social rather than technical dimensions, yet buy into egalitarian narratives of empowerment and enfranchisement that overpromise the effects of computer technologies. Such processes construct computing infrastructures not as value-neutral spaces but as intrinsically democratic spaces, an equally deterministic account that minimizes the need for social resources. For if the popular MCI advertisement is correct—that there are only "minds" in cyberspace—then power and authority are no longer complexly determined by a wide range of social, political, institutional, and technological forces, but by the degree to which ideas—pure ideas—are accepted or not accepted in the marketplace or schoolplace (two environments, incidentally, that are also often constructed as intrinsically democratic spaces). The concept of reintegration functions as a counterweight to such progress narratives because it reminds students that power continuously circulates in the contested and highly political territory of computing infrastructures.

This parameter should resonate with the many teachers who consider popular representations to be an area of great consequence for students. As with the other parameters, this one contributes dominant discourses that have an effect on the activities associated with using a computing infrastructure. But a distinction is that this effect can be more difficult for students to see because of the perceived distance between representations in the public imagination and decisions made in the context of locally operated facilities. This is one reason why the responsive move of technological reconstitution is particularly valuable here: In order to produce counterartifacts that displace the politics of technological regularization, students must be able to make concrete connections that implicate popular representations. Systems analysis is one site where students can more easily make such connections, in large part because of the discrete-entity narratives that discourage an attention to the social resources that computer users need in order to be successful.

## Conclusion

Michael Joyce argues that "Technology aspires toward transparency. Insofar as that aspiration intends to hide its failings, technology, like any unacknowledged representation of power, endangers learning" (65). Students who are critically literate are alert to the fact that computers can be dangerous, although their attentiveness is neither superficial nor unfocused. To put it another way, students should be able to recognize and articulate the ways power circulates in technological contexts. The approach this chapter offers encourages the use of heuristics that can help students develop a meta-discourse for political critique, one that illuminates the dominant discourses associated with the parameters of a critical approach to computer literacy: design cultures, use contexts, institutional forces, and popular representations. But while this approach is effective, I should underscore that it is only one method of critical analysis and therefore inescapably restricted in perspective. Hence, one task for the profession is to develop a full-scale assortment of metadiscourse heuristics with a critical bent. In addition, however, students should also be able to function as more ambitious agents of positive change. In other words, students should be able to function as reflective producers of computer technologies. The next chapter, therefore, focuses on the rhetorical literacies that can support social action on a larger scale.

# 4 / Rhetorical Literacy
## Computers as Hypertextual Media, Students as Reflective Producers of Technology

If English is to remain relevant as the subject which provides
access to participation in public forms of communication, as
well as remaining capable of providing understandings of
and the abilities to produce culturally valued texts, then an
emphasis on language alone simply will no longer do. English
will need to change.

—Gunther Kress,
"'English' at the Crossroads: Rethinking Curricula of
Communication in the Context of the Turn to the Visual"

In "Negative Spaces: From Production to Connection in Composition," Johndan Johnson-Eilola encourages teachers to reconsider what in composition studies counts as a text. Although social construction and postmodernism in composition theory provide important ways to understand texts as inherently social artifacts, he argues, teachers still tend to privilege a vision of composition practice that "remains rooted in relatively concrete, individualist notions of authorship" (17). To support his assertion, Johnson-Eilola distinguishes between writing as production versus writing as connection. In the production paradigm, which usually prevails in composition studies, teachers embrace process models and even the social turn that the discipline has taken, yet they ultimately expect students to produce a thoroughly original text, one in which their own (if intertextualized) ideas and words become the discernable anchor of the discourse. The connection paradigm, in contrast, values the negotiation of contexts, the ability to "write with fragments" (24). In this approach, writers focus on reorganizing and rerepresenting existing (and equally intertextualized) texts—their own included—in ways that are meaningful to specific audiences. An example would be a hypertext that interprets and arranges relevant

135

discussions of copyright for teachers of writing and communication. Johnson-Eilola does not dismiss the production paradigm, but he does find adequate justification for the connection paradigm in a postindustrial culture where linked information packets, not discrete concrete goods, increasingly assume key social and economic value (see also Negroponte; Reich).

Anyone who has been overwhelmed by the sheer volume of information on the Internet knows that the metatext—a heavily linked text that connects other texts and their contexts in imaginative and meaningful ways—has become an invaluable online genre, one that requires in its construction a sophisticated knowledge of audience, purpose, context, and the various organizational schemes that hypertext can support. But the node-link mechanism in hypertext is not the only feature that challenges teachers to expand their idea of what a text (or author) is, for computer-based texts not only accommodate automatic intertextual mechanisms but also encourage writers to function as designers of spatialized literacy environments.

Indeed, the World Wide Web has quickly become a popular instructional site in which rhetoric as it has been traditionally mapped out both illuminates and fails to illuminate the process of creating online texts. Hypermedia design often confounds print-reared teachers trained solely in verbal rhetoric (S. Williams), a fact borne out by two diametrically opposed approaches to what is already becoming a conventional assignment: the Website design project. The first approach asks students to create a Website that conforms to specific technical requirements. Reminiscent of the impoverished version of functional literacy critiqued in chapter 2, a standard assignment directs students to design a project that includes particular site elements: for example, five paragraphs of text, one ordered list, two unordered lists, three graphics, one image map or animated image, three internal links with anchors, three external links, and two manipulations of text attributes. It is the electronic equivalent of the five-paragraph essay assignment. If students are provided a context for their project, it is surely secondary to the correct execution of interface requirements in HTML. On the other end of the spectrum, the second approach emphasizes context but largely abandons all considerations of the medium, as if the technological environment of the Internet provides a neutral space for writers. It is the equivalent of an assignment inviting students to "write about anything." In this situation, students are typically asked to create Websites that demonstrate an awareness of stock concepts in composition: the canons of rhetoric, the elements of argument (logos, pathos, ethos), the rhetorical situation (audience, purpose, occasion). Criteria for evaluation are borrowed from the expository essay, which is to say that teachers focus on such areas as expression (Is the work expressed clearly and efficiently?), organization (Is the work organized logically?), content (Is the work presented thoroughly and accurately?), and context (Is the work addressed appropriately and persuasively to a specific audience for a specific purpose?). The not altogether bad outcome of this second approach is projects that privilege academic print literacies, those that pay homage to a history of rhetoric.

That instructional approaches to the design of online texts might be imagined in antithetical ways should not come as a complete surprise in departments of English, where multiple curricular visions coexist and sometimes conflict. In 1982, James Berlin admonished teachers to understand their roles and responsibilities in epistemic terms: "In teaching writing, we are not simply offering training in a useful technical skill that is meant as a simple complement to the more important studies of other areas" ("Contemporary" 776). Rather, Berlin continued, "We are teaching a way of experiencing the world, a way of ordering and making sense of it" (776). Yet a service-oriented culture in which teachers routinely fixate on vocational preparation thrives. In such a culture, technical considerations provide a natural focal point, especially in light of the facts that employers often organize job descriptions around software skills and programs and that students often expect teachers to offer vocationally serviceable instruction. On the other hand, some teachers are so insulated into the discipline that their investments in rhetoric properly understood limit the manner in which online texts are conceptualized and constructed. As Don Byrd and Derek

Owens explain, "We bring a limited number of formal vocabularies to the new technologies, and instead of exploring how these technologies might create hybrid forms, often we use them to preserve old paradigms of rhetorical construction" (49). Although rhetoric should serve as a linchpin in the education of computer-literate students, redefinitions of rhetoric can take place at the nexus of literacy and technology.

Consider speed as a feature of computer-mediated communication. Readers in electronic environments expect them to be reasonably responsive, so writers must orchestrate the temporal dimensions of online texts. That is, they must become designers of information environments that span time as well as space. But this task involves competencies that transcend the familiar confines of the English curriculum. For example, on the Web, students need a certain level of domain knowledge from computer science in order to produce texts that are optimized for performance. Such technical awareness includes a basic comprehension of the client/server architecture that underlies the Internet, because the configurations of end-user computers (clients) help determine the speed with which texts are delivered over the Internet (via servers). However, a fast text is not necessarily an effective text, so whenever possible speed must be calculated in rhetorical terms, even though a rhetoric of optimization has yet to be worked out. Numerous how-to guides advise students to design Web pages that download quickly, but what does that mean? Ten seconds? Twenty seconds? Thirty seconds? I agree with Jakob Nielsen that online environments can encourage impatience, yet is it so inconceivable that in certain contexts readers might be more or less patient given the nature of their task? In addition, is it so inconceivable that speed might be manipulated to achieve certain rhetorical effects, perhaps in a multimedia transition? The plot thickens as students consider issues of speed in a highly visual medium where images consume the bulk of the bandwidth. If the aforementioned tensions were not complicated enough, students must invent and produce visual representations that negotiate the design constraints of the Internet. This activity

interlaces—and redefines—technical, rhetorical, and visual literacies in ways before not imaginable.

Speed, of course, is not the only feature online that expands
textual parameters, nor are technical, rhetorical, and visual literacies the only literacies that inform the creation of online texts. Lee
Brasseur has characterized electronic spaces as postmodern because in those spaces writers, readers, and software designers all
collaborate on some level in the formation and interpretation of online texts. Nowhere is this more evident than in open hypertexts in
which technical features support the physical collapse of writer-
reader distinctions, although it should be noted that traces of collaboration can be found in almost any computer-mediated environment, as Johnson-Eilola argues in his proposal for a connection
paradigm in composition studies. Yet for student writers, electronic
spaces are also postmodern in a curricular sense. That is, the traditional categories that organize knowledge in academia are too rigid
to explain texts that cast aside rigid genre distinctions. E-mail, for
instance, is a genre that mixes oral and literate practices, and so
because e-mail exchanges are primarily written, the discipline provides a foundation for the study and use of e-mail. However, where
any one discipline thins is in the creation and evaluation of online
texts that incorporate an array of data types and structures, particularly for networked environments.

This chapter assumes that one facet of a computer multiliteracy-
cies program should prepare students to be authors of twenty-first-
century texts that in some measure defy the established purview
of English departments. I start with an overview of interface design, tracing broad shifts in audience, genre, and context that have
helped to move this activity into the territory of writing and communication teachers. Next I sketch out the terrain of rhetorical literacy by relating four parameters from rhetoric to interface design
that constitute a rhetorically literate student: persuasion, deliberation, reflection, and social action. In the final section of the chapter,
I consider computers as hypertextual media, the metaphor of identity that has become inextricably bounded up with the landscape of

rhetorical literacy. Overall, this chapter insists that students who are rhetorically literate will recognize the persuasive dimensions of human-computer interfaces and the deliberative and reflective aspects of interface design, all of which is not a purely technical endeavor but a form of social action.

## A Preliminary Note about Interface Design

Critical work on computer literacy often concludes with a call for action, a call that lays out concrete steps students and teachers might take to respond productively to the politics of technologies. One step frequently recommended is that students should become *producers* and not just *users* of computer-based environments, people who can contribute in unique ways to the design of literacy technologies. In "The Politics of the Interface: Power and Its Exercise in Electronic Contact Zones," Cynthia Selfe and Richard Selfe warn that if teachers fail to prepare students of writing and communication as architects of virtual spaces, "interface design will continue to be dominated primarily by computer scientists and will lack perspectives that could be contributed by humanist scholars" (498). Their warning here is clear: Interface design should be an enterprise the discipline influences because there is so much at stake in the representations of literacy online.

Interface design, however, may be a phrase that some teachers in departments of English are only vaguely familiar with, so let me clarify my use of the phrase. In a traditional sense, interface design concerns the front-end layer of computers that users manipulate in order to accomplish tasks (e.g., the keyboard, mouse, desktop, or the features of end-user applications). But interface design involves much more than that. As Michael Heim explains,

> Interface denotes a contact point where software links the human user to computer processors. This is the mysterious, nonmaterial point where electronic signals become information. It is our interaction with software that creates

an interface. Interface means the human being is wired up.
Conversely, technology incorporates humans. (78)

In other words, the interface is the place where different agents and
contexts are connected to each other: It is where the communicative process is centered, spreading out from that contact point between texts and users. This definition is a sensible one for humanists because it transcends the design of functional screen elements
into psychological and emotional considerations and because, unlike numerous other definitions, it includes social and political dimensions in that it defines human action as an essential element or
condition of interfaces.

The academic roots of interface design can be traced to human-
computer interaction (HCI), an area in computer science that since
the 1950s has devoted itself to improvements in the ways people
relate to computer technologies. In the evolution of computer interfaces—from command-line to menu-driven to graphical—it is not
difficult to spot advances that have made computers easier to operate. In his history of human-computer interaction technologies,
Brad Myers organizes such advances into three categories: basic interactions, computer applications, and software tools and architec-
tures. Advances in basic interactions have included windows, icons,
and other elements that allow for the direct manipulation of software programs. Ben Shneiderman argues that direct manipulation
was a major breakthrough because it allowed cryptic command language syntax to be replaced by relatively straightforward visible
screen objects. As a result, computer applications are now available
for a wide range of users and uses. What is more, multimedia and
gesture-recognition applications accommodate users who are differently abled (Slatin, "Art of ALT"). So for software tools and archi-
tectures, the programs used to create interfaces have been dramatically improved, to the point where utilities have even been created
that allow users to adjust the look and feel of interfaces, a feature
which, as chapter 2 argued, is crucial to a more effective approach
to functional literacy. Anyone who has hand-coded Web pages and

then switched over to a visual HTML editor appreciates the point Myers makes about the level of control that powerful development tools can provide. This is all to say that interface design has evolved out of computer science in at least one significant sense: The audience for computer interfaces is no longer solely, or even primarily, other computer scientists.

Although his history is valuable and useful, Myers stresses the computer side of the human-computer interaction dyad and thus elides other important ways interface design surpasses computer science contexts. Beth Kolko pinpoints one omission when she argues that in networked environments like the Internet, the concept of human-computer interaction should be reimagined as human-computer-human interaction, or HCHI (versus HCI). Kolko also traces technical developments in computer systems, particularly from stand-alone to globally wired machines, but the dynamic she highlights "speaks to more than the representation of objects and environments; it is the representation of people in interactional circumstances" (220). In other words, Kolko is interested in approaches that not only acknowledge the existence of others online but see the human-human relationship as the primary relationship around which interface design practices should revolve. Computers have been networked for decades (B. Myers), yet time and again the limelight remains on individual transactions with machines, a reality that underrates the value of social perspectives in HCI.

For the purposes of this chapter, which do not really deal directly with electronic exchanges, there are other ways for humanists to identify with interface design as an expansive activity. One straightforward avenue would be to enlarge the time-honored definition of software so that it covers electronic texts that are user centered. Most discussions in computer science divide software into two categories: system software, which controls hardware devices, and application software, which allows users to solve problems or accomplish targeted tasks. System software coordinates the relationship between hardware devices and software applications. This intermediary function is rather stable and hence not easily open to reinterpretation. But application software is a different story, at least in the realm of special-purpose programs. When most people think of software, the first things that probably come to mind are word-processing, spreadsheet, database, and e-mail programs, what Marilyn Meyer and Roberta Baber would call general-purpose programs (3–4). These programs do not really fit in here because it is unrealistic to think that students will be able to create them in writing and communication courses. Although students should interrogate the biases of general-purpose programs whenever possible and remap their interfaces to make them as meaningful as possible, it is more likely that our students will produce electronic texts that function as special-purpose programs—programs that solve specific communication problems for specific users. Realistic examples include informational Websites, hypertextual bibliographies, and online documents that serve instrumental purposes. In addition to content, such texts have interfaces, often intricate ones, that must be designed by their authors, our students.

If shifts in genre and audience have turned computer science outward and toward the business of humanists, so too has the realization that human-computer interfaces incorporate not only multiple users, as Kolko notes, but their social settings as well. This can perhaps best be illustrated by an attention to usability, a subfield in HCI concerned with the assessment of interfaces at both formative and summative stages of development. Usability is a complex area, but it can be addressed here by simply contrasting stereotypical descriptions of three basic approaches: heuristic evaluations, tests, and contextual inquiries. Although each of these approaches is profitable in its own right, and especially in combination, they make different assumptions about the scope of interfaces.

As the name implies, heuristic evaluations are conducted by usability experts who analyze an interface against the best practices reported in the HCI literature. In this case, experts speak to one another about the interface, which is limited to the software program. Usability tests attempt to open up this controlled feedback loop. There are too many types of tests to mention, but typically they ask real users (or user surrogates) to perform a set of authentic tasks that can be observed and measured. Here the actions and reactions of the user-tester, which are psychological and emotional and physical, constitute human layers of the interface. Contextual inquires flesh out the human context because they jettison the controlled conditions of tests for the contingencies of user environments. Contextual inquiries attempt to understand a software program as it gets used in actual settings of work. This requires interface designers to obtain access to user sites, see users as collaborators in the design process, understand qualitative approaches to research, and recognize the fact that social, political, and institutional factors shape user actions and interpretations in central ways. This last point is paramount, for in the richly textured sites that users inhabit, human-computer interactions are composed of various cultural and technical forces.

Interface design has historically been the bailiwick of computer scientists, principally those in the area of human-computer interaction. Yet numerous changes have pushed out the boundaries of HCI and expanded the competencies needed to create intelligible interfaces. These changes have altered the ways interface designers must think about audiences (computer users have become heterogeneous), genres (electronic texts have become software programs), and contexts (user sites have become crucial to the signification of interface objects and actions). As should be evident, the competencies such new realities call for are largely rhetorical in nature.

## The Parameters of a Rhetorical Approach

Rhetorical literacy as I envision it here has not been well articulated in the discourse of English studies. As chapter 2 indicated, teachers of writing and communication have concentrated on the assumptions and consequences of functional literacy, if mainly to reject shortsighted educational programs that cater to private interests. But there is an identifiable disciplinary narrative, one teachers continue to write and revise in a digital age in which students must learn to take advantage of computer technologies. Likewise, in chapter 3, I invoked perspectives that are highly recognizable. In fact, it is unremarkable to claim that the values and directions of critical literacy have shaped the discipline in central ways. In the context of computers, critical approaches have provided a much-needed corrective to the emphases often placed on functional skills, as well as a socially comfortable framework. However, if discussions of functional and critical literacy construct a well-established dualism, teachers have just begun to define the parameters for rhetorical literacy, which at least partially mediates this dualism because rhetorical literacy insists upon praxis—the thoughtful integration of functional and critical abilities in the design and evaluation of computer interfaces.

In some measure, Daniel Boyarski and Richard Buchanan rough out aspects of a key parameter that should speak to teachers in departments of English. These two professors of design at Carnegie Mellon University have employed rhetorical studies to better understand effective human-computer interaction. Rhetoric has become indispensable because computer design problems must always be contextualized in social terms. In their words,

> Science is concerned with laws, rules, and other forms of universal regularity. In contrast, human-computer communication is a concrete problem, always situated in a particular environment of human experience. The concreteness of communication reminds us of a truth that is sometimes forgotten when scientists and engineers attempt to project their knowledge in practical application: there is no science of the particular. (32)

Boyarski and Buchanan rightly doubt that a "deductive and predictive science of HCI" can account for the "habits, desires, preferences, and values of the different types of human beings who use computers" (32). So they turn to rhetoric for insight into what orients computer users and encourages them to act—or not act—in specific situations. Toward this end, Boyarski and Buchanan model an approach that formulates interface design as persuasive communication. "HCI is like a persuasive speech" (34), Boyarski and Buchanan argue: "The user is led into the computer system and provided with every support deemed valuable for its use. A balance of reasoning, implied voice, and feeling (haptic as well as emotional) is critical to effective human-computer communication" (34). Such an argument, it should be emphasized, is atypical in a field that has overwhelmingly relied on either system-centered or text-centered models of human-computer interaction (Johnson).

Persuasion is indeed one fundamental parameter in the terrain of rhetorical literacy, and for this reason I want to unpack the persuasive dimensions of HCI in more detail. But once interfaces have been contextualized, understood as discursive technologies, and implicated in value systems, other parameters can be conceptualized. In addition to persuasion, deliberation, reflection, and social action are parameters that illuminate the role of rhetoric. Briefly, deliberation refers to the very real likelihood that in any situation there are no perfect solutions to interface design problems. Interface design problems are ill-defined problems, and therefore require designers to continuously engage in deliberative activities. Reflection could be discussed under deliberation, but because usability is such an important area, I isolate it to extend the analysis. Social action concerns the responsibilities of interface designers, who are in a position to help enact productive societal change. These four parameters—persuasion, deliberation, reflection, social action—delimit the terrain of rhetorical literacy and suggest the qualities of a rhetorically literate student (see table 4.1).

*Persuasion*

There are a number of levels on which interfaces are persuasive, yet only the most obvious ones have been generally recognized. Evidence to substantiate this claim abounds, but I reference captology, the study of computers as persuasive technologies, because this area of inquiry has been formalized in highly visible places (see <http://captology.stanford.edu>). Captologists are interested in the planned effects of computers, so they focus exclusively on those systems that attempt to modify attitudes or behaviors in explicit ways (Fogg). Technologies on the Internet that would engage captologists include Websites that promote safe sex, educate voters,

## Table 4.1
Parameters of a Rhetorical Approach to Computer Literacy

| Parameters | Qualities of a Rhetorically Literate Student |
|---|---|
| Persuasion | A rhetorically literate student understands that persuasion permeates interface design contexts in both implicit and explicit ways and that it always involves larger structures and forces (e.g., use contexts, ideology). |
| Deliberation | A rhetorically literate student understands that interface design problems are ill-defined problems whose solutions are representational arguments that have been arrived at through various deliberative activities. |
| Reflection | A rhetorically literate student articulates his or her interface design knowledge at a conscious level and subjects their actions and practices to critical assessment. |
| Social Action | A rhetorically literate student sees interface design as a form of social versus technical action. |

and calculate the benefits of individual retirement accounts. Phillip King and Jason Tester analyze the landscape of captology and offer these conclusions about its state of affairs: persuasive technologies flourish in certain domains, namely marketing, health, safety, and environmental conservation (32); persuasive technologies primarily target teen and preteen children (33); the physical manifestations of persuasive technologies vary, although the Internet has encouraged the development of systems that can be accessed through personal computers (36); and the persuasive strategies interface designers use are not necessarily novel (37). These observations, notably the first two, help delineate the boundaries of captology, for as researchers in this area fondly assert in no uncertain terms, "not all technologies are persuasive; in fact, only a small subset of today's computing technologies fit this category" (Fogg 27).

But is that really true? I take issue with this assertion and the assumptions it makes about persuasion, and I suspect others will too because persuasion involves symbolic gestures that can operate implicitly and subtly. I applaud captologists for their scholarly efforts, which have advanced persuasion as a quasi-legitimate topic in HCI. Perhaps their greatest contribution has been to challenge interface designers to think about ethics (Berdichevsky and Neunschwander), a matter that cannot be dismissed in even the most impoverished conversations about persuasion. However, the standpoint that captologists have so far adopted is not plausible enough to account for the manifold ways that computer users are influenced in technological environments. William Nothstine and Martha Cooper oppose three perspectives toward persuasion—classical, symbolist, and institutional—that elucidate the concerns I have here. My aim is not to rehearse the nuances of theoretical discussions of persuasion, but to sketch in broad strokes the limitations I see in captology.

The first perspective, the classical, is the one captologists have adopted, but I will urge teachers of writing and communication to consider the explanatory power of the other two perspectives. Nothstine and Cooper write that the "paradigm and rationale of persuasion within the classical perspective," and by classical, they mean Aristotelian, "is the intentional and explicit attempt by an individual to influence matters of civic concern by directly addressing an audience" (506). The salient point to note is that this perspective "lays primary emphasis on strategic—hence, intentional—choices among persuasive strategies" (506). If persuasion is a premeditated and rational enterprise, as captologists maintain, then the job of interface designers is to construct software elements that appeal directly to their audiences. Fair enough.

But what about the unintentional effects of interfaces, as well as the more implicit forms of persuasion? What about, for example, the wildly different worldviews of computer users that have a direct bearing on how interfaces get interpreted? This is where the symbolist perspective enters in, a perspective that "centers on the notion that all persuasion is really to a significant extent self-persuasion, involving the active participation of an audience" (509). Nothstine and Cooper elaborate: "Because all symbols represent interests and motives, from the symbolic perspective all symbols, and all acts of interpretation, are considered inherently persuasive" (509). This perspective shifts the epistemological spotlight toward computer users, whose concerns, values, and skills ultimately determine what interfaces mean, a point Boyarski and Buchanan indirectly arrive at in their formulation of interface design as persuasive speech. The symbolist stance has numerous implications, but a major one is to erode unstudied distinctions between the two basic communication functions of online texts: to inform and to persuade.

The third perspective implicates institutions and thus extends the province of persuasion further still. Nothstine and Cooper stress that the context for the institutional perspective "is the modern society, moderated by mass media, which have become both extraordinarily pervasive and interpenetrated with other institutions, all of them large, enduring social collectives empowered by custom or law to perform important social functions" (511). Although the institutional perspective lacks a fully developed and coherent theory of persuasion, it deals with four interconnected spheres: campaigns, social movements, propaganda, and ideology. The relevant sphere for interface designers is the last one, and what is at issue are the formal and informal ways everyday institutions shape the manner in which computer technologies are developed and used. The keys to the institutional perspective are cultural values, shared myths, and power structures, all of which Nothstine and Cooper underscore because ideological persuasion ordinarily goes unnoticed.

Captologists are headed in the right direction insofar as they foreground persuasion, a move that is still uncommon in HCI. But, in point of fact, computers increasingly support overt persuasive activities, especially on the Internet where the "home-page-as-an-ad proposition" (Singh and Dalal 98) has captured the imagination of countless interface designers. So, on the one hand, it is commonsensical to consider the arguments and evidence that appeal to users and how these might be incorporated into computer interfaces. Some of the most profitable work in this vein has examined credibility issues online (Tseng and Fogg), the ways in which Aristotelian notions of drama can inform interface design practices (Laurel), and the "seductive" qualities of software—those things that connect with the goals and emotions of users (Khaslavsky and Shedroff). However, the symbolist and institutional perspectives suggest the limitations of a strictly classical approach. Persuasion operates on numerous levels, and not just those in the realm of interface designers. Research tells us, for instance, that the beliefs, attitudes, and perceptions of users, which can be deeply subjective and idiosyncratic, help determine the ways, and the extent to which, technological innovations are utilized (Xia and Lee). Research also tells us that Hollywood (Crane), the mass media (Poster), software companies (Spender), government agencies (Birkmaier), professional societies (R. Rosenberg), worksites (De Young), educational institutions (Taylor), and the like exert substantial influence on both technology designers and users.

Two boiled-down examples should make this point concrete. Kathryn Henderson studied the situated practices of engineers and discovered that their visual culture, constructed in part from historically rooted organizational and disciplinary conventions, is not always congruent with the assumptions embodied in computer-graphics design. Similarly, Paul Seesing and Mark Haselkorn emphasized that public perceptions of the year 2000 problem, the so-called millennium bug, were driven at least as much by sensational stories as by more accurate understandings of what interface designers and users needed to do to protect themselves. In short, persuasion permeates technological contexts in both obvious and not so obvious ways, yet those who are rhetorically literate, who understand that persuasion always involves larger structures and forces, will be in a unique position to design agreeable and worthwhile interfaces.

This is not an especially difficult point to make in the classroom. Indeed, in my courses I often use a warm-up assignment that asks students to quickly analyze a Website from classical, symbolist, and institutional perspectives on persuasion. Students read an excerpt from Nothstine and Cooper that outlines the basic assumptions of these three perspectives and then identify concrete instances of the different levels on which persuasion operates in HCI. I usually select a Website for analysis that would appeal to captologists, one in which the attempts at persuasion are easily discernable: My objective is not to dismiss the classical perspective, but to gradually paint a more complicated picture of persuasion for budding interface designers. So we start with overt gestures and proceed toward more subtle forms of persuasion.

For example, I often ask students to analyze a United States government Website that encourages people to become organ and tissue donors (<http://organdonor.gov>). From the classical perspective, the analysis is rather straightforward because there is clearly a deliberate attempt on the part of the government to influence the attitudes and behaviors of its citizens. As students point out, explicit attempts at persuasion can be readily found in the introductory paragraphs, in the highly personal testimonials, in the downloadable resources for family members, and in other site areas. Overall, I am sure captologists would agree that this site is persuasive. But is it as effective as possible? This is the question I pose to students in order to turn the analysis in the direction of the symbolist and institutional perspectives. These perspectives invite students to think about the ways the Web site might—or might not—tap into the concerns, perspectives, and values of potential donors as well as the larger cultural narratives that influence them. Because my students are rarely (if ever) actual registered donors, they are well positioned to discuss some of the implicit modes of persuasion that might be exploited. Although my students have tended to conclude that the site is fairly well designed, they have also noted some missed opportunities, such as more direct appeals to the best of American ideals (e.g., dignity, equality of opportunity, the willingness to engage in shared sacrifice) and ties to religious traditions, which overwhelmingly endorse organ and tissue donation as a selfless act of charity. On the whole, I agree with my students that an attention to ideology could help improve the effectiveness of the Website.

### Deliberation

Deliberation is a parameter that teachers of writing and communication often associate with invention, with Aristotle, and with his special topics—deliberative oratory was a branch of classical oratory that dealt with legislative matters and the future of the Athenian state—but what I want to focus on here is the complexion of interface design problems and the concomitant deliberative activities. Nevertheless, this direction should resonate with teachers because there are similarities in the situations writers and interface designers come up against. Specifically, interface designers, like writers, tackle problems that have multiple, contradictory solutions, some of which are better than others, but none of which is absolutely best. That is, in particular cases, certain solutions could be considered more efficient or effective, persuasive or logical, but such judgments are always truth claims that cannot be proven definitively in the same way a math problem can. So, in essence, solutions to interface design problems are representational arguments that have been arrived at through various deliberative activities, through choices that honor one or another value above others.

I need to expound on this point because a tremendous amount of work in HCI has a rationalistic orientation (Winograd and Flores). Horst Rittel and Melvin Webber have explicated considerable variations in the nature of disciplinary problems. According to them, there are two broad classes of problems—tame and wicked—that are fundamentally different in kind. Tame problems are well-defined problems that can be separated from their contexts and from other problems, and thus easily solved. Scientists and engineers have been frequently enlisted to iron out tame problems, examples of which are provided by Rittel and Webber:

> Consider a problem of mathematics, such as solving an equation; or the task of an organic chemist in analyzing

the structure of some unknown compound; or that of the chessplayer attempting to accomplish checkmate in five moves. For each the mission is clear. It is clear, in turn, whether or not the problems have been solved. (160)

Although tame problems can be enormously complex, their complexities are largely technical in character, as are their solutions. In contrast, wicked problems are more intractable in that they inherently involve social judgments. Rittel and Webber dwell on the fact that wicked problems do not have single solutions, only interim and imperfect resolutions. Adjustments in tax rates, changes in school curricula, procedures to reduce crime—these problems can all be understood, addressed, and resolved in countless ways because there are elusive social dimensions that muddy the causal waters. Hence the label "wicked," a term that was adopted not because wicked problems are "ethically deplorable" in the slightest, but rather because such problems are "'malignant' (in contrast to 'benign') or 'vicious' (like a circle) or 'tricky' (like a leprechaun) or 'aggressive' (like a lion, in contrast to the docility of a lamb)" (160).

Rittel and Webber discuss properties that can help teachers realize that interface design problems are more like wicked than tame problems and that although all projects have intricate technical aspects, mathematical and scientific formalisms are inadequate in socially ambiguous situations. There are too many properties to recount here, so let me limit myself to the first three, which happen to be particularly instructive. First, "There is no definitive formulation of a wicked problem" (161). That is to say, the way one understands a problem suggests, and is suggested by, the possible resolutions. Different interpretations of a problem and its context naturally lead to different decisions and actions, which in turn shed light on, and shape, the problem and its definition. So one does not "first understand, then solve" (162) interface design problems; rather, one constructs interface design problems and their resolutions, which are mutually constitutive, out of discursive processes that require "incessant judgment, subjected to critical argument" (162). The challenge, of course, is to figure out who profits from the various social constructions. Second, "Wicked problems have no stopping rule" (162). This property is well-known in departments of English, for writing and communication projects have no stopping rule either. In tame problems, there are criteria or conditions that signal when acceptable solutions have been reached. Not so with wicked problems. Interface designers finalize projects because "time, or money, or patience" have run out, "not for reasons inherent in the 'logic' of the problem" (162). In the same way that papers are never done, just due, interface designs can always be revisited and reconsidered. Third, "Solutions to wicked problems are not true-or-false, but good-or-bad" (162). Although interfaces are never perfected in objective terms, their effectiveness must still be judged. Yet there are no absolutely correct or false answers to interface design problems. This means that the perspectives of judges "are likely to differ widely to accord with their group or personal interests, their special value-sets, and their ideological predilections" (163); and it means that "assessments of proposed solutions are [therefore] expressed as 'good' or 'bad' or, more likely, as 'better or worse' or 'satisfying' or 'good enough'" (163). Such an assessment context is familiar to even first-time writing instructors, who quickly learn that it is difficult, if not impossible, to assess the work of one student apart from that of another or apart from the intended context of the paper or apart from the biases of the teacher. Thus, as the first three properties of wicked problems suggest, when it comes to interface design problems a more rhetorical and less rational view of things is needed. This kind of deliberation is a hallmark of interface design.

Armed with these theoretic insights, teachers might begin to question whether or not wicked problems can be taken up with any degree of precision. Phrased another way, can interface designers work systematically? The answer to this question is definitely yes, although I should spell out my conception of systematic work, which derives from research on the deliberative practices of experienced writers. In a nutshell, researchers have learned that experienced writers have recourse to rich literacy repertoires that can steer their discursive efforts in productive directions (Flower; Rose;

Sommers). These writers recognize that on some level all communication situations are unique but that ad hoc approaches disregard what has been learned from ambitious research on advanced composition, while rules-based approaches are too inelastic to illuminate the contingencies of situated contexts. So one characteristic of experienced writers is that they deliberate over patterns, structures, and frameworks in strategic ways, treating schematized practices as heuristics, not formulas, which are open to analysis and change. In the same manner, interface designers can approach their tasks with analytic flexibility and aplomb. However, this assumes they have been exposed to rhetorical approaches, which are still relatively rare in HCI. An example of one such approach is the model of persuasively effective communication articulated by Boyarski and Buchanan or their more speculative model of mediation in which human-computer interaction is characterized "as a kind of dialogue focused on the phenomenology of the system" (35). This phenomenological approach presupposes that interfaces can always be multiply interpreted; therefore, interface designers should strive to help users understand all of the possibilities in a system, not one, ostensibly true interpretation of it. Nascent approaches like these are philosophically and methodologically different from traditional approaches in HCI, and their deliberative aspects are wholly consonant with academic programs that champion humanistic perspectives.

In chapter 5, I suggest that one way to relate the parameter of deliberation is to have students design entirely different versions of the same Website. But as a preliminary activity, students can read and respond to case studies that illustrate the ill-defined nature of interface design problems. Two cases I use repeatedly have been posted at a government Website dedicated to the improvement of communication about cancer research (<http://usability.gov>). The first case study discusses the development of CancerNet, a Website that organizes a wide array of cancer information from the National Cancer Institute (NCI) for different types of users: patients and their families, health care providers, and researchers. The second case study discusses the development of LiveHelp, an instant messaging system that helps confused users search and navigate not only CancerNet but also all of the other pages on NCI Websites. What can students learn from these development stories? The stories are instructive in large part because they capture the deliberative aspects of interface design in concrete ways. Specifically, they discuss different prototypes and the rationales behind them as well as reveal instances in which the designers needed to redeliberate over their representations of users and user tasks. Although the case studies are relatively brief, they are enriched on account of the fact that as students read and respond to the cases, they can explore the operational versions of CancerNet and LiveHelp.

*Reflection*

The third parameter, reflection, could be considered a species of deliberation, really, because reflective practices invite students to become researchers of their own activities, in order to improve performance. Reflection as a rhetorical concept can be traced back to ancient times (Liu), though to Plato more than to Aristotle. Indeed, it was conventional for ancient rhetors to reflect upon the impact of an oratory or even to reflect while in an oratorical mode—in which case the reflection amounted to considering refutational points that laid out assumptions or limitations or deficiencies so that an overall argument might be strengthened. But the contemporary scholarship on reflection seems more directly related to interface design, especially the work that Donald Schön and his followers have done to conceptualize reflective practices in professional contexts. This work should still be somewhat recognizable to teachers, however, because it has informed important efforts to apprehend, and express, the dynamics of fruitful writing instruction (Hillocks; Yancey). Although Schön would not have considered himself to be a rhetorician per se—at MIT he was a professor of urban studies and education—his insights have been decidedly rhetorical in that they apply not to a single subject matter but to practices across the disciplines.

A number of interrelated factors motivated Schön to inquire into the epistemology of professional practice. One factor was the erosion of public confidence in the professions that began in the 1960s and that continues today. Schön wrote that "We look to professionals for the definition and solution of our problems, and it is through them that we strive for social progress" (3–4). "In return," he continued, "we grant professionals extraordinary rights and privileges" (4). In spite of that, America has had an increasingly troubled relationship with its professional ranks, one that may not be so easily resolved. Although professionalization is emblematic of a postindustrial culture, the social crises of such a culture—poverty, pollution, urban decay, and so on—seem to be rooted in, or at least resistant to, specialized practices. For example, consider this depiction of the role certain specialists played in the perpetuation of the Vietnam War:

> The nation had been enmeshed in a disastrous war which had caused it to seem at war with itself. The professional representatives of science, technology, and public policy had done very little to prevent or stop the war or to heal the rifts it produced. On the contrary, professionals seemed to have a vested interest in prolonging the conflict. (Schön 9)

Unfortunately, this characterization is an all too accurate one and speaks to a dark side of professionalism: the use of specialized knowledge in ways that interest only or mainly the power elite.

But the public can also lose confidence in its professionals for less insidious and perhaps less obvious reasons. In his research, Schön learned that thoughtful professionals often attribute the erosion of trust in professional judgment, at least in part, to an outdated educational system that fails to prepare individuals for the realities of postindustrial work. "Professionals are called upon to perform tasks for which they have not been educated" (14), Schön reported. Said another way, "Professional knowledge is mismatched to the changing character of the situations of practice—the complexity, uncertainty, instability, uniqueness, and value conflicts which are increasingly perceived as central to the world of professional practice" (14). While schools treat professional knowledge as inherently stable, actual situations of practice (interface design included) tend to be marked by instability, uncertainty, and contingency.

But why should schools be so far off base in this regard? Why, in higher education, are professional practices so frequently viewed in one-dimensional terms? Such questions also occurred to Schön, and he uncovered an answer in his research that should not astonish humanists: The dominant epistemology of practice in the academy has been one of "technical rationality," the belief that "professional activity consists in instrumental problem solving made rigorous by the application of scientific theory and technique" (21). A legacy of positivism and (to a degree) of Deweyan pragmatism, technical rationality has produced a hierarchical model of professional knowledge in which "research is institutionally separate from practice" (26), because "real knowledge lies in the theories and techniques of basic and applied science," not "in the use of theory and technique to solve concrete problems" (27). The overall effect of this binary division has not only been that the so-called "hard" sciences have become more valued than the so-called "soft" sciences, but also that, on a curricular level, students have not had sufficient opportunities to apply or test what they have learned in actual settings of use.

I have witnessed this situation in a course I teach in software documentation writing. Although the computer science students have a rock-solid background in math and computer languages, they typically have not been asked to use Microsoft Word in highly organized ways, let alone to construct user requirements out of qualitative inquiries into authentic worksites. In fact, I have yet to come across more than a handful of students who can talk about field methods for software development, even though these methods have become crucial to interface designers (Wixon and Ramey). This is exactly the kind of intellectual disconnect that prompted Schön to map out a different approach to action in the context of professional practice.

Schön articulated and illustrated his reflective turn in a nicely detailed style, and I will not attempt to summarize his project in its entirety because I could not begin to do it justice here. Nor will I attempt to recount the criticisms of his project, which have been taken up elsewhere (see Newman). Instead, let me broadly bracket interface design with several facets of reflection, in an effort to suggest the power of its rhetoricity. Schön contends that skilled practitioners connect thought and action through dialectical habits. They see themselves, at absolute bottom, as continuous learners sensitive and responsive to the tacit dimensions of their practice. Reflective practitioners understand that professional performance cannot be improved unless taken-for-granted assumptions are examined and challenged. This involves perspectives and processes that encourage practitioners to articulate their professional knowledge at a conscious level and to subject their actions to critical assessment.

Robert Kottkamp has provided a catalogue of concrete strategies that can facilitate reflection at various phases of professional practice. Five of them are already mobilized routinely as pedagogical strategies in writing courses: foregrounding the recursive aspects of composing processes; using various types of journals (e.g., daily journals, learning journals, stop action journals) as a means of reflection; assigning case studies to highlight the multiple options for action inherent in professional situations; capturing literacy events—in transcripts of electronic exchanges, on videotapes—so that the events can be studied later; asking students to use metaphors and metaphorical stories to help them describe, and make sense of, their activities and experiences. Students encounter two additional strategies in internships where they are required to shadow and interview mentors. It is important to note that reflection strategies can support either reflection-in-action (formative reflection) or reflection-on-action (summative reflection), a distinction that was significant to Schön. Although both types of reflection are valuable and should be encouraged, reflection-in-action is potentially more potent because it produces contextualized experiments in which professional practices can be reconsidered, adjusted, and enhanced in real time.

Reflection strategies for interface design have been classified under the rubric of usability, but reflection as a conceptual category shifts the focus from the product (Is the interface usable?) to the process (Is the designer reflective?) in useful ways. Although the properties of interfaces must be constantly tested, students will become empowered only if they are emboldened to confront their design processes in a self-conscious and self-critical manner. Consequently, students in my courses are asked to become more aware of their practices through a Freirian-style heuristic that I incorporate into all usability tests. I appropriated this heuristic from John Smyth, an activist scholar who has promoted reflexivity as an important thrust in teacher education. Smyth lays out four stages of sequential action that can help teachers become reflective practitioners: describing, informing, confronting, and reconstructing. But these very stages can also help students as interface designers articulate, understand, and question the tacit dimensions of their work.

In stage one of my adaptation of the heuristic, students create a personalized narrative that describes their interface design practices. The point of this exercise is to develop a rich, concrete account that can serve as a gateway to analysis. As Smyth insists, "written codification can be a powerful guiding device for practitioners engaging in reflective deliberation" (6). In the second stage, students unpack their narratives, identifying the operational theories and assumptions that inform their interface design practices unconsciously or otherwise. Here, students attempt to move their designing "out of the realm of the mystical, as it were, into a situation in which they are able to begin to see through discussion with others the nature of the forces that cause them to operate in the way they do and how they can move beyond intellectualizing the issues to concrete action for change" (6). People employing such a process, however, must be careful not to reinforce the theory/practice split that reflective practitioners aspire to break down. In the third stage of the heuristic, students are asked to interrogate their operational theories and assumptions. To facilitate this stage, Smyth (7) provides a series of prompts that can be channeled in the direction of interface design: What do my practices say about my assumptions, values, and beliefs about designing interfaces? Where did these ideas come from? What social practices are expressed in these ideas? What is it that causes me to maintain my theories? What views of power do they embody? Whose interests seem to be served by my practices? What is it that acts to constrain my views of what is possible in designing interfaces? Prompts like these can assist students as they seek to problematize cultural norms and personal values, which are often deeply entrenched. In the fourth stage, students attempt to reconstruct their practices in order to enact positive change. Hence, students are urged to revisit their interface design processes from the vantage point of what they have learned from the first three stages, looking for ways to improve performance. Schön once characterized contemplative design as a "conversation with the materials of a situation" (78), and this four-stage heuristic helps students have such a conversation. But its real beauty is that it can overlay any usability test, and thus inject reflective aspects into any interface design project.

### Social Action

Just as reflection opens spaces for questions of agency, so too does the final parameter I want to consider: social action. Social action is not a phrase one hears habitually at HCI conferences, nor is it present with any regularity in the published literature. And yet interface design as social action is an equation that rings true in many respects, some transparent, others more subtle.

The most obvious and discussed articulation is one in which interface designers take an activist stance toward injustices in the world. To illustrate, let me relate an event that took place at the Association for Computing Machinery annual conference on Computer-Human Interaction (CHI). The 1992 CHI conference was held in Monterey, California, just a few days after, and about three hundred miles north of, the riots in Los Angeles that were sparked by the inhumane treatment of Rodney King. Several conference participants felt that it would be professionally irresponsible to ignore the riots, in part because the bleak urban landscape of Los Angeles stood in such stark contrast to the prosperity and flamboyance of Silicon Valley. So the participants organized a last-minute session to formulate an initial response. In "Toward a Guide to Social Action for Computer Professionals," Jeff Johnson and Evelyn Pine summarized the activities and outcomes of this special session, which attracted over three hundred concerned individuals. On the whole, these individuals voiced frustrations and shared ideas for how computer professionals, their employers, and professional organizations might make positive contributions to the fight against social inequality. Most of the suggestions were about education or volunteerism. In the case of the former, it was suggested that computer professionals could, for example, tutor disadvantaged children, companies could donate software to schools, and professional organizations could lobby for increased funding for public education. In the case of the latter, it was suggested that computer professionals could, for example, volunteer in urban libraries (in fact, a frequent comment reported by Johnson and Pine was that literacy is more important than computer literacy); companies could allow employees to volunteer on company time and could reward volunteer work; and professional organizations could develop computer curricula that volunteers could use in educational situations. Other suggestions focused on issues of access to online information services and on affirmative action programs for computer professionals that might increase the hiring, promotion, and wages of women and minorities. It should be clear from these examples that there was no shortage of excellent ideas at the session.

Unfortunately, these ideas remain largely unimplemented, despite the extraordinary efforts of Jeff Johnson, Evelyn Pine, Ben Shneiderman, and Computer Professionals for Social Responsibility (CPSR), a professional organization alert to the social impacts of computers on society. The main outcome of their collective effort was supposed to be a "well-digested, well-organized guide to social action" (Johnson and Pine 24). However, as with so many potential projects in the sciences, the guide was never developed because the principal investigators could not secure a grant. One project that did have some initial traction was the creation of a new submission category for the CHI conference: social action posters. This conference feature encouraged participants to report on social action projects, and there were impressive presentations on undertakings that linked children with volunteer pen-pal scientists, encouraged social responsibility through multidisciplinary team approaches to user-centered design, and prevailed on technical professionals to help schools and community organizations address their information technology challenges. But the poster session eventually fizzled out because of a lack of submissions. Nonetheless, activism endures as a minor theme in interface design communities, although serious discussions and projects should be distinguished from the wild predictions and shameless self-promotions of the celebrity digerati.

If activism is a prominent form of social action, it is also a deep-running pedagogical current in rhetorical studies. Not only do liberatory classroom practices and perspectives exist in abundance, but there have been cogent arguments to extend activist projects to non-university settings. Ellen Cushman, for instance, asks for a "shift in our critical focus away from our own navels, Madonna, and cereal boxes to the ways in which we can begin to locate ourselves within the democratic process of everyday teaching and learning in our neighborhoods" (12). The civic participation Cushman advocates might not appear to be all that different from what the computer professionals suggested after the riots in Los Angeles, but there is a notable distinction: Cushman argues for self-reflexive activities that call into question the subject positions of activists. I suspect the computer professionals did not think to interrogate their own subject positions because such a step was not suggested by their working definition of social action. My take on the normal view in HCI is that social action is like a two-position toggle switch that one can turn on or off at will. Those with strong political sensibilities pursue social action projects, while those without attend to the more or less neutral business of interface design. Social action is so easily compartmentalized because it is an undertheorized concept in HCI. That is, activism has become synonymous with social action. Interface designers are considered to be social actors only if they are involved in projects that deal with unmistakably political issues, such as privacy, free speech, and intellectual property, or if they push socially conscious agendas. Thus, workaday issues and tasks are not usually defined inside the realm of social action.

The consequence is that the influence interface designers wield is often underestimated. To understand the full force of their activities, interface designers need an expanded definition of social action, one that envelopes routine work. There are countless paths toward such an elaboration, but one fruitful course for teachers of writing and communication is through the scholarship of Marilyn Cooper and Michael Holzman. Once again, there are parallels that can be drawn between the contexts of writers and interface designers. Cooper and Holzman argue that "Computers will not end illiteracy. Literacy is not a technology that can be freely transferred from one culture to another, or acquired like an appliance. Writing is not a technique" (xi). To the contrary, these scholars maintain that "Writing is a form of social action. It is part of the way in which some people live in the world. Thus, when thinking about writing, we must also think about the way that people live in the world" (xii). In their interpretation of what it means to write, then, Cooper and Holzman "assert the primacy of the social over that of the technological" (xi).

This is not to say that computers do not contribute to the shape of social realities—indeed, Cooper and Holzman are quick to point out that culture is overdetermined—but that technological activities always take place in larger social environments. The social environments in which interface designers live are highly collaborative, explicitly intertextual, and theoretically centered on real audiences. Interface designers almost always work in teams, and new development methodologies emphasize collective versus individual ownership. For example, in extreme programming (XP), two interface designers sit at a single computer: one person thinks about how to implement a solution, while the other takes under consideration the implications of that solution (Beck). In addition, the materials and not just the methods of interface designers also have social dimensions. Interface designers draw on earlier versions of projects and on competitive products, and they share and reuse source code. The Open Source Initiative (<http://opensource.org>) attests to the seriousness with which interface designers have engaged in the communal development of software. But perhaps the most effective way to set forth an expanded sense of social action is to concentrate on real audiences. Interface designers have power relationships with users that cannot be avoided. Although these relationships remain underdiscussed in HCI, they provide a focus of attention that can help students see that even mundane tasks are a form of social action.

Lynne Markus and Niels Bjorn-Andersen provide a two-dimensional framework that can be used in the classroom to explain the different types of power associated with interface design. The first dimension of the framework maps out the contexts within which power can be exercised, while the second dimension identifies the possible targets of power moves. Power can be exercised in either specific projects or on a policy level, and it can be directed at either issues of facts or values. This two-dimensional framework yields four types of power exercise: technical, structural, conceptual, and symbolic. The technical exercise of power occurs when interface designers disregard the suggestions and insights of users. This can happen unwittingly if design decisions are predicated on a conception of audience that "differs sharply from the views users hold of themselves" (Markus and Bjorn-Andersen 500). The structural exercise of power occurs when interface designers create systems that contribute to user dependence. The classic example is a support system of cryptic error messages that can be deciphered only by highly trained technical professionals. The conceptual exercise of power occurs when interface designers decide on the objectives of computer systems. In the minds of many, this task is not considered to be a type of social action, yet it imposes definitions of the situation and sets the terms under which user activities and issues are understood and discussed. The symbolic exercise of power occurs when the ideals embedded in interfaces influence the attitudes and beliefs of users. This can be observed in the myriad ways computers have encouraged redefinitions of literacy and work. These four types of power—technical, structural, conceptual, and symbolic—illustrate the fact that everyday activities help construct both worldviews and social worlds. Although activism is a conspicuous manifestation of social action, other forms are less apparent because they have become naturalized as standard approaches to interface design. The formidable task for teachers, therefore, is to denaturalize such approaches so that students can see the diverse modes of social action that permeate development contexts in HCI.

Customary approaches tend to construct interface design as a technological endeavor and perpetuate traditional design methodologies based on the principles of scientific management, such as functional analysis, hierarchical decomposition, and task fractionalization (Markus and Bjorn-Andersen 501). Traditional methodologies have their place, yet all too often they obscure the rhetorical aspects of Website design and usability. But customary approaches can be reconstructed with the parameters that comprise the landscape of rhetorical literacy. To be sure, even technically oriented projects have a rhetorical side, which should help teachers incorporate the territory of interface design into writing and communication courses. This side includes persuasion, deliberation, reflection, and social action, four parameters that suggest the qualities of a rhetorically literate student.

### Computers as Hypertextual Media

In 1990, John Slatin in an article in *College English* broadly introduced scores of English teachers to hypertext and contributed to the ways in which the profession has come to understand the World Wide Web, a massive instantiation of hypertextual ideas that was foreshadowed by Vannevar Bush in the 1940s and conceptualized to some extent by Ted Nelson in the 1960s. Slatin began his article with what he called an "embarrassingly simple" observation:

> Hypertext is very different from more traditional forms of text. The differences are a function of technology and are so various, at once so minute and so vast, as to make hypertext a new medium for thought and expression—

the first verbal medium, after programming languages, to emerge from the computer revolution. ("Reading" 870)

This new medium, Slatin declared, "involves both a new practice and a new rhetoric, a new body of theory" (870), all of which he tried to sketch out for a discipline heavily invested in more traditional literacy technologies. Slatin discussed the multiple media available in hypertext documents, their organizational schemes, the types of readers hypertexts tend to construct, and concepts like intertextuality, authority, and interface design. If his point was straightforward enough, however, it was neither uncontroversial nor unproblematic: Revolutionary rhetorics should always be questioned, especially when technology alone is claimed to compel radical social change.

Theorists like Slatin envision the World Wide Web as a new medium requiring a new rhetoric, while others view it more cautiously, retaining certain practices and perspectives derived from the technology of print. The debate over the novelty of hypertext will undoubtedly continue, but what Slatin offered the profession, in addition to timely and provocative arguments, was a well-articulated metaphorical construction. In 1964, Marshall McLuhan called into question communication theories that distinguish between the how and what of communication. His famous adage—the medium is the message—has become palpable in HCI, even though many interface designers still propose that computer interfaces should be transparent (see Horton; Negroponte; Weiser). McLuhan held that the mode of transmission (the medium) can determine the content of communication (the message) as much as the intentions of a sender. In other words, the way we obtain information influences us as much as the information itself. "The medium is the message" was an important, if hyperbolic, aphorism because it energized communication theorists to study the very real imprint of technology on thought and action. Although discussions of computers as hypertextual media can be traced back to at least the 1960s (Press), it was Slatin and other early adopters of hypertext who first encouraged the majority of teachers in departments of English to imagine computers as more than productivity tools or cultural artifacts.

The research literature stresses that the creation of interfaces for hypertextual media frequently places increased demands on writers. As Beverly Kolosseus, Dan Bauer, and Stephen Bernhardt put it, "Hypertext designers must become comfortable with a grammar for text that exists only inside machines, and they must learn to conceptualize texts that exist in layered, multi-dimensional space" (79–80). Crucial to the intellectual switch from writer to designer is a knowledge of the online medium, a point Slatin drives home throughout his article. There are a number of avenues students can take to learn about hypertext, but any approach to rhetorical literacy should consider the ways in which hypertext gets constituted culturally and discursively and how that constitution contributes to the current treatment of this technology in writing and communication courses and in English departments. This consideration is imperative because hypertext design choices are both productively and unproductively shaped by social as well as technological forces. There are three dominant metaphors that define and describe the basic components of the hypertext medium: (nonlinear) texts, (modular) nodes, and (associative) links. These metaphors filter user understandings of hypertext and have real implications for interface design.

### Nonlinear Text

Hypertext systems can potentially contain various combinations of text; the term assumes written words, graphics, and other kinds of media such as animation, audio, and video. The term hypermedia (synonym: interactive multimedia) also includes such expanded notions of text, although the term hypertext is often used generically to refer to hypermedia as well. Whatever the shape of text available in any one system, many claim that what tends to characterize it across applications is a nonlinear quality (Glushko; Horn; Berk and Devlin; Boyle and Ratliff). Nonlinear (hyper) text is commonly contrasted with traditional, linear text, where readers start on the first page of a printed manuscript and turn successive pages until the end. It is also contrasted with other types of electronic texts, such as those created with word-processing programs:

> The word processor treats text like a scroll, a roll of pages sewn together at the ends, and its visual structures are still typographic. A word processor stores its text as a simple sequence of letters, words, and lines. It remembers margins and pagination; it may remember which letters are to be printed in boldface, in Times Roman, or in 14-point type. But a conventional word processor does not treat the text as a network of verbal ideas. It does not contain a map of the ways in which the text may be read. It does not record or act on the semantic structure of the text. A true electronic text does all this, for a true electronic text is not a fixed sequence of letters, but is instead from the writer's point of view a network of verbal elements and from the reader's point of view a texture of possible meanings. (Bolter, *Writing Space* 5)

The metaphor of nonlinearity that is commonly used to characterize such "true" electronic text has both mental and physical components, and some even claim that it adds a certain democratic dimension to user actions: a freedom of movement among, and inscription within, hypertext documents (Bush; Nelson).

The mental component attempts to overcome the linearity of print by allowing users to write their own versions of texts by making navigational choices in the act of reading. Jay Bolter explains that

> The reader of an electronic text functions like the writer of a genre text, or like a poet in the Greek oral tradition. At the very least, the electronic reader is dropping into slots episodes that he or she selects from the preconceived materials of the author. The reader becomes a writer because

> the reader too is putting together symbols to form a text.
> Instead of letters or words, the unit symbols may be sen-
> tences, paragraphs, or sections, but they are symbols none-
> theless, capable of defining different texts by rearrange-
> ment. ("Literature" 33)

Writing by rearrangement allows users to create endless versions of
texts in ways that are meaningful to them and their current tasks
and in ways that are not generally encouraged by traditional, linear
texts whose organizations have been solely defined by authors. As
George Landow and Paul Delany argue, because individuals experience hypertext "as an infinitely decenterable and recenterable system," they make their "own interests the de facto organizing principle (or center) for the investigation at the moment" (18).

The physical component of nonlinear writing attempts to overcome the fixity of print by allowing users to modify the texts they
encounter in the act of reading or to add entirely new texts, nodes,
and links to existing hypertext applications. By contributing to the
content of hypertexts, users collaborate more substantially in the
act of writing—an act some theorists claim complicates traditional
notions of authorship, literacy, and unified textual meaning (see
Heim; Landow; Moulthrop). Conservative examples of such physical writing exist in hypertext systems that allow users to augment
existing material by creating annotations and establishing bookmarks. These user-generated webs overlay structures and contents
provided by interface designers, creating customized spaces that
are seemingly more useful for individuals and groups. More ambitious examples exist in hypertext systems that support a wide range
of collaborative activities, from group brainstorming, writing, and
project planning to negotiating and critiquing lines of argument
(see Adelson and Jordan; Irish and Trigg; Selber, McGavin, Klein,
and Johnson-Eilola).

Despite the ongoing claims that nonlinear writing automatically or inherently provides users with a substantial degree of textual freedom, this enthusiasm is being tempered. As Jay Bolter con-
cedes,

The rhetoric of hypertext—and all of us who work in hypertext are guilty of this exaggeration—tends to be a rhetoric of liberation. We sometimes talk as if the goal of electronic writing were to set the reader free from all the arbitrary fixity and stability of print culture. In fact hypertext simply entangles the reader in nets or networks of a different order. (qtd. in Tuman 76)

Although the profession has been relatively slow to recognize this new form of entanglement, because the metaphor of nonlinearity complies with our best intentions to empower computer users, a reexamination of this metaphor reveals the "seduction" of its geometry (M. Rosenberg).

According to Martin Rosenberg, nonlinear systems such as hypertext still "create rhetorics entrapped in the necessarily logocentric geometry of regulated time and space" (2). Such geometrical space can restrict movement, for example, by locating users within highly contextualized and historicized textual landscapes. In fact, the degree to which these landscapes might aid navigation at least partially corresponds to the ways users come to accept or reject an interface designer's way of knowing. In hypertext applications that contain a central author-generated text around which user actions revolve, "readers/writers can situate themselves in the whole relatively easily by thinking back to where they fall along in the table of contents, the global master-plan, the historical project" (Johnson-Eilola, "Hypertext"). Authors of such hypertexts project grids of possibility that influence user actions in central ways: they structure graphs that map the hierarchies of included information; construct tables of contents and headings that distinguish topics as primary, secondary, tertiary, and so on; and determine which places in a system constitute centers or homes. From these vantage points, users inherit authorial perspectives on how best to approach online information, and their movements from place to place are at least influenced, if not occasionally determined, by the imposed structures. As Johndan Johnson-Eilola explains, "hypertext doesn't construct a generic sort of space in which users are free to move about as they wish free of any ideological baggage. Every space is ideological, every act of writing and/or reading a hypertext is political" ("Hypertext"). Although a site on the Web might allow users to write and read using personal and associative patterns, these patterns are still constrained, for better and worse, by the geometry of the site's structure. The metaphor of nonlinearity, which encourages students and teachers to associate notions of user freedom with the technology of linking texts, masks the often substantial constraints associated with navigating online information regulated by temporal and/or spatial structures and conventions.

### Modular Nodes

Like hardware devices that constitute points on a local area network (LAN) topology, nodes represent points in a hypertext-based network structure of text. These points are commonly viewed as holders of information, virtual spaces that users traverse and/or create while writing and reading in this environment; they also provide addresses for any included links. Nodes can be limited to a word, sentence, or graphic, but they commonly contain information that supports a single concept (much like a written paragraph). Regardless of size, what commonly defines nodes is their ability to link or be linked to other points in a hypertext system. Metaphors commonly used to characterize them are numerous: for example, "page, card, unit, chunk, topic, article, nugget, link destination, frame, record, document, file, event, sequence, segment, passage, entity, component, view" (Berk 551). Although these tropes filter and delimit user experiences in different ways, they all function as container metaphors that influence the shape of text in hypertext.

According to George Lakoff and Mark Johnson, container metaphors impose boundaries on space. They are used, consciously or not, to impose an in-out orientation on physical and natural objects in the world: for example, I am either in my house or out of my house; in the woods or out of the woods. Importantly, even when a boundary is not suggested—in this case, by the walls of a home or clearing in a forest—territory is still marked so that space has both an inside and bounding surface (29). Lakoff and Johnson suggest that defining territory in this manner "is an act of quanti-fication. Bounded objects, whether human beings, rocks, or land areas, have sizes. This allows them to be quantified in terms of the amount of substance they contain" (30). In hypertext, interface de-signers often regulate and measure the content of nodes by employ-ing modular design strategies. As a goal, these strategies help writ-ers develop meaningful chunks of text that are easily represented and understood on a single computer screen. In terms of meta-phoric possibilities, the concept of modularity has strong connec-tions with structured programming techniques developed by com-puter scientists in the early 1970s.

Structured programming techniques employ "a limited number of control structures, top-down design, and module independence" to reduce complexity in the design and maintenance of computer programs (Capron 219). As opposed to using large numbers of GOTO statements, for instance, this approach encourages develop-ers to use control structures that make reading code more sequen-tial and therefore easier to diagnose, maintain, and update. By using top-down or hierarchical design, developers reduce basic program functions to subfunctions or modules that are as manageable and discrete as possible. Like sections in a book chapter or entries in an outline, these modules include logically related statements that sup-port larger, discursive goals. Once inserted into a program, modules execute a particular function in a hierarchy of relations defined by programmers.

One method for evaluating the design and effectiveness of structured programs measures the coupling between modules and the amount of cohesion within single modules (Capron 220). Cou-pling refers to the degree of interdependence that exists among modules. Ideally, relationships between modules should be "weak" so that they operate independently and so that changes made to any one module will not affect the others. Cohesion refers to the "inter-nal strength" of a module, the degree of interrelationship that exists among its internal elements. Ideally, the relationship between inter-nal elements should be "strong" so that each element relates to the performance of only one function. Importantly, a module should only have one entry and one exit, single points from which its function is executed and ended. Delimiting single entry and exit points helps developers track program logic.

The influence of structured programming techniques on writing has been examined by Henrietta Nickels Shirk. In her discussion of the parallels between the histories of computer programming and technical writing, she notes that

> the recent history of Technical Writing closely parallels the development of many design methodologies in the software side of the computer industry. These methodologies (specifically, those for visually presenting programming information) have had far-reaching effects on documentation both within and outside the computer industry. Not only have graphics and page design been influenced by software design techniques, but these in turn have created some widespread metaphorical assumptions about documentation. (306)

While technical writers have acknowledged the often valuable influences of structured programming techniques on both paper-based and hypertext documents, an important consideration remains primarily undiscussed in HCI: Because computer and human languages differ in important ways, the techniques and principles that programmers use for writing elegant code may not necessarily translate well for students writing hypertexts. In fact, these techniques and principles can reduce the rhetorical complexity of interface design tasks and encourage a distorted view of how language operates in cultural contexts.

In structured programming, developers can create modules that are independent (or contain weak coupling) by specifying inputs and outputs that determine how meaning is made in particular environments. Once these inputs and outputs are specified, the instructions programmers code are interpreted by a given computer in exact ways, and the meaning of these instructions is therefore fixed. In human language, however, writers cannot determine the effect of an environment on communication or communicative acts. Ferdinand de Saussure and structuralist thinkers after him have demonstrated how the relations between signifiers (sounds) and signifieds (concepts) in language are arbitrary, and that signs are only identifiable in relation to what they are not in a larger community of signs. In other words, language does not simply reflect fixed, universal concepts in nature but is composed of relations based on difference. Poststructuralist thinkers have further complicated this notion by arguing that, if signs are only understood in relation to each other, and therefore always involve every other sign in the system, then meaning is never fully present in any instance of language. Poststructuralism provides interface designers with insights into the contingent nature of human language, or the multiple and contradictory meanings associated with texts.

When working with human as opposed to programming language, therefore, the metaphor of modularity is necessarily constituted in less rigid ways. Instead of constructing chunks of code that contain some absolute meaning and therefore execute only one function, writers in hypertext work with language that by its very nature cannot represent only one possible meaning and that may take on different, even contradictory meaning depending on how and when users access particular nodes. So rigid notions of modularity in HCI may encourage popular design advice that reduces students' understanding of the ways users make meaning with text in hypertext. For example, interface designers are commonly advised to map explicitly the logical relations between nodes in a network structure of text. Both the goal and challenge of such an activity is to create semantically meaningful chunks of text that users can understand regardless of their previous locations in a system. Like modular chunks of code that operate independently of an entire program, nodes of text in hypertext are supposed to be meaningful to a range of users either in isolation or in the context of a particular reading. But if we assume that users at least partially make meaning in the act of writing and reading hypertext (or any text for that matter), as opposed to neutrally understanding some predetermined meaning identified by interface designers, then our notions of modularity appropriated from HCI need expansion or modification: A text considered amodular in any one reading could be considered quite modular in a different or new reading because node relevance would depend significantly on the perspectives of users. Though it is clearly valuable to borrow metaphors from HCI that help student writers design hypertexts, such borrowing should consider the potentially harmful consequences of conflating the interpretive habits of humans and machines.

*Associative Links*

Links in hypertext represent relations between nodes in a network structure of text and physically connect these relations to form complex webs of meaning that users can traverse. Some hypertext systems allow designers to designate link types, which describe the kind of relationship that exists between nodes. For example, Edward Fox, Qi Fan Chen, and Robert France describe links that connect commentaries with the texts to which they refer, definitions with the words they define, spreadsheets with sum totals in reports they support, and digitized photographs with the people they portray. Consistently designed, link types help users identify the wide range of textual relationships that are possible in any one hypertext system. Regardless of type, however, what commonly defines a link is its ability to point in at least one direction, from a source node to a target node, and to be actuated by users. Common paper-based metaphors for the term link include "library card catalogs, footnotes, cross-references, sticky notes, commentaries, indexes, quotes, and anthologies" while computer-based metaphors include "linked note cards, popup notes, linked screens or windows, stretch text (outlines), semantic nets, branching stories, relational databases, and simulations" (Horn 30–33). Although the term *link* is commonly used to describe the mechanism that joins nodes together, at the core of this metaphor and others is the notion that such links, and the relations they connect, are associative: that they represent, and can thus map, the workings and organization of human memory (Conklin; Parunak).

The idea of associative networks forms the earliest conceptual basis for hypertext, and the promise of this technology seems largely tied to its ability to support personal ways of writing, reading, and structuring texts. Vannevar Bush, writing in the 1940s in response to the limitations that he saw in print-based indexing systems designed to handle increasingly vast and varied amounts of information, considered linking to be the central quality of the memex, the precursor to computer-based hypertext systems:

> It affords an immediate step, however, to associative indexing, the basic idea of which is a provision whereby any item may be caused at will to select immediately and automatically another. This is the essential feature of the memex. The process of tying two items together is the important thing. (103)

Assuming that the human brain works by association, Bush argued that such an ability would allow scientists and scientific communities to work more naturally, to pursue and replicate thought processes common to their day-to-day work.

Building upon Bush's description of, and assumptions informing, the memex, Ted Nelson also urged an ambitious vision of hypertext, a *docuverse* containing all the world's literature online that could be connected and reconnected in an infinite number of ways. Central to this project, and to others in the hypertext community that employ World Wide Web resources, is the notion that print-based texts often fail to encourage nonlinear writing and reading, and therefore associative thinking. Nelson provides two general arguments to support his claim: The technology of print "spoils the unity and structure of interconnection" and "forces a single sequence for all readers which may be appropriate for none" (1/14). The former observation has also been made in social thought associated with rhetorical and writing studies. Notions of intertextuality, multivocality, and decenteredness that privilege a kind of textual openness—where every text at least always refers to other related texts and contexts—underscore Nelson's concerns about the textual closeness encouraged by the technology of print. The latter claim about print's inability to accommodate diverse, complex, and multiple audiences has been discussed, at least in spirit, in the literature on audience analysis. For example, in their overview of common approaches to structuring printed functional documents for varied audiences, Melissa Holland, Veda Charrow, and William Wright advise that writers may need to develop separate documents that correspond to the different reading goals that audiences bring to reading tasks. And textbooks in technical writing have long noted how certain segments of reports are often designed to meet the needs of different readers.

However, even if writers can seemingly find ways of successfully structuring printed texts for different audiences or creating entirely separate texts for all audiences, these tasks still assume that writers can clearly identify some unified meaning for texts and that readers of an intended audience learn, problem-solve, and make meaning in the same ways. But, as Janice Redish notes,

> Meaning does not reside in the text of a document; it exists only in the minds of communicators who produce documents and readers who use documents. Because each reader is an individual with his or her own knowledge, interests, and skills, a text can have as many meanings as it has readers. (22)

Of course, this is also true of a fixed text; much hypertext theory assumes incorrectly that fixed texts always address a monadic, static, unified reader. Still, one promise of hypertext is that it can provide users with greater and perhaps even different opportunities in which to explore information and make meaning from texts by way of personal associations: Their writing, reading, and thinking patterns are made explicit and ultimately support individual learning styles and problem-solving strategies. Applications that provide such potentially customized learning spaces exist not only in corporate sites but in educational settings as well.

Despite the pedagogical promise of mapping user associations in hypertext, applications commonly privilege links or connections generated by teachers at the (unconscious or conscious) expense of those generated by students. An example of such an instance is outlined by David Jonassen, who describes hypertext-based tools for evoking semantic networks from subject-matter experts that can be used to shape a novice learner's understanding and experience of some new information. According to Jonassen and cognitive theory, as individuals go through life they develop schemata or mental models that organize their experiences and that help them understand and interpret new knowledge domains. The more associations that individuals can form between old and new knowledge, the better their understanding of that new knowledge is likely to be. One pedagogical assumption of such a position is that learning requires individuals to instantly restructure their schemata in response to new experiences. Another is that, in the process of learning, a novice's knowledge structure (or semantic network) increasingly resembles, to varying degrees, that of an expert's ("Semantic" 144). Ultimately, according to Jonassen, "the instructional process may be thought of as the mapping of subject matter knowledge (usually that possessed by the teacher or expert) onto the learner's knowledge structure" (144).

As opposed to supporting associative ways of learning, hypertext can paradoxically become a technology that unwittingly positions students in relatively passive rather than active roles. At the extreme, one could argue that the automation of expert knowledge in virtual space, combined with the authority often attributed to hypertext (and other "technologies of progress") in Western culture, encourage computer-based instructional approaches that actually limit rather than enrich student learning. In terms of Paulo Freire's banking concept of education, "in which the students are the depositories and the teacher is the depositor" (58), novices may be simply asked to reproduce the knowledge of an expert, which can at least be partially mapped and captured in hypertext systems. In this way, interface designers and other experts contributing to these systems centrally shape a subject area and the manner in which learners approach that area pedagogically and epistemologically:

> It follows logically from the banking notion of consciousness that the educator's role is to regulate the way the

world "enters into" the students. His [or her] task is to
organize a process which already occurs spontaneously,
to "fill" the students by making deposits of information
which he [or she] considers to constitute true knowledge.
(Freire 63)

Although hypertext can encourage associative work, it can also
support literacy practices that discourage students from pursuing
this type of personal inquiry. In fact, as Alister Cumming and Gerri
Sinclair argue,

If teachers are prompted to determine the content and
uses of hypermedia, following conventional practices, it is
probable that the potential uses of hypermedia will be reduced to task routines which are not, fundamentally, unlike those now occurring in classrooms using less sophisticated media. (322)

Interface designers frequently rely on the metaphor of association as
evidence of user control, but such a reliance may unintentionally
mask the potential of hypertext to support control by experts rather
than students.

The metaphors that define and describe texts, nodes, and links,
then, encourage developments and uses of hypertext along particular axes of interest, and so the realms from which these metaphors
are appropriated should therefore be considered in any rhetorical
approach to computer literacy. To provide students with the theoretical lenses needed for such considerations, a crucial pedagogical
activity is to conceptualize metaphor as a social force, that is, as a
trope that filters and delimits experience, functions as a heuristic
device, and helps constitute what a culture considers knowledge.
From this epistemic viewpoint, metaphors are not simply stylistic
devices or reducible to literal expressions without cognitive loss.
Rather, as with other forms of language, they play a central role in
how meaning is made discursively. And, because terrains mapped
metaphorically are marked by preferred sets of beliefs and perspec-

tives, they represent a useful area in which to examine social influences in HCI.

There are many theories that articulate how metaphors operate semantically, but Max Black's interactive view provides an account that highlights their filtering quality. According to Black, metaphors contain two constituent halves: a principal and subsidiary subject (or what I. A. Richards has termed a *tenor* and *vehicle*). A subsidiary subject filters our experience of a principal subject by providing contexts that impose an extension or change of meaning; this occurs when individuals attempt to connect or reconcile the realms of thought summoned by what a metaphor juxtaposes (73). As I demonstrated in the previous discussion, it is not difficult to identify subsidiary subjects that commonly influence the design and use of hypertext. And they each invoke a different "system of associated commonplaces" (74) or set of cultural connections. According to Black, these connections might include "half-truths or down-right mistakes (as when a whale is classified as a fish); but the important thing for the metaphor's effectiveness is not that the commonplaces be true, but that they should be readily and freely evoked" (74). Thus, this filtering process relies on cultural myths as well as on more accurate understandings of the relationships between things juxtaposed in metaphorical constructions. This is an important point that should be stressed to students.

Although metaphors for hypertextual media may be both productive and unproductive, as well as rich in contradiction, they are always significantly influential. Through these tropes and other social, political, and ideological forces, teachers help articulate forms to hypertext, mapping a wide range of potential uses within the territory of rhetorical literacy. However, as cartographer Dennis Wood notes, the making of these maps is never innocent—certain interests are always served through representational gestures. Because the effectiveness of metaphors is a direct result of their selectivity, they work to naturalize certain cultural perspectives on how hypertext might be best designed and employed. Teachers should therefore help students become critical readers of the metaphors that are commonly used to represent human-computer interfaces, a task that requires paying attention to their "absences" as well as "presences" (Wood).

## Conclusion

Rhetorical literacy concerns the design and evaluation of online environments; thus students who are rhetorically literate can effect change in technological systems. Students should not be just effective users of computers, nor should they be just informed questioners. Although these two roles are essential, neither one encourages a sufficient level of participation. In order to function most effectively as agents of change, students must also become reflective producers of technology, a role that involves a combination of functional and critical abilities. Teachers who are responsible for helping students become rhetorically literate might feel nervous about this prospect, and indeed interface design is a brave new world for many humanists. However, interface design can be understood as largely a rhetorical activity, one that includes persuasion, deliberation, reflection, social action, and an ability to analyze metaphors. The key for teachers is to be flexible in their perspectives on literacy. As Kathleen Welch argues, "electric rhetoric is not a destroyer of literacy, as is commonly thought. It is, instead, an extension of literacy, a thrilling extension," one that "will bring about many important changes and may bring about good changes" (157). These changes include not only new definitions of literacy but also different decisions about who should have a say in the design of literacy technologies. The time is ripe for students and teachers in departments of English to have their say.

# 5 / Systemic Requirements for Change

> Technology must be sociotechnical rather than technical, and
> a technology must include managerial and social supporting
> systems necessary to apply it on a significant scale. Most highly
> original inventions have usually involved social as well as
> technical innovation.
>
> —Harvey Brooks,<br>"Technology, Evolution, Purpose"

One cannot overestimate what is required to implement, operate, and maintain a computer literacy program that prepares students in the multiple ways that I have outlined in the previous chapters. The requirements are numerous and subject to local conditions. Still, local circumstances cannot be the only consideration. In fact, any attempt to enact change may be most effective when the effort to do so is guided by an imaginative framework that illuminates the broad requirements associated with a more productive vision of computer literacy, because teachers of writing and communication have come to recognize that systematic efforts frequently yield more insightful results. Although I will offer such a framework, I encourage teachers to think of it as an imperfect heuristic rather than as a rigid prescription for action.

The purpose of this chapter is to help teachers envision a full-fledged program that integrates and emphasizes functional literacy, critical literacy, and rhetorical literacy in ways that are effective and professionally responsible. Its tone takes on a sort of informed practicality in that the chapter respects the existing research and the expertise of teachers about their institutional settings while offering real suggestions for how to go about imagining a computer multiliteracies program. I suspect very few departments of English have such a program, yet after reading this chapter, teachers should have some idea about how to develop one, even if their departments do not have a specialist in literacy and technology on the faculty, and even if some department members are rather fearful of technology.

I begin with a necessary detour through theories of change, arguing that a systemic perspective is especially needed in technological contexts. Some believe that the most important part of a computer literacy program is the technology itself, but a systemic perspective reminds teachers that any change initiative requires an attention to many different aspects of an educational system, not just one (if important) piece of it. Moreover, a systemic perspective stresses that there is no final end point at which change is fully and finally realized. Rather, because change is a function of numerous interrelated forces—some stable, some not—it is fragile and requires ongoing consideration and commitment. Which is why it is so important for English departments to formalize computer literacy programs, in order to ensure that teachers of writing and communication are sufficiently supported and recognized for the vital work that they do.

Toward this end, the chapter conceptualizes the requirements needed for systemic change as an assemblage of nested contexts, a conceptualization in which an increasingly broad set of forces is implicated and no single context can be understood in isolation from the others. As figure 5.1 illustrates, the innermost context involves technical requirements and from there the requirements spiral outward, from pedagogical to departmental contexts and beyond. Importantly, this figure is not a set of concentric circles with technology as a common center (a techno-centric model). Rather, it is a representation that situates technology in contexts that are ever more social in nature.

Although table 5.1 does not model the spiral shape of nested contexts, it does summarize the requirements needed for systemic change and the approaches I put forward to address them. Both the requirements and approaches are far from exhaustive, but they provide a sense of what is needed to realize computer literacy programs that encourage multiple literacies.

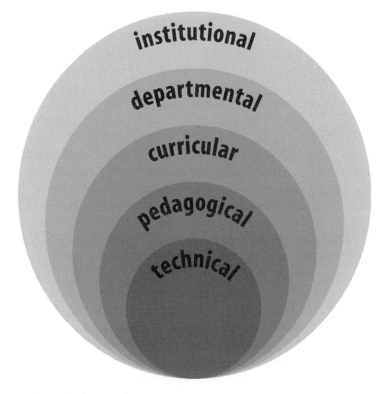

Fig. 5.1. The nested contexts in a computer multiliteracies program

## Assumptions about the Nature of Change

Numerous theories attempt to explain how change takes place in educational settings. There are theories that come at it from the top-down, and there are theories that come at it from the bottom-up (R. Morgan). There are theories that understand change as a process that can be modeled in a series of sequential stages: for example, evaluation, initiation, implementation, and routinization (Hage and Aiken). There are theories that posit effective communication as the key to educational change. That is, meaningful change cannot take place unless the stakeholders are involved and agree that

**Table 5.1**
Systemic Requirements for Change in Technological
Contexts

| Requirements | Approaches |
| --- | --- |
| Technical | (1) Shape computer-related infrastructures on campus through participation in official discussions about technological requirements. (2) Use technical exigencies as a way to raise questions about current practices that do not support the needs of students and teachers in writing and communication courses. |
| Pedagogical | (1) Scaffold instruction that leverages well-known contexts and gradually releases certain responsibilities to technologically competent students. (2) Use (ungraded) diagnostic measures to learn about the technological experiences and attitudes of students. (3) See pedagogy and technology as coextensive and mutually constitutive, which requires teachers to become thoughtful designers of technological environments. |
| Curricular | Conceptualize the tripartite framework of functional literacy, critical literacy, and rhetorical literacy as a fractal that can be applied in ever smaller scales to the curricular components of academic programs. That is, apply the framework (1) to curricula as a whole, (2) to specific courses, and (3) to individual assignments. |

*Continued on the next page*

## Table 5.1 *Continued*

| Requirements | Approaches |
| --- | --- |
| Departmental and Institutional | (1) Demonstrate that humanists can help a university construct better alternatives to computer literacy. (2) Hire, retain, and value tenure-line faculty members whose primary scholarly work resides at the nexus of literacy and technology. (3) Provide ongoing professional development opportunities for faculty and graduate students. (4) Provide easy access to technological environments that have been designed to support the work of writing and communication teachers. (5) Account for the fact that technology adds real layers of complexity to any project. (6) Recognize the fact that technology work typically contains a measure of professional risk for teachers, which is often unforeseen. (7) Hold open forums in which people who might be affected by the computer literacy initiatives have opportunities to voice their perspectives. (8) Recognize the fact that successful computer literacy programs require significant ongoing expenditures. (9) Encourage administrators to clearly and continuously communicate their support for the computer literacy initiatives of writing and communication teachers. |

change is needed (Wiggam). David Dill and Charles Friedman review the extensive literature on innovation and change in higher education and report that the majority of theoretical approaches can be located across four frameworks: planned change models, which focus on the change process in and of itself; conflict models, which focus on the social conditions that lead to conflict, a significant catalyst for change; diffusion models, which focus on the ways innovations migrate from creation to use in social systems; and complex organization models, which focus on the variables that characterize social systems as a whole and the systemic change those variables can encourage. I will argue in this section that systemic perspectives are particularly important in the context of computer literacy.

The problem with so many approaches to change is that they reduce a system to its parts but ultimately neglect the relationship of the parts to the whole. But like literacy itself, change involves the interconnected workings of numerous different elements in a loosely coordinated fashion. Although partition is a valuable analytic tool, piecemeal approaches can assign too much causal weight to a single factor and not enough to the highly interactive, complex, and contingent network of forces that constitute human activity systems. In educational settings, technology is often seen as the primary intervention in a system where a variety of interrelated interventions are needed to achieve change. Almost everyone who works with computers has extolled their benefits at one point or another, yet it is highly unlikely that computer technologies, all on their own, will engender the kinds of social, political, and pedagogical reform the profession is interested in.

The part-oriented, reductionist outlook on change is not hard to come across, especially in discussions of educational technologies. For example, Diana Oblinger and Anne-Lee Verville state that "technology is inexorable" (47). In their article "Information Technology as a Change Agent," Oblinger and Verville contend that "fundamental technological change ultimately begets significant structural change, regardless of whether the affected participants choose to join or resist the movement" (54). Their deterministic account of the dynamics of change in higher education identifies four technological trends that will transform research and instructional activities: digitization, data storage, processing power, and universal communications. Digitization techniques, according to Oblinger and Verville, provide a universal "language" for effective communication worldwide, one that "makes the once improbable entirely possible" (48). Data-rich materials (hypermedia) provide more powerful educational experiences. The speed and power of personal computers provide super capabilities, which greatly increase productivity and efficiency. And global connectivity radically alters patterns of access and control. Given such developments, these researchers claim, computers will inevitably and universally change the educational process, and for the better. Never mind the activities of students and teachers and program administrators, never mind the histories of departments and institutions, and never mind the politics and economics of higher education—put computers in universities, and wonderful things will happen.

The impulse to envision computers as autonomous agents of change is understandable on some level, in part because educators tend to be hopeful and overly optimistic professionals. Not only that, but computer technologies, under certain circumstances and in certain contexts, *have* contributed in unique and impressive ways to educational endeavors and assisted the progress of positive change. Examples of this situation are not hard to imagine: ESL students who do not like to participate in face-to-face conversations because they are self-conscious about their oral skills come alive in electronic conferences; traditional students who are technologically savvy decenter authority in the classroom by helping other students —and their teachers—design sites on the World Wide Web; and nontraditional students who must hold down a job and/or care for family members further their education through courses and programs offered online. However, in each of these instances, it is also not hard to imagine a set of counter forces that could cancel out such desirable outcomes. For example, the dominant discourses in online conversations could still manage to silence ESL students who are communicative-apprehensive learners (or, for that matter, students who avoid combative interactions). Teachers could feel threatened by technologically savvy students and thus could reassert their authority in ways that are counterproductive. The design of online courses and programs could include synchronous components that conflict with the work schedules or family commitments of nontraditional students, which would make it difficult, if not impossible, for them to participate. And these forces—discourse, authority, instructional design—are just some of the forces that help determine the interactions and experiences associated with computers. That is why a systemic outlook is essential, to provide more accurate perspectives on the change process per se and on the vast complex of interconnected factors that might aid (or impede) the adoption of more expansive articulations of computer literacy.

Systemic approaches offer teachers a conceptual frame of reference that shifts attention away from oversimplified cause-effect relationships, often between just two variables, and toward networked conceptions in which causation is considered to be a mutual, multiple, and contingent phenomenon, one that can be difficult to trace or pin down. There are numerous theoretical variations on this theme. In fact, Lars Skyttner discusses no less than a dozen different systems theories and their presuppositions, dynamics, and applications. However, some systems theories, it should be noted, are throwbacks to Newtonian classical science and thus do not conceptualize change in ways that are structurally complex. For example, Val Rust distinguishes between closed systems frameworks and open systems frameworks. Closed systems, which are "rigidly controlled" and "deterministic" in character (43), are insulated from their social contexts. Consequently, change is harder to realize in closed systems, in part because decisions are made at the top, in a unilateral fashion, and because the objectives and goals of such systems are prescribed, with little to no room for self-direction. Rust notes that schools in totalitarian states, highly centralized democratic states, and those affiliated with certain fundamentalist religions typically fit this category. In contrast, open systems, which are "pluralist" and "complex" in character (42), are responsive—and vulnerable—to their social contexts, so change is easier to realize, if less predictable. Moreover, those in open systems have opportunities to contribute to the objectives, directions, and workings of such systems. Rust notes that public schools in decentralized democratic states, nontraditional schools, and artistic educational communities typically fit this category. The distinction between closed and open systems is an important one in that it reminds teachers that not all systems-oriented approaches recognize micropolitical actions or broader social forces.

Although systems theories vary in numerous and notable ways, there are several shared principles of open systems that can shed light on change processes in university settings: educational systems are nested in communities and the larger society; educational systems themselves are composed of multiple systems; educational systems are greater than the sum of their parts; change in one part of an educational system affects the other parts; and educational systems organize and mutate over time (see Banathy; Hanson). There are more principles, but these should be adequate for the purposes here because they suggest three key points. First, that open systems operate on different hierarchical levels means that teachers must look well beyond their own classroom contexts, in both upwards and downwards directions, as they contemplate and work toward the kinds of changes they would like to see. Second, that change is a function of the (uneven) interaction of a multitude of variables means that change should always be associated with more than one factor, no matter how potent a particular factor might appear to be. Third, that open systems are living systems, constantly in flux, means that the direction of change can be difficult to predict and that the forces that encouraged change at one historical point might not encourage it at another. Change, therefore, is not something that is achieved once and for all but must be constantly nurtured and tended, especially in schools where there is an inclination to reproduce the status quo.

So what does any of this have to do with computer literacy? To start, the nature of change in open systems adumbrates the complexity of the task before teachers who want to encourage the multiple literacies discussed in this book. I am optimistic that effective change can be brought about, but it will not happen overnight, nor will it happen on a meaningful scale unless there is commitment and cooperation from more than a few interested individuals. Furthermore, expansive computer literacy programs will require routine maintenance. Inertia is in the direction of reductive functional approaches, and conservative winds can buffet even the best-laid plans. For this reason, computer literacy programs must be institutionalized in ways that allow them to be revisited, freshened up, and renewed, as a matter of course, on theoretical, practical, and administrative levels. Finally, teachers will need to pay attention to far more than technical requirements. Although these should be considered, other parts of the educational system will be equally important to any prospects for change. Thus, the sections that follow consider not only technical requirements but also pedagogical, curricular, departmental, and institutional requirements.

## Technical Requirements

In one respect, an obvious place to start is with the technical requirements intimated by my multilayered version of computer literacy. For example, the functional layer implies access to—and control over—technologies that can support the educational goals of students, help them manage their computer-based activities, and help them resolve their technological impasses. The critical layer implies access to computer technologies for the purposes of critique, and not just one platform: Students need to be able to study different instantiations of the same system, in order to compare and contrast the various politics of technological contexts. And the rhetorical layer implies access to robust computer environments that can support the technical side of interface design, which includes the collaborative production of rapid prototypes and visual images, not to mention actual interfaces that function. Given these requirements, I could attempt to outline a specific set of technical parameters, one that could be used in any English department. However, such an approach would fall prey to the narrow functional perspectives that I criticized in chapter 2, those that totalize literacy as a neutral skill that can be transferred cross-culturally to achieve universal results. To avoid such a backslide, I will instead encourage teachers to influence the technological infrastructure on their campuses, so that it might support the development of multiple computer literacies from a humanistic perspective. As I will suggest, this can be accomplished through both official and unofficial means.

The area of technical requirements is the most obvious area, yet in some ways it is also the hardest one to talk about in general terms. That is because any attempt to pinpoint technical requirements should consider the local standards and approaches students come into contact with across their curricular experiences. Why should this be so? Because it makes sense to tap into mature resources and to minimize the number of systems students must learn to operate, assuming that the standards and approaches are workable in writing and communication courses. For example, my institution has a set of technical requirements for all students in distance education courses, and whenever possible I adhere to these requirements because Penn State has decided to put all of its credit courses online, ensuring that they will be available not only to distance education students but also to approximately eighty thousand resident students across twenty-four campuses. However, this accommodation sometimes compels me to make adjustments because the technical requirements do not always support the computer literacies I encourage. For example, the requirements call for a fifteen-inch monitor (800 × 600 resolution). Although 800 × 600 pixels is a standard size for Web pages, the monitor size is simply too small for many interface design tasks. The small size of the monitor also makes it difficult for students to manage multiple application spaces at once, which is an important functional activity. I also deviate from the standard in the CD-ROM requirement. The technical requirements do not call for a CD-ROM drive, the assumption being that students can download university-approved software over the network and that they have ample personal server space. But CD-ReWritable (CD-RW) drives, which have become commonplace, provide a relatively inexpensive method for students to use to archive, backup, and share information (one CD can hold up to 650 megabytes of information, the equivalent of more than 450 floppy disks). I stray from the standard technical requirements in other ways, but the majority of the requirements seem to serve the purposes of students and teachers in my department reasonably well.

It should come as no surprise, however, that teachers of writing and communication are not at the top of the list when universities consult with their faculty and staff about technical requirements, even those connected to literacy. That is why some departments of English have decided to go it alone, to administer their own facilities in which students have access to computer-based environments that have been designed with the objectives of the profession in mind by teachers who understand such environments not as computational spaces but as discursive spaces. There is an enormously rich and deep literature on the technical issues associated with the design of computer-based facilities, and I will not discuss these issues here, for they have been well rehearsed in recent years in books, articles, and conference presentations. Rather, the point I want to make is that even departments that are ambitious enough to operate their own facilities must be alert to larger technological contexts.

Indeed, in the world of networked computers, no individual computer facility is an island unto itself: English departments almost always count on such institutional resources as Internet backbones, remote access services, databases and directories, administrative applications, Usenet news (Netnews) servers, high performance systems (e.g., videoconferencing systems), university firewalls, and more. Although this infrastructure should be leveraged, it must also be taken into account because institutional infrastructures can present certain challenges to students and teachers. For example, university firewalls provide a needed measure of protection from security threats, but systems administrators will be the first to admit that firewalls can also block legitimate network uses. On another— and no less important—level, departments must be mindful of the technical policies of their institutions, which frequently include computer usage agreements, Web publishing guidelines, guidelines on the distribution and use of electronic surveys, and institutional positions on intellectual property, online privacy, and the use of university data about, or stored in, its online environments (e.g., Web server statistics). The efficacy of institutional policies should be scrutinized, but such policies must also be taken seriously because some of them are a matter of law and because negligent departments can jeopardize student access to important resources.

If universities are not quick to consult humanists on technical issues, then teachers of writing and communication must look for ways to enter the conversations that shape the technical infrastructures on their campuses. And of course there are different routes into those conversations, both official and unofficial. An example of an official route are the feedback mechanisms used to collect software suggestions from academic computer users. Sometimes these mechanisms are as simple as an e-mail address one can send questions and comments to, or a Web-based form that seeks specific reactions but also provides a field for open-ended responses. However, feedback mechanisms can be more elaborate and encourage teachers and (sometimes) students to assist in the development of software programs. At my institution, for example, there was a call for participation to contribute to the development of our student portal, a site students can personalize and use to organize their digital world. I responded to this call because I wanted to use the portal in my technical writing courses. One of my standard assignments asks students to assemble a research guide for other students in their major. This assignment requires writers to think concretely about audience, purpose, and context of use, but also to collaborate, evaluate print-based and online resources, abstract and organize them in meaningful ways, and compile the resources into a usable format that can be employed for research purposes. I wanted to update this assignment by asking students to design disciplinary portals for other students in their major, a task that would begin to disclose the issues associated with interface design (portal features are not created from the ground up, but chosen from design libraries). Yet what I discovered through various beta tests was that an online portal cannot be shared because access to it on any level requires a unique password that must remain secure, the same password students use to access their e-mail accounts or to transfer files to their personal server spaces. So through standard feedback protocols I lobbied the developers to create a read-only path into student portals. This path, I suggested, could allow read-only access to anyone online anywhere, or just to users in the Penn State system, or just to users the portal owner identified, or to nobody at all. Students would decide who has access to their online portal and when. The portal developers took me seriously because I made time to participate in their usability tests and because my suggestions had the potential to increase the value of the portal system by an order of magnitude in that they would extend the system from personal to social realms. At the same time, my suggestions promised to help create an environment for students and teachers in writing and communication courses that is more pedagogically friendly.

Before I provide an example of an unofficial route into conversations about technical requirements, I want to detour through an example of an official route with some unofficial dimensions that can help students grasp the overall concept of multiple computer literacies. Universities typically operate a number of e-mail forums (via mechanisms including listserv lists and/or Usenet newsgroups) that anyone in the university community can join in order to stay abreast of technical developments on campus. There are forums that focus on products, vendors, and service providers, announcements (e.g., network outages and emergencies), security issues, technical policy issues, development issues, and the like. I suspect that very few teachers actually subscribe to such forums, in part because they are unaware of them: New faculty are rarely told that these forums exist, let alone which ones might be particularly pertinent. Moreover, busy teachers typically depend upon computer support personnel who monitor these forums to forward any crucial messages. However, although e-mail forums of a technical nature all too often function as one-way communication channels that an elite few use to broadcast technical decisions made in a relatively autonomous fashion, this does not have to be the case. Indeed, e-mail forums constitute a form of computer-supported cooperative work that has productively anchored the campuswide systems that ensure that anyone has opportunities to contribute to discussions of technical requirements. But on a subsequent level, such forums can serve as sites that can be used to introduce alternative visions of computer literacy.

For example, students could be asked to join a forum and study its discourse from functional, critical, and rhetorical perspectives. Recall that one parameter of a functional approach is social conventions: Students should be able to decipher the discursive codes that have been adopted in socialized network spaces. Toward that end, students could study the online discourse to discern its authorized patterns: the kinds of topics that are taken up, the appeals that seem to be successful, the unwritten rules for participation, and so on. The instructional objective is to help students learn ways to successfully enter the online conversations they hope to participate in and shape. Students could then turn a critical eye toward that same discourse. What are the social forces that regulate the discussion? Who is able to speak and why? Are there legitimate topics that have been shut down or avoided? Such questions encourage students to interrogate the dominant discourses, to explore power relations in electronic spaces that are frequently touted as egalitarian. Lastly, students could examine the interface configuration of the e-mail forum itself. Students who are rhetorically literate can effect change in technological systems, and they can do so by being invited to investigate both the different software options available to forum administrators and the potential consequences of those options for users and their conversations. Laurie Cubbison provides an accessible example of such an investigation in her analysis of the configuration possibilities in a listserv header file. I have students read her article for a thoughtful discussion of the available options and then examine an actual listserv list to see how administrator choices might have played out. Another possibility is for teachers to include students in the process of configuring e-mail forums used in writing and communication courses. Although e-mail forums for the discussion of technical requirements are not created to be research sites, they can help introduce the concept of multiple literacies in surprisingly useful ways.

To return to the heart of the matter, unofficial routes into conversations about technical requirements can be found in the interstices of routine practices, especially in technical exigencies conducive to discussions and debates on matters of institutional policy. The heated controversy over Napster, a peer-to-peer environment students have used to freely exchange copyrighted musical works, opened spaces not only for discussions of ethical and legal issues but also for computer usage policies. In the face of Napster, Gnutella, Freenet, and other peer-to-peer applications, universities have been compelled to enter into conversations about the appropriate use of network resources, as student computers are turned into servers that transfer large files over university networks. Although most universities have taken a conservative stance on Napster-like programs because of concerns over copyright law suits, the controversy has enabled conversations about who determines computer usage policies, which do not always have a basis in law, and what counts as productive computer activities. In fact, I have used the Napster controversy to start electronic conversations that fruitfully blur the dividing line between so-called proper educational activities and student interests.

But technical exigencies on a more local level can also provide unofficial opportunities to talk about—and influence—technical requirements. For example, almost all of the universities I have been associated with have, at one point or another, conducted an unscheduled sweep of departmental computers to ferret out software programs that have been illegally installed by faculty and graduate students. Whether these sweeps are considered to be unwarranted intrusions or mere annoyances, hardly ever are they viewed as occasions in which technical standards might be discussed or challenged. I am aware of one sweep in an English department that turned up numerous illegal copies of a bibliographic software program and a file conversion program. In such a situation, the impulse is to condemn the guilty parties and admonish them to follow the rules in the future, to only use software programs that have been obtained via approved channels. However, this situation also created an opportune time to revisit standard desktop configurations and to reconsider the computer resources faculty and graduate students need in order to be productive.

As I mentioned earlier, there will always be different valid answers to the question of technical requirements, answers that will reflect specific considerations of local circumstances. So the best concrete advice is to keep a vigilant eye out for ways to influence the computer culture on a campus. There are both official and unofficial routes into conversations about technical requirements. Often, though not exclusively, official routes can be found through university sponsored e-mail lists and mechanisms designed to solicit usability feedback from academic computer users. Unofficial routes are less predictable but can be constructed out of technical exigencies that necessitate, or are conducive to, larger discussions of policies, standards, and conventions. Although change often comes at a glacial pace in academia, it comes nonetheless, and teachers who are attentive and judicious can be instrumental in the formation and evolution of technological infrastructures.

## Pedagogical Requirements

If technical requirements is one obvious area of consideration, another is the pedagogical requirements that might support a more productive vision of computer literacy. After all, as Henry Giroux (*Teachers*) reminds us in his work on teachers as transformative intellectuals, and as scores of teachers already know through first-hand experience, pedagogy represents one of the most immediate and direct ways for teachers to encourage (or discourage) educational change. The three requirements I discuss in this section have to do with teachers, students, and pedagogical facilities and resources, although all of them involve micropolitical action on the part of teachers. More specifically, the requirements call on teachers to be courageous enough to experiment with technology in the classroom, even if that experimentation makes them rather uncomfortable, and even if it positions them as novices to some degree; to evaluate the technological experiences and attitudes of students by means of self-assessment surveys, hands-on activities, and technology narratives; and to understand pedagogy and technology as coextensive and mutually constitutive, an understanding that requires teachers to become reflective designers of the technological facilities and resources they employ.

When it comes to pedagogical requirements, the good news is that more comprehensive approaches to computer literacy do not necessarily require completely new pedagogies. Although I will discuss three essential pedagogical aspects, it is safe to say that on some level there are objectives and methods already in place that apply to almost any subject matter or instructional situation. Mike Markel has taken commentators in the distance education literature to task for their not infrequent claim that online education demands wholly novel pedagogical approaches. One of his main points, which seems to me irrefutable, is that most teachers share certain goals that transcend individual classroom contexts, online or off. For example, most writing teachers want their students to learn how to learn; reason rhetorically, creatively, and analytically; collaborate productively; locate and assess information; and communicate information clearly and persuasively to different audiences (216–17). This list is not meant to be comprehensive, but to suggest that certain time-tested goals can carry over into new media contexts (e.g., we want our students to be able to reason rhetorically, whether they are composing expository essays or designing Websites). In addition, Markel argues, what teachers do both inside and outside the classroom is not necessarily refigured in extreme ways as courses are moved online. That is, writing teachers have similar sorts of responsibilities in either online or on-site contexts—among them, to prepare well-organized instructional materials, to provide prompt and supportive feedback, to stay current with the field, to help students with their projects, and to motivate students (218–19). The argument here, and it is a sensible argument, is that some practices remain effective across different pedagogical situations. The corrective Markel provides should hearten experienced teachers who have been led to believe that they are foundationless when it comes to teaching about and with computers.

If completely new pedagogies are not required, however, that is not to say that established practices and perspectives will be totally sufficient. Consider the role and authority of teachers who work with technologically competent students. Authority in the post-modern classroom has been redefined as an unstable relationship, one that is reprocessed continuously in the unequal interactions between students and teachers. The interests of students are presumably served when teachers use their authoritative capacities to encourage emancipatory outcomes. But in the context of computer literacy, the grounds for teacher authority have been partially reframed in ways that could make some established teachers rather uncomfortable. I suspect Mary Warnock is one of those teachers. In her essay entitled "Good Teaching," she declares that "One very obvious source of authority for teachers is that they are older than their pupils and therefore know more and have more entitlement to speak of what they know" (18). This perspective, which maintains that there is a "natural hierarchy" (18) in the classroom, presupposes that "Teachers should have the ability to speak as 'authorities' about whatever it is that they teach" (19). Warnock not only sees knowledge as relatively stable, but she avoids computers because younger generations frequently know more about them than older generations. To be sure, technology is one of the few areas where one can find an inverse relationship between age and expertise.

*Positioning Teachers as True Learners*
Given the fact that students are often more conversant with technological issues than their teachers, teachers must be disposed to classroom settings that position them as true learners. One frequent assertion in the discourse on critical pedagogy is that teachers should become colearners in instructional activities, but this usually means that teachers should learn about, respect, and value the backgrounds and interests that have come to shape the literate practices of their students. This assertion does not often mean, as far as I can tell, that teachers should take up topics they have not yet mastered. However, how many teachers in departments of English could be considered content experts in the domain of interface design? Usability testing? Digital literacy? Visual literacy? Computer-supported cooperative work? Not enough to cover the courses, that is for sure. I, for one, do not consider myself to be an

expert in all of the domains related to computer literacy, so I tell my students, at the start of each semester, that I will probably only be able to answer about half of their technical questions and that when it comes to the other half we will need to find the answers together. I realize that this is a moderately low-risk gesture for someone in my position: a white, male, tenure-line faculty member whose ethos is bolstered by such unambiguous markers of status. Still, teachers must find ways to comfortably introduce precarious topics and to effectively communicate to students that it is not only acceptable but desirable, at least on some level, for their teachers to become real colearners.

There is no one best approach to this task, but any method will probably involve scaffolded instruction that integrates novel and familiar practices. For example, teachers in a technical writing course could begin their unit on job-search materials with the standard resume assignment, which should be relatively straightforward and provide a rhetorical anchor. From there teachers could introduce scannable resumes, resumes that are still print-based but designed to be scanned and fed into highly searchable database systems. Scannable resumes bridge media contexts and raise provocative discussion questions about how machines versus people "read" texts. The final extension of the assignment could introduce Web resumes, which are only available online and which capitalize on the unique affordances of the Internet. At this point, low-tech teachers could begin to feel out of their element, but the preliminary instruction, if it is sound and cogent, should infuse confidence and enable students and teachers to explore together the mechanics and rhetorical dynamics of online environments. It should not be overly difficult for teachers to imagine other ways to scaffold novel and familiar activities.

*Evaluating Student Experiences and Attitudes*
Another pedagogical move that should be contemplated is the employment of diagnostic measures. In 1990, when I first integrated computers systematically into my courses as a graduate student at Michigan Technological University, it was almost always the case

that students in the humanities department knew relatively little about computers. Students worked with computers in a variety of capacities, but these were normally limited to the rather predictable undertakings associated with the composition and production of reports and papers. It was not that difficult to gauge where any class was as a whole: Very few of my students actually owned their own computers, and their experiences, for the most part, were defined by the software programs that had been consistently installed across campus, which were not always the applications prized in the humanities. So programs like Daedalus, Storyspace, PageMaker, Prose, HyperCard, and PREP Editor were undeniably puzzles to most of my students. They were all more or less beginners, and I was pretty much right there with them at the starting gate. Now, more than a decade later, it is much more difficult to quickly assess the technological experiences of students. Although today there are very few absolute beginners, there is quite a continuum of competencies in writing and communication classrooms, from students who are just familiar with basic software programs to those who are experienced programmers. In a sense, this range of competencies is not unlike the wide disparity in writing abilities teachers invariably find among their students.

I use three (ungraded) diagnostic measures to learn about the technological experiences of my students. In large courses with a wide variety of majors, I use all three, but there are times when fewer measures are sufficient, such as in specialized courses with students I have taught before (e.g., students in our technical writing minor or with an emphasis in rhetoric or publishing). The first diagnostic measure is a simple survey students fill out right away. This survey lists the different technologies that will be employed in the course and asks students to self-assess their experiences with these technologies. For example, in the most recent version of my course on the rhetoric of the Internet, my survey lists the following applications, in rank order of importance for pedagogical purposes: Internet Explorer, Microsoft Word, PSU WebMail, Dreamweaver, Photoshop, Acrobat, Inspiration Pro, Media Player, WS FTP, Xnews, and EndNote Bibliography. For each of these applications, students rate their experiences on a scale of one to five, with one being "not experienced at all" and five being "highly experienced." The data I collect can be vague and imprecise, but it provides an initial sense of the technological baseline in the course.

The second diagnostic measure, which I learned from Thomas Barker of Texas Tech University, concentrates on a technology that will be central to the course. The point of this hands-on measure is twofold. First, I want to learn more about what students specifically know and can do. Second, I want students to be introduced to certain software features and the systematic ways we will make use of them. So in my course on the rhetoric of the Internet, for example, students are asked to try out the features in Microsoft Word that they will need in order to complete their first major written assignment, a guide to electronic citizenship at Penn State. Produced by students for students, this guide is a highly designed booklet that explains the rights and responsibilities of those who use the technological infrastructures on campus. To begin the diagnostic measure, I distribute three items to each student: a copy of a booklet that was created in a previous semester; a chronological checklist of the software features students will be asked to engage (e.g., style sheets, tables, footnotes); and the Microsoft Word file that contains the sample booklet. The third item includes a twist: I have stripped out the design aspects and instead embedded high-level instructions for how the various text elements should be treated (e.g., "Using a style sheet, format the following heading in 12 point Helvetica Bold, upper case"; "Put the following data points into a table"; "Put the following citation into a footnote"). Students work in pairs and with online documentation to recreate the sample booklet, using their checklist of software features to chart progress and record questions and comments. The final step is to print the files and compare the output to the original, to see how well the students did. However, one cannot tell from a printout, for example, if students actually used a style sheet to format headings or the table function as opposed to the tab key to line up data points or the footnote function to insert citations. To determine if the appropriate software features were used—and used in an effective manner—the Microsoft Word files must be collected and examined.

The third diagnostic measure moves away from the realm of practical experience and into psychological and social realms. Narratives provide a means for encouraging students to articulate their perspectives toward technology, which in turn can help teachers better understand the ways students approach computers. I have experimented with technology narratives for several years, but Barbara Duffelmeyer provides a research-based discussion that vividly illustrates their instructional benefits. The details of this diagnostic measure are uncomplicated: In a brief essay, students are asked to reflect upon their technological experiences and to put those experiences into a broader cultural framework. Students are free to approach this assignment as desired, although I offer invention prompts to provoke analysis and not just description. For example, I ask students to characterize their attitudes and expectations in relation to computers, but students must also attempt to account for their personal views in social terms: What are the cultural factors that have shaped your perspectives? Be sure to think about the ways various technologies have been represented in your household, in your schools, in the media, and in advertisements. The objective of such a prompt, as Duffelmeyer explains, is to tease out the extent to which students "support, challenge, or even demonstrate an awareness of prevailing discourses about technology" (290). This information is valuable in that the connections between language and practical experience are not always made clear in technological contexts.

Duffelmeyer studied the technology narratives of students in six computer-intensive sections of a writing course that focuses on argument. The narratives averaged around 350 words and produced three types of information, which I will summarize only superficially to suggest the value of the narratives. Duffelmeyer learned, first of all, that the students tended to express one of three attitudes toward technology. Of the 140 students who completed a narrative, 37 percent had overly positive attitudes, 11 percent had overly negative attitudes, and 52 percent had mixed attitudes that suggested a more nuanced awareness of the effects of computers. This statistic surprised me, and it belies the stereotype teachers often have of students as uncritical users of technology. Duffelmeyer also learned that students in each of the three categories had different perceptions of the role external forces played in the development of their technological attitudes. For example, students with overly positive attitudes had "bootstrap" mentalities of self-reliance and independence; students with overly negative attitudes felt powerless and blamed themselves, teachers, schools, and other factors; and students with mixed attitudes acknowledged societal influences but understood that such influences can vary dramatically from context to context. This insight discloses the varied perspectives on agency that contribute to the technological attitudes of students. In addition, Duffelmeyer's data "revealed common words or characteristic expressions that students use to describe their experiences and trace their individual chronologies with computer technology" (295). Language choices provided an additional clue into the psychological and social ways technological attitudes get constructed and assisted Duffelmeyer in her quest as a researcher to humanize her students and to fairly represent their stories. Note that as a diagnostic measure, the interpretation of technology narratives does not depend upon rigorous qualitative research methods. Teachers can glean useful information from even a quick review of the narratives.

### Understanding Pedagogy and Technology as Coextensive and Mutually Constitutive

The final aspect I want to discuss is pedagogical facilities and resources. Mike Markel is right when he argues that one obligation of teachers, whatever the context, is to prepare well-organized materials that are understandable to students. Syllabi, handouts, and assignment sheets should all be clear and helpful, and teachers should be prepared to elucidate such materials if needed. But I do not draw the sharp distinction that he does between pedagogy and technology. Says Markel: "Even though I realize that facilities can, in fact, influence pedagogy in significant ways, I argue that pedagogy is essentially separate from facilities and resources" (214). To support his argument, Markel describes a progressive exercise on multiculturalism that is indeed student-centered in the very best sense of that phrase. He then reaches this conclusion: "The important characteristic of active, student-centered education is what students are asked to do—how they engage the material—not whether the media used are digital or analog" (215). Leaving aside the issue of whether media are, in fact, neutral, I want to pursue another point: In a digital age, pedagogies, facilities, and resources have become increasingly intertwined.

It is true that teachers have always been designers of instructional environments. Teachers select textbooks, sequence assignments, develop handouts, forge interactions, rearrange classroom spaces, and so on. But I differentiate between these usual types of activities, which remain constant, and the development of online pedagogical spaces, a relatively new task that requires teachers to become designers of facilities and resources. Brad Mehlenbacher provides a concrete example that clarifies this distinction. In "Technologies and Tensions: Designing Online Environments for Teaching Technical Communication," Mehlenbacher describes the Technical Communication Virtual Campus, an environment he created on the Internet to support his technical communication courses. This integrated online space contains five areas: a virtual library, Web resources, a listserv list, electronic course materials, and a MOO.

The virtual library is more like a "special reference room" than a comprehensive library because it "privileges certain types of research and marginalizes others" (222). That is, in this area of his virtual campus, Mehlenbacher provides access to source materials that represent the profession in ways that are consistent with the intellectual directions of his department. This task requires an interface design that reflects those directions. The Web resources area is dedicated to the subject of human-computer interaction and includes pointers to exemplary Web pages and to databases devoted to HCI research. The main design task here also relates to the interface, but because this area is so dynamic, Mehlenbacher established protocols to help him decide when and where to add new resources. The listserv list is a discussion forum that connects students, teachers, and technical writers in the "research triangle" area of North Carolina (Mehlenbacher teaches at NC State). It is one thing to create a listserv for student use and quite another to have a deep knowledge of the technical options, their potential to influence pedagogical activities, and the ethical and legal issues associated with the use of messages that have been posted to online forums with different histories, technical configurations, and discussion contexts. Mehlenbacher runs a moderated list that enables students, researchers, professionals, and other teachers to interact, but the forum design intentionally creates a low-risk atmosphere for students.

The area for electronic course materials houses syllabi and handouts for four different courses in technical writing. If the content in this area is conventional enough, however, larger issues of ownership, authorship, and the distribution of electronic instructional materials have complicated the design situation. Therefore, this area of the virtual campus has been designed as an intranet that is only available to students at NC State. The final area, the TechComm-MOO, contains various technical features that support both synchronous and asynchronous communication. There is a library, which contains online reference works and gopher slates that can be used to take notes. There is a lecture hall, which contains a conch to silence the room, a queue to store questions for the speaker, a slide projector to display extended texts, and a tape recorder to record lectures. And there are several discussion rooms, which contain information desks, pathways to hypertext documents, and bulletin boards that can be used to post messages. These technical features have all been designed by Mehlenbacher and his students to support either conventional or experimental pedagogical activities.

The areas of this virtual campus that most dramatize my argument are the listserv list and the MOO space. These facilities and their resources must be designed and incorporated into courses in ways that are instructionally useful. Teachers who put their hard-copy syllabi on the Internet exploit it as a publication vehicle. This approach is absolutely fine, and not without its advantages. But teachers who pursue an expansive approach to the study and practice of computer literacy will find that the ability to design effective online spaces is an indispensable and inseparable aspect of their pedagogical repertoire. To be fair to Markel, his overall point—that certain enlightened instructional practices can rise above particular classroom settings—is not only valid but crucial, and that is why I included it in the introduction to this section. However, it is important to emphasize that there are no technological facilities or resources that are pedagogically neutral (just ask any teacher who has relied on the default settings of a software program). Moreover, pedagogical perspectives are not fully formulated in a vacuum, but affected in the context of specific instructional circumstances. For example, lectures are not considered to be particularly student-centered. Still, I have not entirely ruled them out because sometimes I discover that a brief lecture or two would be quite helpful, to explain concepts or make historical connections or fill in background information. In situations where I have decided to lecture, it is clear to me that students, course materials, and other resources have shaped my pedagogical perspectives. I will also admit that I often have different expectations for student work that will be published on the Web. Unfortunately, the public nature of the Web has encouraged me to revive some of the regressive assessment practices of current-traditional rhetoric. That is, in selfishly worrying over the fact that certain online projects could reflect poorly upon me as a teacher, at times I have overemphasized issues of correctness. This regrettable move has reminded me that pedagogy and technology can become interconnected in ways that are unanticipated.

The pedagogical requirements outlined in this section are not radical and should not present barriers or inhibit in any way the development or improvement of computer literacy programs. For many teachers, the first pedagogical requirement will probably be the most troublesome one. There is simply too much to know about computers in functional, critical, and rhetorical terms; not only that, this knowledge can be a swiftly moving target. So it is easy to feel underprepared as a teacher of computer literacy. Nevertheless, teachers should be able to alleviate their anxieties on some level with scaffolded instruction that leverages well-known contexts and gradually releases certain responsibilities to technologically competent students. The second pedagogical requirement should be less troublesome. Diagnostic measures are inexact, yet it seems irresponsible to ignore the full spectrum of possible technological experiences and perspectives in the classroom. Computer users nowadays differ in not only numerous but subtle ways, so the variations between students can be difficult to judge, at first glance, in any one course. However, the diagnostic measures I have discussed can serve as an effective and expeditious technological orientation. What is more, technology narratives can serve as a broader introduction to students as writers. The third pedagogical requirement asks teachers to see pedagogy and technology as coextensive and mutually constitutive. The implication of such a dialogic view is that teachers must become more sophisticated designers of the technological environments they employ. This design sophistication will not be achieved instantaneously, but through a steady and continuous process of self-education. Hence, in a later section I discuss the importance of professional development opportunities.

### Curricular Requirements

Computer literacy is one of those rare areas that so thoroughly permeate the arbitrary divisions inside all universities. On my campus, for example, computer literacy initiatives can be found in almost every academic department, not to mention in the interdisciplinary institutes that have managed to attract funded research projects. As well, there are many higher-level units at Penn State that provide a variety of technical and educational support services to the entire university community: the Center for Academic Computing, the Center for Educational Technology Services, the Center for Excellence in Teaching and Learning, the Office of Telecommunications,

Library Computing Services, and so forth. So across my campus, and across most others, there is a panoply of sites and contexts within which computer literacy has become an institutionalized concern. There is also a wide array of informal channels students use in order to learn about computers. Students often learn invaluable things from roommates, from other students in their courses, from Internet-based discussion forums, from software documentation, and from trial-and-error experiences. These informal channels can be extraordinarily productive because students typically acquire information in the framework of actual problems.

If significant resources are already in place, it might seem like duplication to add computer literacy to English studies as well. After all, students can take courses in other departments and make the most of institutional initiatives that have been paid for with tuition dollars and student technology fees. Although students should be exposed to such outside perspectives and opportunities, teachers of writing and communication cannot afford to let others fully define what it means to be computer literate, for the reasons I articulated in chapter 1. If humanists are not directly involved in technology education, it is unlikely that students will be exposed in systematic and sustained ways to the chameleon-like nature of computers and their alternative social configurations and metaphorical constructions. I am convinced that students will learn a considerable amount about computers from the usual suspects and sources. However, I am much less certain that the dominant perspectives will inspire students to cultivate a broader and more balanced sense of computer literacy, one that embraces multiple mindsets, lenses, practices, and voices. In order for the development of an expanded sense of computer literacy to become a distinct possibility, the interests of humanists will need to become more visible as a formalized contribution at all curricular levels. Thus, in this section, I discuss how teachers can integrate functional literacy, critical literacy, and rhetorical literacy into curricula as a whole, into specific courses, and even into individual assignments.

But before I discuss specific curricular configurations, let me make some general points. First, any viable attempt will probably involve several teachers and courses. Simply said, it is not possible to cover the entire complex of issues and practices in a single class or semester. I have tried overly ambitious approaches, and the results have been uniformly poor. The main problem is that students find it difficult to separate the most important things to remember from the disposable particulars. This problem leads to my second point: The curriculum will need to be articulated in strategic ways. Put in different terms, some courses will need to be coordinated in certain respects so that the experiences of students are coherent and meaningful from one semester to the next. Although micropolitical undertakings play an important role in most serious efforts to reform the status quo, curricula will not permit positive change without the collective action and wisdom of teachers and administrators. The objective is to orchestrate a flexible set of educational experiences that somehow or another encompass the multiple computer literacies I have discussed. Note that these experiences could include targeted courses from outside departments if those courses have been thoughtfully designed. Such courses can emphasize other humanist perspectives and help to distribute the curricular workload. For example, I regularly advise students to enroll in two courses offered in the Science, Technology, and Society (STS) program: "Technology and Human Values" and "The History of Women in Science." These courses cover relevant material in ways that complement the educational efforts of the English department.

The final point is that these educational efforts should ultimately be reflected in official course catalogs. Course catalogs are a notoriously weak strut in the support systems of academic advisers. Not only are the course descriptions much too generic, but defunct courses often remain listed because the course approval process can be so arduous and unpleasant. Still, course catalogs constitute an official curricular transcript, one that can help define teachers of writing and communication as either inside or outside the domain of computer literacy. For example, at Penn State, there is a liberal arts course called "Quantitative Methods for Humanists," whose catalog description reads as follows: "Computational techniques for language analysis, including text representation, file manipulation, utilities, with consideration of stylistic, content, linguistic, and literary applications." That most advisers cannot make heads or tails of this description is unfortunate because the course itself has evolved into something that has very little to do with quantitative methods: it is in fact an introduction to the principles of Web design. But the overall effect of such outmoded descriptions (there are others) is that students have not come to see the English department as an academic unit that is central to the scholarly investigation of computer technologies. Thus, in one attempt to reverse this trend, my department has supported the development of a new course called "Writing for the Web." This title should be self-explanatory, and the course description should signal to students and their advisers that computer literacy does indeed fall squarely within the territory of English studies.

In regard to curricular configurations, there are a number of sound ways to translate the notion of multiple computer literacies into an intelligible program of study. Although in the abstract there is no one best approach to this translation task, conceptually the tripartite framework of functional literacy, critical literacy, and rhetorical literacy operates like a fractal (a fractal is a geometric shape that can be subdivided mathematically into parts that approximate a reduced copy of the whole). This framework is fractal-like in that it can be applied in ever smaller scales to the curricular components of academic programs. That is, the framework can be applied to curricula as a whole, to specific courses, or even to individual assignments. This extensibility should help teachers imagine and ramp up tightly integrated initiatives.

### The Design of the Curriculum as a Whole

In terms of the curriculum as a whole, a program could offer at least one course in each of the three areas. The stand-alone course in functional literacy might foreground the five parameters discussed in chapter 2: educational goals, social conventions, specialized discourses, management activities, and technological impasses. Although courses in functional literacy can be found at nearly all universities—with titles like "Introduction to Computers," "Computer Applications for the Liberal Arts," or "Writing with Computers"—these courses tend to be organized around hardware components and software skills and programs. The challenge is to offer a contextualized course that focuses on the functional issues that remain most important as old versions of hardware and software are inevitably replaced by new ones. Let me outline one particular version.

To build a consequential context for functional instruction, I teach a course that starts with the educational goals of the other classes students are enrolled in. We arrange the various types of goals into rough categories and then discuss where computer technologies might or might not be able to assist students. For the instances in which computers can be helpful, we investigate specific software functions and the ways those functions can be customized for personal use. In the next phase of the course, students examine the social conventions and specialized discourses associated with the technologies that can support their most important educational goals. This phase does not involve vocabulary tests but activities that ask students to become modestly knowledgeable about two different cultures. The first culture is disciplinary, and the activities are meant to illuminate the conventional practices in a field that will need to be accommodated on some level. Two of the assignments I routinely use ask students to analyze the discourse patterns on disciplinary listserv lists and the content patterns on disciplinary Websites. The second culture is interdisciplinary, and the activities are meant to illuminate the specialized discourses that have been designed into the software programs students have come to depend upon. In this case, I often ask students to trace appropriated language back to its offline context and to report on what that context might teach computer users. This research exercise is useful, for example, because programs like Adobe PageMaker and Adobe PageMill usually make more sense to students once they have read about the function and history of pasteboards in graphic arts production (the pasteboard metaphor is central to these and other design programs).

Integrated into both phases of the course are discussions of management activities and technological impasses. There are points in the course where issues related to these two functional parameters naturally come up, and when those issues arise we take considerable time out to discuss particular situations as well as more general considerations. For example, I do not want to receive twenty-four e-mail attachments that have all been named "Assignment One," so before the first draft of assignment one is due, we develop a meaningful scheme that students should use to organize and name all course files. This situation also opens a window on the need to track revisions electronically and to back up work consistently. Likewise, I do not want to answer the same technical questions over and over again—and besides, students are better served not when they are supplied with direct answers but when they are encouraged to exploit help resources in systematic ways. Thus, individual questions become problems for the entire class to solve, and my job is to situate those problems in a larger conceptual structure so that students can learn how to resolve their own technological impasses more independently. Chapter 2 provides an example of one heuristic that teachers can use to help students work through performance-oriented impasses. Another approach would be to make the analysis of help resources a formal aspect of the course, on the grounds that students cannot become effective troubleshooters unless they understand the conventions and constraints of such resources. In the appendix to their book on computer documentation, Thomas Duffy, James Palmer, and Brad Mehlenbacher provide an in-depth questionnaire students can use to evaluate the design of online help systems. In my course, students use this instrument to interrogate the major design features of a key resource and to draw conclusions about when to turn to online help rather than other forms of assistance.

The stand-alone course in critical literacy would concentrate on the politics of computer technologies. What specifically do I mean by politics? As the discussion in chapter 3 should make clear, I basically mean, in the words of Langdon Winner, the "arrangements of power and authority in human associations as well as the activities that take place within those arrangements" (22). Hence, the main objective of the course would be to shine a bright beam of light on the non-neutral dimensions of computers and their non-neutral contexts of production and use. In an entire course dedicated to critical literacy, there should be ample time to entertain a rather involved heuristic as well as other approaches. So when critical literacy is the primary focus, I adopt a technology reader that comes with a full complement of discussion questions and assignments (see Hawisher and Selfe; Vitanza; Yagelski). Although the course starts with articles and activities that ease students into the idea that computers instantiate values and align with preferred sets of perspectives, the main intellectual focus models this idea in an orderly and concrete fashion.

To begin the modeling process, I ask students to read the piece by Bryan Pfaffenberger that supplies the metadiscourse heuristic for critical literacy sketched out in chapter 3. This piece is more challenging than most of the essays reprinted in technology readers and draws much more heavily on theory, but I have learned not to underestimate my students, who can handle difficult texts reasonably well as long as they have been sufficiently contextualized. So before students start in on the piece, we consider the constitutive aspects of language, because in Pfaffenberger's conception of power, discourse is what lends technological artifacts their sustained force in social settings. As the heuristic gets employed, a simplification tactic is to isolate its three component parts: technological regularization, technological adjustment, and technological reconstitution. That is, I first ask students to find clear examples for each of the eleven regularization strategies: exclusion, deflection, differential incorporation, compartmentalization, segregation, centralization, standardization, polarization, marginalization, delegation, and disavowal. These examples then provide the context for thinking through the indirect response strategies of technological adjustment (countersignification, counterappropriation, and counterdelegation) and the direct response strategy of technological reconstitution (antisignification). The anticipation of reintegration strategies reassembles the heuristic and highlights its recursive nature.

To some, this heuristic might seem overly academic or cumbersome, but its explanatory power is undeniable. The typology of regularization strategies is quite exhaustive: If there are other ways technologies can be political, these are derivative or minor in comparison. The same can be said for the redressive social processes, which provide a comprehensive set of useful responses to the politics of technologies. Although the heuristic's theoretical nomenclature can be tricky, it functions as a shared grammar system that helps students become critically literate. Students who are new to the unconventional notion that technologies and their contexts are biased will appreciate an introduction that operates by political stereotypes; they provide a way to simplify complex ideological ideas. However, once students become more comfortable, the theoretical nomenclature helps them to make fine distinctions between different types of political gestures and responses. The other good thing about the heuristic is its pedagogical flexibility. It can be used either in isolation or as part of a larger project. I like to incorporate the heuristic into a recommendation report assignment that asks students to analyze issues of technology access on campus. In this assignment, the role of the heuristic is to help students articulate persuasively the nature and scope of the problem. After the problem has been clearly and cogently defined, students conduct primary research in order to recommend solutions. Because the heuristic is so flexible in instructional terms, it can be integrated into critical literacy courses at all levels, from first-year writing courses to graduate seminars.

The stand-alone course in rhetorical literacy would explore new media environments and the implications of those environments for English studies. Ideally, the course would reimagine computer users and critics as interface designers and computer tools and artifacts as hypertextual media. This shift is additive because functional and critical abilities contribute in a central and obvious manner to the design of human-computer interfaces. The course could also be considered additive in that it builds on rhetorical concepts that should be at least somewhat familiar to student writers: persuasion, deliberation, reflection, and social action. Although these concepts should not be allowed to limit the ways students come to understand new media, rhetoric provides a sound humanistic foothold in a rapidly expanding area that often seems to be fascinated more by the marvels of technology than by the social challenges of the tasks at hand.

There are a number of different lines of attack that teachers can take in order to develop a course in rhetorical literacy. For departments without an established curricular location for new media studies, perhaps the best approach would be to pilot a course in a slot dedicated to special topics in English. We have such a slot for experimental courses at both the undergraduate and graduate levels, and I presume most other programs do as well. Another place is in advanced courses that have been broadly defined. For example, my department currently has several courses on the books where students could legitimately examine and produce multimedia texts from a rhetorical perspective. In the undergraduate curriculum, these courses include "Studies in Genre," "The Editorial Process," "Advanced Technical Writing," "Rhetorical Theory and Practice," "Current Theories of Writing and Reading," "Rhetorical Approaches to Discourse," "Problems in Critical Theory and Practice," and "Authors, Texts, Contexts." Courses in graduate curricula are generally more open and flexible, so any course that covers contemporary theories and practices in rhetoric, composition, or technical communication should accommodate teachers who want to focus on human-computer interactions. Eventually, however, any experimental efforts will need to become more established, so that teachers of writing and communication are seen as unmistakable providers of technology education on campus.

The course itself could be productively organized in many diverse ways: There is no imperative need to work through the rhetorical concepts exactly as they have been laid out in chapter 4. The main idea is to underline the unique perspectives of humanist scholars and teachers. Of course, these perspectives should be left wide open to challenge and critique, for as I have argued, traditional maps of rhetorical theory do not illuminate every design aspect of online environments. Still, a focus on persuasion, deliberation, reflection, and social action produces a very different kind of course than do other disciplinary emphases. For example, on my campus, computer scientists primarily understand Web design as a technical problem, business types primarily understand Web design as a marketing or management problem, and librarians primarily understand Web design as an archiving problem. In turn, the courses these individuals teach stress directions and features that are congruent with their disciplinarily determined perceptions of the Web. This characterization is not an unfair distortion but a fairly obvious observation about the role disciplinary blinders play in all knowledge construction activities. Similarly, the priorities and perspectives in English studies encourage humanists to primarily understand Web design as a discursive problem, one that inherently involves interpretation, negotiation, and collaboration in both contexts of production and consumption. As a result, rhetoric has become the overarching framework for our course in Web design.

When I teach the course, I start with an historical overview of the major development models that have been reported in the literature on human-computer interaction: system-centered, text-centered, and user-centered (Johnson). The overview does not march steadily through a chronological list of famous computer scientists or notable technical advancements but instead looks more historiographically at the models in order to trace out the cultural, political, and economic contexts within which HCI has operated as an applied field. This tack enables me to highlight some of the social forces that have widened the domain of interface design to include the beliefs and concerns of humanists. It also helps me introduce the concept of deliberation, because it is a short intellectual step from the notion that technology history is a contested site to the notion that technology itself is a contested site. The course continues with deliberation and the other rhetoric concepts as we look more closely at user-centered approaches to interface design, the characteristics of reflective practitioners, and the requirements of actual design projects. To this end, I have employed service learning projects to call attention to the rhetorical aspects of Web design. So, whenever possible, I encourage our teachers to commission assignments with local agencies or businesses.

In a commissioned assignment, students work closely with a client to develop a Website that has consequences outside the classroom. The interactions between the students and the client hold the key to a productive educational experience that emphasizes persuasion, deliberation, reflection, and social action. For example, in my course, a first step is to meet with the client in order to learn more about his or her needs and contexts. Students actually meet regularly with the client, but the initial meetings are crucial because their main purpose is to increasingly disclose the rhetorical complexity of the design situation. Consequently, in one early activity, students work with the client to develop a thick description of the ways in which, and the settings in which, the Website will be employed. This persuasion task introduces students to the interpretive frameworks of users and to the nontechnological factors that could influence their online behaviors. After a full design plan has been completed (see Selber, Johnson-Eilola, and Mehlenbacher for a discussion of design plans), students are divided into six teams and asked to rapidly produce a prototype. This deliberation task drives home the point that interface design problems are ill-defined problems with multiple suitable solutions. I maintain a focus on the deliberative aspects of HCI by asking the class to select out the most promising aspects of the six prototypes and develop two entirely different Websites for the client.

The many points at which students interact with the client reinforce the concept of reflection. Students do not work in a vacuum but constantly test their beliefs and formative designs with the help of the client. These usability situations make it clear to students that the contingent nature of interface design will require them to become continuous and gracious learners. In fact, on some level it is usually impossible to completely reconcile the different assumptions of clients and students (and of students and students), a situation I exploit as a recursive way to return to issues of persuasion and deliberation. Finally, in the case of nonprofit agencies, it is fairly self-evident that interface designers are social actors, although I make sure to draw out the less obvious power relationships between interface designers and users as well as any intertextual circumstances. However, the nature of work in business settings does not necessarily encourage students to see broader implications. So in commissioned assignments for businesses, I explicitly introduce the four types of power exercise outlined in chapter 4 (technical, structural, conceptual, and symbolic), drawing on concrete examples from earlier commissioned assignments. This discussion considers the political decisions that confront interface designers and the concomitant opportunities for influencing users in even mundane decision-making situations.

*The Design of Specific Courses*

Functional literacy, critical literacy, and rhetorical literacy can also be mobilized in specific courses. In fact, I can envision a new survey course called "Multiliteracies for a Digital Age" that would cover all three areas in ways that are less in-depth but that more closely demonstrate the interrelationships between functional, critical, and rhetorical literacies. As with most new courses, version one will probably involve a certain amount of trial and error, as teachers attempt to orchestrate novel instructional experiences that speak to students and take advantage of local resources. One could certainly organize a valuable course around service-learning projects, which can integrate functional and critical considerations with rhetorically focused design activities. On a functional front, the projects themselves could suggest the software features and disciplinary contexts that should be studied, and technical questions and other functional issues could be handled and conceptualized as the projects unfold. On a critical front, the Pfaffenberger heuristic could be used to conduct usability evaluations that look at the politics of project designs. But to more deeply engage with the educational issues, I would also require students to write up some critical commentary that reflects on the overall experience of participating in a service-learning project.

However, this course would not have to be organized around

commissioned assignments at all. For example, its theme could be identity and the Internet, and the instructional activities could invite students to construct multiple online identities in different types of technological environments and to critique the design functions of those environments in terms of their tendencies and constraints. Moreover, the course would not have to center exclusively on the Web or other Internet technologies. For example, the policies, procedures, and physical spaces that shape technology development and use on a campus represent ideologically complex artifacts that can be exploited for the purposes of literacy education. In this case, students might be asked to reimagine such artifacts from a more humanistic standpoint.

### *The Design of Individual Assignments*

At the most micro-level, the three-part framework could be presented in an individual assignment in almost any course. For obvious reasons, it probably makes sense for apprehensive teachers to get started with a new assignment that fits as comfortably as possible into an old framework. It also seems sensible to locate the assignment toward the end of the course, to allow time for teachers to establish a positive ethos before students embark into comparatively untested instructional territory. In the earlier section on technical requirements, I mentioned that listserv lists could be used to help students come to terms with the concept of multiple computer literacies. More specifically, I suggested that students could be asked to join an e-mail forum and study its discourse from functional, critical, and rhetorical perspectives. This might be a good first assignment for teachers who are not quite ready to deal with the multimedia dimensions of the Web.

But for those teachers who are prepared, redesign projects might be the best pedagogical vehicle in courses where only a single assignment attends to technological issues. As the name suggests, redesign projects do not require students to develop brand new Websites from scratch, a task that could conceivably span the space of several assignments. Rather, students redesign the content and structure of existing Websites in ways that make them more compatible with whatever perspectives are being studied. So, for example, in a course on feminist rhetorics, students could redesign Websites from various feminist perspectives; in a course on African American literacies, students could redesign Websites from various African American perspectives; and in a writing course that takes a cultural studies approach, students could redesign Websites from various social-cultural perspectives. The real genius of such redesign projects is that they are easily scalable: Students can revise any or all aspects of a Website, and the redesigns themselves can range from rough conceptual prototypes to highly finished products.

In addition, an integrated assignment I like to use in my technical writing courses asks students to create Web-based tutorials for undocumented pieces of software that can be downloaded via the Internet and used in campus computer labs. The functional and rhetorical facets of this assignment should be apparent, but for the critical component, my students write elaborative reference materials that explain the ethical and legal issues associated with the use of shareware, freeware, and applications in the public domain, three different software classifications for inexpensive or free programs, which students at my institution tend to search out. Although I have broadly described some example assignments that incorporate functional literacy, critical literacy, and rhetorical literacy, teachers should not let these few examples limit their pedagogical imaginations. Indeed, there must be countless ways to effectively join together multiple computer literacies via individual assignments.

To summarize, English departments will need to craft multi-leveled curricular approaches in order to organize meaningful instructional experiences for students. These approaches should be strategically articulated as well as clearly represented in course catalogs and other official sites that help communicate who shares in the responsibility for educating computer literate students. Thinking in fractal terms about the tripartite framework of functional literacy, critical literacy, and rhetorical literacy can help teachers figure out how to structure coherent and comprehensive curricula. Although the exact nature of curricula will vary from program to program, it is safe to say that curricular configurations should be diversified in that they include a wide range of teachers, courses, and assignments that explicitly concentrate on computer literacy. The only danger I see is at the level of curricula as a whole: The stand-alone courses could fail to make the connections clear between the different types of computer literacies. That is why these in-depth courses must be related to some degree, and perhaps taken after a survey course that introduces and interrelates functional, critical, and rhetorical literacies. Of course, the problem of how to productively sequence courses and assignments is one that will be solved differently in every specific situation, so even this rather small suggestion should not go untested. Moreover, although I did not really talk about it, not every possible assignment or course requires access to computer technologies, especially in the area of critical literacy. Students can surely learn some valuable things about technology in offline contexts.

## Departmental and Institutional Requirements

This final section discusses two sets of requirements together because the substantial amount of support teachers will need in order to be successful must be deeply embedded in institutional as well as departmental structures. It is possible for unsupported teachers to accomplish impressive things both inside and outside the classroom. Indeed, it goes without saying that isolated and underappreciated teachers everywhere perform small educational miracles on almost a daily basis. Furthermore, early adopters of instructional technologies, who think and work outside the box in ways that are professionally risky, have made essential pedagogical contributions with little to no assistance or encouragement from official university quarters. Nevertheless, it remains a fact that high-quality programs in computer literacy cannot be built or sustained on the backs of unsupported teachers. What is needed, without a doubt, are significant departmental and institutional structures that value and support teachers in career-sustaining ways and that consider graduate students, who represent the future of the workforce, to be a special responsibility when it comes to technology education.

Although this section brings together departmental and institutional requirements, it is still a comparatively short section because support issues for teachers experimenting with technology have already been fairly well discussed in the literature on innovation and change in higher education and in the increasing number of articles in English studies that discuss actual computer literacy initiatives. In English studies, teachers of writing and communication repeatedly report that they either grossly underestimated the extent to which various types of support systems would be needed or deliberately bypassed repressive institutional structures in ways that were pedagogically fruitful but created an enormous amount of additional work, such as running a server, developing a software program, or administering a computer-supported writing facility. For these and other reasons related to issues of equity and status, the profession has focused a great deal of attention on tenure and promotion when it is connected to work in computer literacy (see Katz, Walker, and Cross; Lang, Walker, and Dorwick). In fact, as I mentioned in chapter 1, both the National Council of Teachers of English and the Modern Language Association have sensible guidelines that should help departments and institutions fairly evaluate any faculty work with technology. So there is no real need for me to discuss in detail the well-rehearsed concerns associated with tenure and promotion, which are legitimate and not to be minimized.

If some departmental and institutional requirements have been forged in the crucible of tenure and promotion, others have been illuminated in literature reviews that report on what researchers have learned about the nature of innovation and change in higher education. In his review of the literature, Donald Ely discusses eight conditions for technological change that facilitate the smooth progress of reform in educational settings. These conditions, which were first directed toward library contexts and then studied in a variety of education-related contexts, encapsulate the vast majority of support issues facing teachers of writing and communication who work with technology. I will run through the eight conditions rather quickly because they have already been talked about in published research and because so many of them are obvious.

The first condition is that there must be a significant amount of dissatisfaction with the status quo. Teachers, program administrators, department heads, and upper administrators should all sincerely believe that the dominant approaches to technology education on campus are impoverished, if not harmful, and that humanist perspectives can help a university construct better alternatives. The second condition is that those who are centrally involved in the change process itself must have the requisite knowledge and skills needed to get the job done. This means that English departments and upper administrators should be prepared to hire, retain, and value tenure-line faculty members whose primary scholarly work resides at the nexus of literacy and technology. It also means that professional development opportunities should be made available to everyone involved in the process, for technology is such a dynamic area. The third condition is that sufficient resources must be made available to support the change initiatives. Departments and institutions should provide easy access to robust technological environments that have been explicitly designed to support the work of writing and communication teachers. The fourth condition is that sufficient time must be made available for exploration and innovation. This means that everyone should account for the fact that technology adds real layers of complexity to any project, pedagogical or otherwise.

The fifth condition is that incentives must exist for the participants involved in change initiatives. Departments and institutions should recognize the fact that technology work typically contains a measure of professional risk for teachers, which is often unforeseen. The sixth condition is that broad-based participation must be expected and encouraged. Departments and institutions should hold open forums in which students and teachers who might be affected by the change initiatives have genuine opportunities to voice their opinions and perspectives, ask questions, and obtain information about the administrative and instructional aspects of any new policies, procedures, or technological developments. The seventh condition is that there must be a high level of commitment on the part of key stakeholders. Department heads and upper administrators should recognize the fact that successful computer literacy programs require significant ongoing expenditures. The eighth condition is that strong leadership must be evident. Department heads and upper administrators should find ways to clearly and continuously communicate their support for the change initiatives, and certain faculty members should be asked to take on more responsibility.

These eight conditions may not be totally exhaustive, but departments that achieve many of them will probably experience a high degree of sustained success. Dissatisfaction with the status quo, knowledge and skills, resources, time, rewards and incentives, participation, commitment, and leadership—these are not optional programmatic elements that can be safely overlooked or rationalized away. Rather, such departmental and institutional support structures will be crucial in all phases of any approach that attempts to invent or reimagine an ambitious curriculum that encompasses multiple computer literacies. As Ely points out, the eight conditions also function as a heuristic that can be applied in different ways at various stages of a project.

In initial stages, the conditions could be phrased as questions that can help an English department size up its support situation. Is there a significant amount of dissatisfaction with the status quo? Does the faculty possess the requisite competencies? Are sufficient resources available? After conducting a thorough needs assessment, a department would be in a better position to determine a judicious course of action, which could include inaction until the proper support structures have been put into place. In development stages, the conditions could serve as a checklist to help ensure a favorable outcome. If support structures atrophy over the duration of a project, its chances of success are sure to diminish appreciably. Thus, as teachers become engrossed in project work they must continue to monitor their levels of institutional and departmental support. Finally, once a project has been completed the conditions could be used to help teachers assess the settings of implementation. Change does not magically take care of itself, nor does a reformed curriculum automatically have positive effects. Although teachers can do much to encourage change, many will need a tremendous amount of support in order to be productive in actual pedagogical situations.

Professional development for faculty members is one of two areas on which I want to briefly elaborate. Ely discusses the importance of professional development opportunities, yet English departments frequently fail to move beyond ad hoc approaches. Informal conversations, guest speakers, and brown bag lunches can certainly infuse energy and confidence into a faculty, and by all means departments should look to capitalize on whatever occasions might be profitable. However, there is no substitute for a carefully crafted program for faculty professional development. What might such a program look like? One of the richest descriptions I have found was sketched out by Stephen Bernhardt and Carolyn Vickrey, who argue for "coherent approaches to faculty development that rely on natural learning within full social and technological contexts" (332). By *natural learning* they mean that programs "must prominently include helping individuals form productive relationships with technology, relationships that are self-sustaining, that grow and are nurtured within communities of learners, and that embed rewards in enhanced individual performance and accomplishments" (332). Given this objective, Bernhardt and Vickrey outline five components that are crucial to an environmental model of professional development: the program provides easy access to appropriate technology in offices and classrooms, so that faculty have convenient places in which to learn and work and so that technology is readily available in the primary spaces where faculty conduct most of their business on campus (339); the program provides adequate technical support, so that faculty do not have to become computer technicians or network specialists (341); the program offers targeted workshops and classes, so that faculty can learn to use technology in contextual ways that appeal to humanist scholars and teachers (344); the program provides released time and recognition of accomplishment, so that faculty involvement is truly valued, not just highly recommended (348); and the program builds a learning community, so that faculty can share experiences, compare notes, collaborate, and generally learn from each other (349). Creating a professional development program that contains these five component parts would indeed represent a significant departmental investment, but one that should yield powerful intellectual dividends.

The other area on which I want to briefly elaborate is technology education for graduate students, something that is not entirely unrelated to faculty professional development. Two data points lead me to believe that many graduate programs could be doing a better job in this important area. I cited the first in chapter 1: According to a survey of writing program administrators conducted by Sally Barr Ebest, only one-fourth of all students in graduate programs in rhetoric and composition have an opportunity to teach in computer-supported writing facilities (68). The second data point also derives from systematic research: When Catherine Latterell studied the pedagogical education of students in 50 percent of the graduate programs that Stuart Brown, Theresa Enos, and Paul Meyer identified in their comprehensive article, "Doctoral Programs in Rhetoric and Composition: A Catalog of the Profession," she learned from her examination of purpose statements, course descriptions, course materials, orientation materials, and handbooks for graduate teaching assistants that many TA education courses function largely as skills-based practica that deal only with the most immediate needs and concerns of those who are teaching for the very first time. In such a pragmatic context, technology education understandably takes a back seat to other, less-avoidable matters. If these two research studies are not persuasive enough, consider the place of graduate students in the overall power structure of an English department. Although graduate students typically have the most innovative and ambitious technological projects, they also typically have the least amount of influence over the distribution of departmental resources. The consequence is that graduate students tend to be poorly outfitted in not only an intellectual but material sense.

Bernhardt and Vickrey articulate what must be done to remedy this situation:

> A department that honestly wished to create change through
> technology would need to begin by looking at the distribu-
> tion of knowledge, status, power, and money, and to cre-
> ate a change initiative that worked both ends toward the
> middle, trying to align power, authority, and money with
> knowledge and vision. (339)

This might seem like a tall order, especially given the tensions between stasis and change that are so evident in academic settings. Yet
departments of English cannot afford to shirk their responsibilities
when it comes to educating the next generation of humanist scholars and teachers. That is why any professional development programs that are created for faculty members should be equally available to graduate students (and vice versa): Doing so would offer one
way to begin the realignment process suggested by Bernhardt and
Vickrey, and it would add value to the educational experiences of
faculty, who might just learn a thing or two from their junior colleagues, the colleagues that tend to be the most innovative and ambitious when it comes to computer literacy initiatives. At the same
time, technology education for graduate students is so important as
to warrant a more direct and considerable departmental investment,
which can be made in a wide variety of ways. Let me broadly describe two initiatives to suggest what some of those ways might be.

The first initiative, which has not yet been fully implemented
in my department, is modeled off of a program at Penn State that
matches technologically competent undergraduate students with
faculty members who need help learning how to employ computers in classroom settings. These students, who are officially called
Technology Learning Assistants, receive academic credit to tutor
faculty as they move aspects of their resident instruction into online
environments. Although faculty are the supposed beneficiaries of
the program, it is the students who are really stretched because they
must learn not only about the technology but also about how it
might be best applied in specific disciplinary domains. I am working to replicate this program in our department at the graduate level,
which should help in the task of creating a learning community. In

my version of the program, a graduate student would work twelve to sixteen hours per week as a technology learning assistant in lieu of teaching one course. Given this block of time, which is not unsubstantial, a graduate student could assist several different faculty members who have put in a departmental request for pedagogical help with technology. The student would first meet with the faculty members to learn about their needs and interests, and then take time to explore pedagogical possibilities and even lead the faculty members through any needed technology training sessions, which could be either formal or informal depending on the circumstances. The student and faculty members would then work together to produce online materials and environments that could conceivably be shared with the entire department. This type of initiative obviously represents a win-win investment in that everyone involved should reap some very real benefits. But because a department will only be able to fund a limited number of graduate students as technology learning assistants, I want to mention an initiative that is broader in its reach.

At Penn State, all graduate students from any academic department can earn a noncredit Teaching with Technology Certificate. This certificate is awarded by the graduate school and is supported by the Center for Academic Computing and the departments that have chosen to participate. We decided to participate because the certificate provided an impetus for us to get more serious about technology education. As the departmental representative for English, I help graduate students negotiate the process of earning the certificate, which is relatively straightforward. They first contact me so that we can go over the requirements as well as the criteria that will be used for assessment. In order to earn the certificate, a graduate student creates an online teaching portfolio that includes a philosophy-of-teaching statement that focuses on the role of technology in education; a professional home page that includes a curriculum vitae; evidence of online course materials that are available outside of the classroom; evidence that technology has been integrated into actual teaching situations, including evaluative reflections on how things went; evidence that multiple media have been

integrated into actual teaching situations; and evidence of the use
of technology that can support progressive pedagogical methods.
Once we have looked at these requirements, many of which are
flexible given that they can be fulfilled in several different ways, we
create an educational plan that leads to student success.

Because the certificate is a noncredit initiative, there are no
prerequisites or curricular conditions that must be satisfied, so advanced graduate students can, in theory, proceed to develop their
online portfolios at their own pace. However, most graduate students are not quite ready to proceed without help, so I variously
provide them with reading lists, advise them to enroll in appropriate seminars, encourage them to sit in on appropriate teaching
methods courses, advise them to enroll in technology training sessions, and subscribe them to a listserv list associated with the certificate so that they can ask questions and learn from each other.
Once a graduate student has pulled together a draft of his or her
online portfolio, it gets reviewed by me and by an instructional designer in the Center for Academic Computing. After the portfolio
has been revised to our satisfaction, I convene a small departmental committee that takes one last look at its contents, being sure
to keep in mind the assessment criteria that students have been
given. The final portfolio is sent from the English department to
the graduate school, where it must also be approved. Because a
teaching-with-technology certificate can be so deceptively difficult
to earn, many of the graduate students who initially sign on eventually withdraw from the process. I think this is absolutely fine, for
I want the certificate to signify a considerable educational achievement. But for those graduate students who are serious, the institutionalized nature of the initiative commits the English department
to continuous improvement in the quality of its opportunities for
technology education and support.

Effective computer literacy programs cannot be produced and
perpetuated with shoestring resources, lofty promises, or the best of
intentions, and the grit and determination of individual faculty
members can only go so far. Significant departmental and institutional investments must be made in support structures that will

make it possible for a critical mass of teachers to do their very best work, because teaching about and with computers can be such a demanding and vexing proposition. The support structures teachers may need will vary in every specific situation. However, it is a safe assumption that many of the eight conditions for educational change that Ely listed out will probably be involved. Although it is difficult to rank-order the importance of these conditions, creating a coherent program for faculty professional development will unquestionably be a critical step for any English department. Such programs should take in graduate students, but because graduate students represent a special responsibility, departments should also be sure to create educational opportunities that specifically address the needs and concerns of those who represent the future of the profession.

## Conclusion

It is often claimed that computers have produced an enormous number of positive changes in higher education, changes that have vastly improved the social as well as instructional landscape that students and teachers inhabit. The trouble with such an unqualified claim is that it grants a level of autonomy to technology that simply does not exist. Although computers have the potential to assist the progress of positive change, they have just as much potential to help ensure the status quo. This is not to say that computers are neutral, but rather that teachers who are committed to a progressive agenda for education must pay attention to far more than technology. One way to do that, as this chapter argues, is to conceptualize the requirements needed for systemic change as a set of nested contexts, a nest that starts with specific technological features and from there spirals outward to include pedagogical, curricular, departmental, and institutional spheres. I assume that departmental and institutional support systems will provide teachers with the theoretical background they will need in order to be alert to the social, political, and economic issues that are inextricably bound up with technology development and use.

# Epilogue

**I**t is axiomatic that computer technologies, in this day and age, permeate educational settings. This deep diffusion seems to reach into every corner of the university, leaving very few activities, individuals, or structures entirely unaffected. Departments of English are especially touched by the ubiquity of technology, for there is so much at stake in the representations of literacy online and in the manifold ways human values become instantiated in technological environments.

If students are to become agents of positive change, they will need an education that is comprehensive and truly relevant to a digital age in which much of the instructional agenda seems to be little more than indoctrination into the value systems of the dominant computer culture. In its attempt to provide students with an appropriate and worthwhile education, the profession has preferred to focus on critical concerns instead of functional concerns, a move that is understandable for humanists—even indispensable in that it can serve as a corrective to popular misconceptions about the role of technology in society. However, all too often such an approach simply replaces one literacy with another; it fails to expose students to the wide array of literacies they will need in order to participate fully and productively in the technological dimensions of their professional and personal lives. I realize that most approaches to functional literacy are utterly impoverished, but that does not change the fact that students must still learn to work with computers in effective ways. Moreover, an attentiveness to critical literacy does not guarantee that students will develop the rhetorical perspectives needed to design online texts and environments. The bottom line is that functional, critical, and rhetorical literacies, as I have mapped them out in this book, should all be crucial aspects of any computer literacy program that professes to be both valuable and professionally responsible. Indeed, students will require direct, repeated, and integrated contact with the particulars of all three literacies in order to become well-rounded individuals equipped with a keen and judicious sense of the technological world around them.

And it is certainly the responsibility of writing and communication teachers to help students develop this sense. As I have argued, there is a heavy price to be paid for leaving technology education entirely to those outside of the humanities. Numerous departments and units within a university will at once be involved in various types of computer literacy initiatives. However, few if any of these initiatives will seriously foreground cultural, political, and rhetorical frameworks. The effects of this situation are many and not very good: Computer literacy programs that focus on technical matters will not prepare students to think and work in a contextually and socially sensitive manner, will not encourage conceptions of literacy that align with the values and perspectives of writing and communication teachers, and will not help to alleviate the inequalities and inequities that can be perpetuated, unintentionally or otherwise, through the use and development of technology. In addition, a technical focus contributes to the marginalization of English departments by defining them as less than central to important educational activities in a digital age.

I opened chapter 1 with an epigraph from Neil Postman: "Technology education is not a technical subject. It is a branch of the humanities" (191). My hope is that I have convinced teachers of writing and communication that Postman is right in this regard. Humanists often have estranged or uncomfortable relationships with technology, yet neither indifference nor paralysis are acceptable options nowadays. In fact, an important role for English departments is to help position human-computer interaction as essentially a social problem, one that involves values, interpretation, contingency, persuasion, communication, deliberation, and more. In instructional situations in which such matters are properly emphasized, I am certain that teachers of writing and communication will discover that they have a great deal of expertise to contribute to computer literacy initiatives.

Works Cited

Index

# Works Cited

Adelson, Beth, and Troy Jordan. "The Need for Negotiation in Cooperative Work." *Sociomedia: Multimedia, Hypermedia, and the Social Construction of Knowledge*. Ed. Edward Barrett. Cambridge: MIT P, 1992. 469–92.

Allen, Brockenbrough S., and Robert P. Hoffman. "Varied Levels of Support for Constructive Activity in Hypermedia-Based Learning Environments." *Designing Environments for Constructive Learning*. Ed. Joost Lowyck, Thomas M. Duffy, and David H. Jonassen. New York: Springer, 1993. 261–90.

*The American College Teacher: National Norms for 1998–1999 HERI Faculty Survey Report*. Summer 1999. Higher Education Research Institute, UCLA Graduate School of Education. 15 Feb. 2002 <http://www.gseis.ucla.edu/heri/heri.html>.

Anderson, John R. *Language, Memory, and Thought*. Hillsdale: Erlbaum, 1976.

Apple, Michael W. *Teachers and Texts: A Political Economy of Class and Gender Relations in Education*. New York: Routledge, 1989.

Arnow, David. "The Iliad and the WHILE Loop: Computer Literacy in a Liberal Arts Program." *Proceedings of the Twenty-Second ACM Technical Symposium on Computer Science Education, San Antonio, 7–8 March 1991*. New York: ACM, 1991. 78–81.

Aronowitz, Stanley. "Looking Out: The Impact of Computers on the Lives of Professionals." *Literacy Online: The Promise (and Peril) of Reading and Writing with Computers*. Ed. Myron C. Tuman. Pittsburgh: U of Pittsburgh P, 1992. 119–37.

Aronowitz, Stanley, and Henry A. Giroux. *Postmodern Education: Politics, Culture, and Social Criticism*. Minneapolis: U of Minnesota P, 1991.

Baker, Ronald L. "A Comprehensive Integrated Computing Curriculum for End-Users." *Education and Computing* 6 (1990): 47–53.

Baldauf, Ken. Interview with Bob Edwards. *National Public Radio*. PBS. Washington, DC. 12 Nov. 1999.

Banathy, Belah H. *Systems Design of Education: A Journey to Create the Future*. Englewood Cliffs: Educational Technology Pub., 1991.

Bannon, Liam J., and Susanne Bodker. "Beyond the Interface: Encountering Artifacts in Use." *Designing Interaction: Psychology at the Human-Computer Interface*. Ed. John M. Carroll. Cambridge: Cambridge UP, 1991. 227–53.

Barger, Robert Newton. "Computer Literacy: Toward a Clearer Definition." *T.H.E. Journal* Oct. 1983: 108–12.

Barker, Thomas. "The Empowered User: A New Approach to Software Documentation." *Proceedings of the Forty-First Annual Conference of the Society for Technical Communication, Minneapolis, 15–18 May 1994.* Arlington, VA: STC. 5–7.

Barrett, Edward, ed. *Sociomedia: Multimedia, Hypermedia, and the Social Construction of Knowledge.* Cambridge: MIT P, 1992.

Bartholomae, David. "Inventing the University." *Perspectives on Literacy.* Ed. Barry M. Kroll, Eugene R. Kingten, and Mike Rose. Carbondale: Southern Illinois UP, 1988. 273–85.

Batson, Trent. "Historical Barriers to Intelligent Classroom Design." *Approaches to Computer Writing Classrooms: Learning from Practical Experience.* Ed. Linda Myers. Albany: State U of New York P, 1993. 1–18.

Baym, Nancy K. "The Emergence of Community in Computer-Mediated Communication." *Cybersociety: Computer-Mediated Communication and Community.* Ed. Steven G. Jones. Thousand Oaks: Sage, 1995. 138–63.

Bazerman, Charles. *Constructing Experience.* Carbondale: Southern Illinois UP, 1994.

Beck, Kent. *Extreme Programming Explained: Embrace Change.* Boston: Addison, 2000.

Belsey, Catherine. *Critical Practice.* London: Routledge, 1980.

———. *The Subject of Tragedy: Identity and Difference in Renaissance Drama.* New York: Routledge, 1985.

Ben-Ari, Mordechai. "Constructivism in Computer Science Education." *Proceedings of the Twenty-Ninth ACM Technical Symposium on Computer Science Education, Atlanta, 26 February–1 March 1998.* New York: ACM, 1998. 257–61.

Berdichevsky, Daniel, and Erik Neunschwander. "Toward an Ethics of Persuasive Technology." *Communications of the ACM* 42 (1999): 51–58.

Berghel, Hal. "Cyberspace 2000: Dealing with Information Overload." *Communications of the ACM* 40 (1997): 19–24.

Berk, Emily. "A Hypertext Glossary." *Hypertext/Hypermedia Handbook.* Ed. Emily Berk and Joseph Devlin. New York: McGraw, 1991. 535–54.

Berk, Emily, and Joseph Devlin. "What Is Hypertext?" *Hypertext/Hypermedia Handbook.* Ed. Emily Berk and Joseph Devlin. New York: McGraw, 1991. 3–7.

Berlin, James A. "Contemporary Composition: The Major Pedagogical Theories." *College English* 44 (1982): 765–77.

———. *Rhetorics, Poetics, and Cultures: Refiguring College English Studies.* Urbana: NCTE, 1996.

Bernhardt, Stephen A., and Carolyn S. Vickrey. "Supporting Faculty Development in Computers and Technical Communication." *Computers and Technical Communication: Pedagogical and Programmatic Perspectives.* Ed. Stuart A. Selber. Greenwich: Ablex, 1997. 331–52.

Berthoff, Ann E. "The Problem of Problem Solving." *College Composition and Communication* 22 (1971): 237–42.

Birkmaier, Craig. "Limited Vision: The Techno-Political War to Control the Future of Digital Mass Media." *NetWorker: The Craft of Network Computing* 1 (1997): 36–52.

Bizzell, Patricia. "The Prospect of Rhetorical Agency." *Making and Unmaking the Prospects of Rhetoric: Selected Papers from the 1996 Rhetoric Society of America Conference.* Ed. Theresa Enos. Mahwah: Erlbaum, 1997. 37–42.

Black, Max. "Metaphor." *Philosophical Perspectives on Metaphor.* Ed. Mark Johnson. Minneapolis: U of Minnesota P, 1981. 63–82.

Bodner, George, Michael Klobuchar, and David Geelan. "The Many Forms of Constructivism." The ACS Piaget, Constructivism, and Beyond Symposium, Dallas, 29 Mar.–2 Apr. 1998.

Bolter, J. David. "Literature in the Electronic Writing Space." *Literacy Online: The Promise (and Peril) of Reading and Writing with Computers.* Ed. Myron C. Tuman. Pittsburgh: U of Pittsburgh P, 1992.

———. *Turing's Man: Western Culture in the Computer Age.* Chapel Hill: U of North Carolina P, 1984.

———. *Writing Space: The Computer, Hypertext, and the History of Writing.* Hillsdale: Erlbaum, 1991.

Borgmann, Albert. *Technology and the Character of Contemporary Life: A Philosophical Inquiry.* Chicago: U of Chicago P, 1984.

Bowen, William. "The Puny Payoff from Office Computers." *Computers in the Human Context: Information Technology, Productivity, and People.* Ed. Tom Forester. Cambridge: MIT P, 1989. 267–71.

Boyarski, Daniel, and Richard Buchanan. "Exploring the Rhetoric of HCI." *Interactions* Apr. 1994: 24–35.

Boyle, Craig, and Kelly Ratliff. "A Survey and Classification of Hypertext Documentation Systems." *IEEE Transactions on Professional Communication* 35 (1992): 98–111.

Brand, Stewart. *The Media Lab: Inventing the Future at MIT.* New York: Viking, 1987.

Brandt, D. Scott. "Constructivism: Teaching for Understanding of the Internet." *Communications of the ACM* 40 (1997): 113–17.

Brasseur, Lee. "Visual Literacy in the Computer Age: A Complex Perceptual Landscape." *Computers and Technical Communication: Pedagogical and Programmatic Perspectives.* Ed. Stuart A. Selber. Greenwich: Ablex, 1997. 75–96.

Braverman, Harry. *Labor and Monopoly Capital: The Degradation of Work in the Twentieth Century.* New York: Monthly Review, 1974.

Brecher, Deborah L. *The Women's Computer Literacy Handbook.* New York: New American Library, 1985.

Brooks, Harvey. "Technology, Evolution, Purpose." *Technology and Man's Future.* Ed. Albert H. Teich. New York: St. Martin's, 1981. 294–320.

Brown, John Seely. "Process Versus Product: A Perspective on Tools for Communal and Informal Electronic Learning." *Computers in Education 5–13.* Ed. Ann Jones and Peter Scrimshaw. Philadelphia: Open UP, 1988. 303–22.

Brown, Lin. "Human-Computer Interaction and Standardization." *StandardView* 1 (1993): 3–8.

Browning, Graeme. *Electronic Democracy: Using the Internet to Influence American Politics.* Wilton: Pemberton, 1996.

Bruckman, Amy, and Mitchel Resnick. "The MediaMOO Project: Constructionism and Professional Community." *Constructionism in Practice: Designing, Thinking, and Learning in a Digital World.* Ed. Yasmin Kafai and Mitchel Resnick. Mahwah: Erlbaum, 1996. 207–21.

Bruffee, Kenneth A. "Social Construction, Language, and the Authority of Knowledge: A Bibliographic Essay." *College English* 48 (1986): 773–90.

Burke, Kenneth. *A Grammar of Motives.* Berkeley: U of California P, 1945.

Burns, Hugh. "Teaching Composition in Tomorrow's Multimedia, Multinetworked Classrooms." *Re-Imagining Computers and Composition: Teaching and Research in the Virtual Age.* Ed. Gail E. Hawisher and Paul LeBlanc. Portsmouth: Boynton, 1992. 115–30.

Bush, Vannevar. "As We May Think." *Atlantic Monthly* 176.1 (1945): 641–649. Rpt. in *From Memex to Hypertext: Vannevar Bush and the Mind's Machine.* Ed. James M. Nyce and Paul Kahn. New York: Academic, 1991. 85–107.

Byrd, Don, and Derek Owens. "Writing in the Hivemind." *Literacy Theory in the Age of the Internet.* Ed. Todd Taylor and Irene Ward. New York: Columbia UP, 1998. 47–58.

Capron, H. L. *Computers: Tools for an Information Age.* Redwood: Benjamin, 1990.

Carroll, John M., and Wendy A. Kellogg. "Artifact as Theory-Nexus: Hermeneutics Meets Theory-Based Design." *Proceedings of the 1989 ACM Conference on Human-Computer Interaction, Austin, 30 April–4 May 1989.* New York: ACM, 1989. 7–14.

Cassell, Justine, and Henry Jenkins, ed. *From Barbie to Mortal Kombat: Gender and Computer Games.* Cambridge: MIT P, 1998.

Conklin, Jeff. "Hypertext: An Introduction and Survey." *IEEE Computer* Sept. 1987: 17–41.

Cook-Gumperz, Jenny. "Literacy and Schooling: An Unchanging Equation?" *The Social Construction of Literacy.* Ed. Jenny Cook-Gumperz. Cambridge: Cambridge UP, 1986. 17–44.

Cooper, Marilyn M., and Michael Holzman. *Writing as Social Action.* Portsmouth: Boynton, 1989.

Cooper, Marilyn M., and Cynthia L. Selfe. "Computer Conferences and Learning: Authority, Resistance, and Internally Persuasive Discourse." *College English* 52 (1990): 847–69.

Crane, David. "In Medias Race: Filmic Representations, Networked Communication, and Racial Intermediation." *Race in Cyberspace*. Ed. Lisa Nakamura, Beth E. Kolko, and Gilbert B. Rodman. New York: Routledge, 2000. 87–115.

Cubbison, Laurie. "Configuring LISTSERV, Configuring Discourse." *Computers and Composition* 16 (1999): 371–81.

Cumming, Alister, and Gerri Sinclair. "Conceptualizing Hypermedia Curricula for Literary Studies in Schools." *Hypermedia and Literary Studies*. Ed. Paul Delany and George P. Landow. Cambridge: MIT P, 1990. 315–28.

Cushman, Ellen. "The Rhetorician as an Agent of Social Change." *College Composition and Communication* 47 (1996): 7–28.

Davis, Philip. "How Undergraduates Learn Computer Skills: Results of a Survey and Focus Group." *T.H.E. Journal* 26 (1999): 68–71.

Davis, Philip, and Reuben Hersh. *Descartes' Dream: The World According to Mathematics*. Boston: Houghton, 1986.

De Young, Laura. "Organizational Support for Software Design." *Bringing Design to Software*. Ed. Terry Winograd. New York: ACM, 1996. 253–67.

Dijkstra, Sanne. "Instructional Design Models and the Representation of Knowledge and Skills." *Educational Technology* June 1991: 19–26.

Dill, David D., and Charles P. Friedman. "An Analysis of Frameworks for Research on Innovation and Change in Higher Education." *Review of Educational Research* 49 (1979): 411–35.

Doheny-Farina, Stephen. *The Wired Neighborhood*. New Haven: Yale UP, 1996.

Dombrowski, Paul, ed. *Humanistic Aspects of Technical Communication*. Amityville: Baywood, 1994.

Dougherty, William V. "Computer Expertise: What Expectations Should We Have of New Teachers?" *NASSP Bulletin* Jan. 2000: 72–77.

Dreilinger, Daniel, and Adele E. Howe. "Experiences with Selecting Search Engines Using Metasearch." *ACM Transactions on Information Systems* 15 (1997): 195–222.

Duffelmeyer, Barbara Blakely. "Critical Computer Literacy: Computers in First-Year Composition as Topic and Environment." *Computers and Composition* 17 (2000): 289–307.

Duffy, Thomas M., James E. Palmer, and Brad Mehlenbacher. *Online Help: Design and Evaluation*. Norwood: Ablex, 1992.

Ebest, Sally Barr. "The Next Generation of WPAs: A Study of Graduate Students in Composition/Rhetoric." *Writing Program Administration* 22 (1999): 65–84.

Ellsworth, Elizabeth. "Why Doesn't This Feel Empowering? Working Through the Repressive Myths of Critical Pedagogy." *Feminisms and Critical Pedagogy*. Ed. Carmen Luke and Jennifer Gore. New York: Routledge, 1992. 90–119.

Ely, Donald P. "Conditions that Facilitate the Implementation of Educational Technology Innovations." *Journal of Research on Computing in Education* 23 (1990): 298–305.

Ertmer, Peggy A., and Timothy J. Newby. "Behaviorism, Cognitivism, Constructivism: Comparing Critical Features from an Instructional Design Perspective." *Performance Improvement Quarterly* 6 (1993): 50–72.

Faigley, Lester. "Competing Theories of Process: A Critique and a Proposal." *College English* 48 (1986): 527–42.

———. "Subverting the Electronic Notebook: Teaching Writing Using Networked Computers." *The Writing Teacher as Researcher: Essays in the Theory and Practice of Class-Based Research.* Ed. Donald A. Daiker and Max Morenberg. Portsmouth: Boynton, 1990. 290–311.

Feenberg, Andrew. *Critical Theory of Technology.* New York: Oxford UP, 1991.

Fertig, Scott, Eric Freeman, and David Gelernter. "Lifestreams: An Alternative to the Desktop Metaphor." *Proceedings of the 1996 ACM Conference on Human-Computer Interaction, Vancouver, 13–18 April, 1996.* New York: ACM, 1996. 410–11.

Flax, Jane. *Thinking Fragments.* Berkeley: U of California P, 1990.

Flores, Mary J. "Computer Conferencing: Composing a Feminist Community of Writers." *Computers and Community: Teaching Composition in the Twenty-First Century.* Ed. Carolyn Handa. Portsmouth: Boynton, 1990. 106–17.

Flower, Linda. *The Construction of Negotiated Meaning: A Social Cognitive Theory of Writing.* Carbondale: Southern Illinois UP, 1994.

Fogg, B. J. "Persuasive Technologies." *Communications of the ACM* 42 (1999): 27–29.

Foucault, Michel. *Discipline and Punish: The Birth of the Prison.* New York: Random, 1979.

Fox, Edward A., Qi Fan Chen, and Robert K. France. "Integrating Search and Retrieval with Hypertext." *Hypertext/Hypermedia Handbook.* Ed. Emily Berk and Joseph Devlin. New York: McGraw, 1991. 329–55.

Franke, Richard H. "Technological Revolution and Productivity Decline: The Case of US Banks." *Computers in the Human Context: Information Technology, Productivity, and People.* Ed. Tom Forester. Cambridge: MIT P, 1989. 281–90.

Freire, Paulo. *Pedagogy of the Oppressed.* New York: Herder, 1970.

Freire, Paulo, and Donaldo Macedo. *Literacy: Reading the Word and the World.* New York: Bergin, 1987.

Gee, James. *Social Linguistics and Literacies: Ideology in Discourse.* New York: Falmer, 1990.

Gilroy, Faith D., and Harsha B. Desai. "Computer Anxiety: Sex, Race, and Age." *International Journal of Man-Machine Studies* 25 (1986): 711–19.

Giroux, Henry A. "Literacy and the Politics of Difference." *Critical Literacy: Politics, Praxis, and the Postmodern.* Ed. Colin Lankshear and Peter L. McLaren. Albany: State U of New York P, 1993. 367–77.

———. *Teachers as Intellectuals: Toward a Critical Pedagogy of Learning.* New York: Bergin, 1988.

Glasersfeld, Ernst von. "Constructivism in Education." *The International Encyclopedia of Education Research and Studies.* Ed. Torsten Husen and T. Neville Postlethwaite. New York: Pergamon, 1989. 162–63.

Glushko, Robert J. "Seven Ways to Make a Hypertext Project Fail." *Technical Communication* 39 (1992): 226–30.

Gomez, Mary Louise. "The Equitable Teaching of Composition with Computers: A Case for Change." *Evolving Perspectives on Computers and Composition Studies: Questions for the 1990s.* Ed. Gail E. Hawisher and Cynthia L. Selfe. Urbana: NCTE, 1991. 318–35.

Grabill, Jeffrey T. "Utopic Visions, The Technopoor, and Public Access: Writing Technologies in a Community Literacy Program." *Computers and Composition* 15 (1998): 297–315.

Green, Kenneth C., and Steven W. Gilbert. "Academic Productivity and Technology." *Academe* Jan.–Feb. 1995: 19–25.

Greenberg, Saul, ed. *Computer-Supported Cooperative Work and Groupware.* New York: Harcourt, 1991.

———. "Designing Computers as Public Artifacts." *International Journal of Design Computing* Volume 2 (1999–2000): 38 pars. 20 Feb. 1992 <http://www.arch.usyd.edu.au/kcdc/journal/IJDC2/files/dcnet/sub18/index.html>.

Greene, Stuart, and John M. Ackerman. "Expanding the Constructivist Metaphor: A Rhetorical Perspective on Literacy Research and Practice." *Review of Educational Research* 65 (1995): 383–420.

Haas, Christina, and Christine M. Neuwirth. "Writing the Technology That Writes Us: Research on Literacy and the Shape of Technology." *Literacy and Computers: The Complications of Teaching and Learning with Technology.* Ed. Cynthia L. Selfe and Susan Hilligoss. New York: MLA, 1994. 319–35.

Hadjerrouit, Said. "A Constructivist Framework for Integrating the Java Paradigm into the Undergraduate Curriculum." *Proceedings of the Sixth ACM Joint Conference on Integrating Technology into Computer Science Education, Dublin, 18–21 August 1998.* New York: ACM, 1998. 105–7.

Hage, Jerald, and Michael Aiken. *Social Change in Complex Organizations.* New York: Random, 1970.

Handa, Carolyn. "Designing a Computer Classroom: Pedagogy, Nuts, and Bolts." *Approaches to Computer Writing Classrooms.* Ed. Linda Myers. Albany: State U of New York P, 1993. 103–18.

Hansen, Craig J. "Networking Technology in the Classroom: Whose Interests

Are We Serving." *Electronic Literacies in the Workplace: Technologies of Writing.* Ed. Patricia Sullivan and Jennie Dautermann. Urbana: NCTE and *Computers and Composition,* 1996. 201–15.

Hanson, Barbara Gail. *General Systems Theory: Beginning with Wholes.* Washington, DC: Taylor, 1995.

Harasim, Linda M. "Networlds: Networks as Social Space." *Global Networks: Computers and International Communication.* Ed. Linda M. Harasim. Cambridge: MIT P, 1993. 15–34.

Harris, Joseph. *A Teaching Subject: Composition Since 1966.* Upper Saddle River: Prentice, 1997.

Hawisher, Gail E. "Research Update: Writing and Word Processing." *Computers and Composition* 5 (1988): 7–27.

Hawisher, Gail E., Paul LeBlanc, Charles Moran, and Cynthia L. Selfe. *Computers and the Teaching of Writing in American Higher Education, 1979–1994: A History.* Norwood: Ablex, 1996.

Hawisher, Gail E., and Charles Moran. "Electronic Mail and the Writing Instructor." *College English* 55 (1993): 627–43.

Hawisher, Gail E., and Cynthia L. Selfe. *Literacy, Technology and Society: Confronting the Issues.* Upper Saddle River: Prentice, 1997.

Hayes, Dennis R. "Digital Palsy: RSI and Restructuring Capital." *Resisting the Virtual Life: The Culture and Politics of Information.* Ed. James Brook and Ian A. Boal. San Francisco: City Lights, 1995. 173–80.

Heim, Michael. *The Metaphysics of Virtual Reality.* New York: Oxford UP, 1993.

Heinssen, Robert K., Carol R. Glass, and Luanne A. Knight. "Assessing Computer Anxiety: Development and Validation of the Computer Anxiety Rating Scale." *Computers in Human Behavior* 3 (1987): 49–59.

Henderson, Kathryn. "The Visual Culture of Engineers." *The Cultures of Computing.* Ed. Susan Leigh Star. Cambridge: Blackwell, 1995. 196–218.

Herndl, Carl G. "The Transformation of Critical Ethnography into Pedagogy, or the Vicissitudes of Traveling Theory." *Nonacademic Writing: Social Theory and Technology.* Ed. Ann Hill Duin and Craig J. Hansen. Mahwah: Erlbaum, 1996. 17–33.

Hillocks, George. *Teaching Writing as Reflective Practice.* New York: Teachers College P, 1995.

Hiltz, Starr Roxanne. *The Virtual Classroom: Learning Without Limits via Computer Networks.* Norwood: Ablex, 1994.

Hiltz, Starr Roxanne, and Murray Turoff. "Structuring Computer-Mediated Communication Systems to Avoid Information Overload." *Communications of the ACM* 28 (1985): 680–89.

Holland, Melissa V., Veda R. Charrow, and William W. Wright. "How Can Technical Writers Write Effectively for Several Audiences at Once?" *Solving*

*Problems in Technical Writing.* Ed. Lynn Beene and Peter White. New York: Oxford UP, 1988. 27–55.

Holmevik, Jan Rune, and Cynthia Haynes. *MOOniversity: A Student's Guide to Online Learning Environments.* Boston: Allyn, 2000.

Hooper, Paula K. "'They Have Their Own Thoughts': A Story of Constructionist Learning in an Alternative African-Centered Community School." *Constructionism in Practice: Designing, Thinking, and Learning in a Digital World.* Ed. Yasmin Kafai and Mitchel Resnick. Mahwah: Erlbaum, 1996. 241–53.

Horn, Robert E. *Mapping Hypertext: Analysis, Linkage, and Display of Knowledge for the Next Generation of On-Line Text and Graphics.* Lexington: Lexington Inst., 1989.

Horton, William. "Let's Do Away with Manuals . . . Before They Do Away with Us." *Technical Communication* 40 (1993): 26–34.

Hourigan, Maureen M. *Literacy as Social Exchange: Intersections of Class, Gender, and Culture.* Albany: State U of New York P, 1994.

Howard, Rebecca Moore. "Sexuality, Textuality: The Cultural Work of Plagiarism." *College English* 62 (2000): 473–91.

Howard, Tharon. "Designing Computer Classrooms for Technical Communication Programs." *Computers and Technical Communication: Pedagogical and Programmatic Perspectives.* Ed. Stuart A. Selber. Greenwich: Ablex, 1997. 289–309.

———. "WANS, Connectivity, and Computer Literacy: An Introduction and Glossary." *Computers and Composition* 9 (1992): 41–58.

Hull, Glynda. "Hearing Other Voices: A Critical Assessment of Popular Views on Literacy and Work." *Literacy: A Critical Sourcebook.* Ed. Ellen Cushman, Eugene R. Kintgen, Barry M. Kroll, and Mike Rose. New York: Bedford, 2001. 660–83.

Huot, Brian. "Computers and Assessment: Understanding Two Technologies." *Computers and Composition* 13 (1996): 231–43.

Irish, Peggy M., and Randall H. Trigg. "Supporting Collaboration in Hypermedia: Issues and Experiences." *The Society of Text: Hypertext, Hypermedia, and the Social Construction of Knowledge.* Ed. Edward Barrett. Cambridge: MIT P, 1989. 93–106.

Jay, Gregory, and Gerald Graff. "A Critique of Critical Pedagogy." *Higher Education under Fire: Politics, Economics, and the Crisis of the Humanities.* Ed. Michael Berube and Cary Nelson. New York: Routledge, 1995.

Johnson, David C., Ronald E. Anderson, Thomas P. Hansen, and Daniel L. Klassen. "Computer Literacy—What Is It?" *The Information Age Classroom: Using the Computer as a Tool.* Ed. Terence R. Cannings and Stephen W. Brown. Irvine: Franklin, 1986. 38–41.

Johnson, Jeff, and Evelyn Pine. "Toward a Guide to Social Action for Computer Professionals." *SIGCHI Bulletin* 25 (1993): 23–27.

Johnson, Robert R. *User-Centered Technology: A Rhetorical Theory for Computers and Other Mundane Artifacts.* Albany: State U of New York P, 1998.

Johnson-Eilola, Johndan. "Accumulation, Circulation, and Association: Economies of Information in Online Spaces." *IEEE Transactions on Professional Communication* 38 (1995): 228–38.

———. "Hypertext and Print Culture: Some Possible Geometries for Cyberspace." Conference on College Composition and Communication Convention. Sheraton Harbor Island Hotel, San Diego. 1–3 Apr. 1993.

———. "Negative Spaces: From Production to Connection in Composition." *Literacy Theory in the Age of the Internet.* Ed. Todd Taylor and Irene Ward. New York: Columbia UP, 1998. 17–33.

Johnson-Eilola, Johndan, and Stuart A. Selber. "Policing Ourselves: Defining the Boundaries of Appropriate Discussion in Online Forums." *Computers and Composition* 13 (1996): 269–91.

Jonassen, David H. *Computers in the Classroom: Mindtools for Critical Thinking.* Englewood Cliffs: Prentice, 1996.

———. "Semantic Network Elicitation: Tools for Structuring Hypertext." *Hypertext: State of the Art.* Ed. Ray McAleese and Catherine Green. Oxford: Intellect, 1990. 142–52.

———. "Thinking Technology: Toward a Constructivist View of Instructional Design." *Educational Technology* 30 (1990): 32–34.

Jones, Steve, ed. *Doing Internet Research: Critical Issues and Methods for Examining the Net.* Thousand Oaks: Sage, 1999.

Joyce, Michael. *Of Two Minds: Hypertext Pedagogy and Poetics.* Ann Arbor: U of Michigan P, 1995.

Kafai, Yasmin B. "Learning Design by Making Games: Children's Development of Design Strategies in the Creation of a Complex Computational Artifact." *Constructionism in Practice: Designing, Thinking, and Learning in a Digital World.* Ed. Yasmin Kafai and Mitchel Resnick. Mahwah: Erlbaum, 1996. 71–96.

Kalmbach, James. "Computer-Supported Classrooms and Curricular Change in Technical Communication Programs." *Computers and Technical Communication: Pedagogical and Programmatic Perspectives.* Ed. Stuart A. Selber. Greenwich: Ablex, 1997. 261–74.

Katz, Seth, Janice Walker, and Janet Cross, ed. "Tenure and Technology: New Values, New Guidelines." *Kairos* 2.1 (1997) <http://english.ttu.edu/ kairos/2.1>.

Kay, Alan. "Computers, Networks, and Education." *Scientific American* Sept. 1991: 138–48.

———. "User Interface: A Personal View." *The Art of Human-Computer Interface Design.* Ed. Brenda Laurel. Reading: Addison, 1990. 191–207.

Kay, Robin H. "Bringing Computer Literacy into Perspective." *Journal of Research on Computing in Education* 22.1 (1989): 35–47.

Kemp, Fred. "Computer-Mediated Communication: Making Nets Work for Writing Instruction." *The Dialogic Classroom: Teachers Integrating Computer Technology, Pedagogy, and Research.* Ed. Jeffrey R. Galin and Joan Latchaw. Urbana: NCTE, 1998. 133–50.

———. "Who Programmed This? Examining the Instructional Attitudes of Writing-Support Software." *Computers and Composition* 10 (1992): 9–24.

Khaslavsky, Julie, and Nathan Shedroff. "Understanding the Seductive Experience." *Communications of the ACM* 42 (1999): 45–49.

Kiesler, Sara, Jane Siegel, and Timothy W. McGuire. "Social Psychological Aspects of Computer-Mediated Communication." *American Psychologist* 39 (1984): 1123–34.

King, Phillip, and Jason Tester. "The Landscape of Persuasive Technologies." *Communications of the ACM* 42 (1999): 31–38.

King, Raymond E., and Michael D. McNeese. "Human-Computer Anxiety and Phobia: A Consideration of Foundations and Interventions." *Proceedings of the IEEE Fourth Annual Symposium on Human Interaction with Complex Systems, Dayton, 22–25 March 1998.* Piscataway: IEEE, 1998. 205–8.

Kiper, James D., and Cathy Bishop-Clark. "Abstraction, Design, and Theory in Computer Science: A Liberal Arts Course." *Computer Science Education* 6 (1995): 93–110.

Kling, Rob. "Behind the Terminal: The Critical Role of Computing Infrastructure in Effective Information Systems Development and Use." *Challenges and Strategies for Research in Systems Development.* Ed. W. W. Cotterman and J. A. Senn. New York: Wiley, 1992. 365–413.

Kling, Rob, and Tom Jewett. "The Social Design of Worklife with Computers and Networks: A Natural Systems Perspective." *Advances in Computers.* Vol. 39. Ed. Marshall C. Yovits. San Diego: Academic, 1994. 239–93.

Knabe, Kevin. "Apple Guide: A Case Study in User-Aided Design of Online Help." *Proceedings of the 1995 ACM Conference on Human-Computer Interaction, Denver, 7–11 May 1995.* New York: ACM, 1995. 286–87.

Knoblauch, C. H. "Literacy and the Politics of Education." *The Right to Literacy.* Ed. Andrea A. Lunsford, Helene Moglen, and James Slevin. New York: MLA, 1990. 74–80.

Kolko, Beth. "Erasing @race: Going White in the (Inter)Face." *Race in Cyberspace.* Ed. Lisa Nakamura, Beth Kolko, and Gilbert B. Rodman. New York: Routledge, 2000. 213–232.

Kolosseus, Beverly, Dan Bauer, and Stephen A. Bernhardt. "From Writer to Designer: Modeling Composing Processes in a Hypertext Environment." *Technical Communication Quarterly* 4 (1995): 79–93.

Kottkamp, Robert B. "Means for Facilitating Reflection." *Education and Urban Society* 22 (1990): 182–203.

Kress, Gunther. "'English' at the Crossroads: Rethinking Curricula of Communication in the Context of the Turn to the Visual." *Passions, Pedagogies, and Twenty-First Century Technologies*. Ed. Gail E. Hawisher and Cynthia L. Selfe. Logan: Utah State UP and NCTE, 1999. 66–88.

Kretovics, Joseph R. "Critical Literacy: Challenging the Assumptions of Mainstream Educational Theory." *Journal of Education* 167 (1985): 50–62.

Kreuzer, Terese. "Computers on Campus: The Black-White Technology Gap." *Journal of Blacks in Higher Education* 1 (autumn 1993): 88–95.

Lakoff, George, and Mark Johnson. *Metaphors We Live By*. Chicago: U of Chicago P, 1980.

Landow, George P. *Hypertext: The Convergence of Contemporary Critical Theory and Technology*. Baltimore: Johns Hopkins UP, 1992.

Landow, George P., and Paul Delany. "Hypertext, Hypermedia, and Literary Studies: The State of the Art." *Hypermedia and Literary Studies*. Ed. George P. Landow and Paul Delany. Cambridge: MIT P, 1991. 3–50.

Lang, Susan, Janice Walker, and Keith Dorwick, eds. "Special Issue: Tenure 2000." *Computers and Composition* 17 (2001): 1–115.

Lanham, Richard. *The Electronic Word: Democracy, Technology, and the Arts*. Chicago: U of Chicago P, 1993.

Lankshear, Colin. "Ideas of Functional Literacy: Critique and Redefinition of an Educational Goal." *New Zealand Journal of Educational Studies* 20 (1985): 5–19.

Latterell, Catherine G. "Training the Workforce: An Overview of GTA Education Curricula." *Writing Program Administration* 19 (1996): 7–23.

Lauer, Sister Janice. "Heuristics and Composition." *College Composition and Communication* 21 (1970): 396–404.

Laurel, Brenda. *Computer as Theatre*. Reading: Addison, 1993.

LeBlanc, Paul. *Writing Teachers Writing Software: Creating Our Place in the Electronic Age*. Urbana: NCTE and *Computers and Composition*, 1993.

Leister, Jenni. "Promoting Gender Equity in Computer Literacy." *Proceedings of the Twenty-First ACM Conference on User Services, San Diego, 7–10 November 1993*. New York: ACM, 1993. 292–96.

Lester, James C., Patrick J. Fitzgerald, and Brian A. Stone. "The Pedagogical Design Studio: Exploiting Artifact-Based Task Models for Constructivist Learning." *Proceedings of the 1997 International Conference on Intelligent User Interfaces, Orlando, 6–9 January 1997*. New York: ACM, 1997. 155–62.

Leto, Victoria. "'Washing, Seems It's All We Do': Washing Technology and Women's Communication." *Technology and Women's Voices: Keeping in Touch*. Ed. Cheris Kramarae. New York: Routledge, 1988. 161–79.

Levine, Kenneth. "Functional Literacy: Fond Illusions and False Economies." *Harvard Educational Review* 52 (1982): 249–66.

"Life on the Internet Timeline." *PBS Online.* 20 Feb. 2002 <http://www.pbs.org/internet>.

Liu, Yameng. "Rhetoric and Reflexivity." *Philosophy and Rhetoric* 28 (1995): 333–49.

Lyman, Peter. "What Is Computer Literacy and What Is Its Place in Liberal Education?" *Liberal Education* 81.3 (1995): 4–15.

MacLean, Allan, Richard M. Young, and Thomas P. Moran. "Design Rationale: The Arguments Behind the Artifact." *Proceedings of the 1989 ACM Conference on Human-Computer Interaction, Austin, 30 April–4 May 1989.* New York: ACM, 1989. 247–52.

Mahoney, Michael. "Software as Science—Science as Software." International Conference on the History of Computing, Paderborn, Germany, 5–7 Apr. 2000.

Marakas, George M., and Daniel Robey. "Managing Impressions with Information Technology: From the Glass House to the Boundaryless Organization." *Impression Management and Information Technology.* Ed. Jon W. Beard. Wesport: Quorum, 1996. 39–50.

Marcus, George E., and Michael M. J. Fischer. *Anthropology as Cultural Critique: An Experimental Moment in the Human Sciences.* Chicago: U of Chicago P, 1986.

Markel, Mike. "Distance Education and the Myth of the New Pedagogy." *Journal of Business and Technical Communication* 13 (1999): 208–22.

Markus, M. Lynne, and Niels Bjorn-Andersen. "Power over Users: Its Exercise by System Professionals." *Communications of the ACM* 30 (1987): 498–504.

Markussen, Randi. "Constructing Easiness—Historical Perspectives on Work, Computerization, and Women." *The Cultures of Computing.* Ed. Susan Leigh Star. Cambridge: Blackwell, 1996.

Martin, W. Allen. "Being There Is What Matters." *Academe* Sept.–Oct. 1999: 32–36.

Martocchio, Joseph J. "Effects of Conceptions of Ability on Anxiety, Self-Efficacy, and Learning in Training." *Journal of Applied Psychology* 79 (1994): 819–25.

Marvin, Carolyn. *When Old Technologies Were New: Thinking about Electric Communication in the Late Nineteenth Century.* New York: Oxford UP, 1988.

McComiskey, Bruce. *Teaching Composition as a Social Process.* Logan: Utah State UP, 2000.

McGowan, Matthew K., and Larry Cornwell. "Measuring Computer Literacy Through the Use of Proficiency Exams." *Journal of Computer Information Systems* 40 (1999): 107–12.

McLaren, Peter. "Literacy Research and the Postmodern Turn: Cautions from the Margins." *Multidisciplinary Perspectives on Literacy Research.* Ed. Judith L.

Green, Richard Beach, Michael L. Kamil, and Timothy Shanahan. Urbana: NCRE/NCTE, 1992. 319–39.

McLaughlin, Margaret L., Kerry K. Osborne, and Christine B. Smith. "Standards of Conduct on Usenet." *Cybersociety: Computer-Mediated Communication and Community.* Ed. Steven G. Jones. Thousand Oaks: Sage, 1995. 90–111.

McLuhan, Marshall. *Understanding Media: The Extensions of Man.* New York: Penguin, 1964.

Mehlenbacher, Brad. "Technologies and Tensions: Designing Online Environments for Teaching Technical Communication." *Computers and Technical Communication: Pedagogical and Programmatic Perspectives.* Ed. Stuart A. Selber. Greenwich: Ablex, 1997. 219–38.

Meyer, Marilyn, and Roberta Baber. *Computers in Your Future.* Indianapolis: Que, 1997.

Mirel, Barbara. "Applied Constructivism for User Documentation: Alternatives to Conventional Task Orientation." *Journal of Business and Technical Communication* 12 (1998): 7–49.

Moran, Charles. "Access: The 'A' Word in Technology Studies." *Passions, Pedagogies, and Twenty-First Century Technologies.* Ed. Gail E. Hawisher and Cynthia L. Selfe. Logan: Utah State UP and NCTE, 1999. 205–20.

Morgan, Robert M. "Educational Reform: Top-Down or Bottom-Up?" *Systemic Change in Education.* Ed. Charles M. Reigeluth and Robert J. Garfinkle. Englewood Cliffs: Educational Technology Pub., 1994. 43–50.

Morgan, Wendy. *Critical Literacy in the Classroom.* New York: Routledge, 1997.

Moulthrop, Stuart. "The Politics of Hypertext." *Evolving Perspectives on Computers and Composition Studies: Questions for the 1990s.* Ed. Gail E. Hawisher and Cynthia L. Selfe. Urbana: NCTE and Computers and Composition, 1991. 253–71.

Mountford, S. Joy. "Tools and Techniques for Creative Design." *The Art of Human-Computer Interface Design.* Ed. Brenda Laurel. Reading: Addison, 1990. 17–30.

Myers, Brad A. "A Brief History of Human-Computer Interaction Technology." *Interactions* 5 (1998): 44–54.

Myers, Greg. "The Social Construction of Two Biologists' Proposals." *Written Communication* 2 (1985): 219–45.

Nardi, Bonnie A., and Vicki L. O'Day. *Information Ecologies: Using Technology with Heart.* Cambridge: MIT P, 1999.

Negroponte, Nicholas. *Being Digital.* New York: Knopf, 1995.

Nelson, Theodor Holm. *Literary Machines 90.1.* Sausalito: Mindful, 1990.

Nesbitt, Jim, and Jim Barnett. "Software Giant's Dominance Goes Beyond Issues of Antitrust Law." *Newhouse News Service.* 22 Feb. 2002 <http://newhousenews.com/archive/story1a060200.html>.

Newman, Stephen. *Philosophy and Teacher Education: A Reinterpretation of*

*Donald A. Schön's Epistemology of Reflective Practice.* Brookfield: Ashgate, 1999.

Nielsen, Jakob. "Be Succinct!" *Alertbox.* 15 Mar. 1997. 22 Feb. 2002 <http://www.useit.com/alertbox/9703b.html>.

*The 1999 National Survey of Information Technology in Higher Education.* Oct. 1999. The Campus Computing Project. 1 Mar. 2003 <http://www.campuscomputing.net>.

Noble, Douglas. "Computer Literacy and Ideology." *Teachers College Record* 85 (1984): 602–14.

Norman, Donald A. *The Design of Everyday Things.* New York: Doubleday, 1988.

Norman, Donald A., and James C. Spohrer. "Learner-Centered Education." *Communications of the ACM* 39 (1996): 24–27.

Nothstine, William L., and Martha Cooper. "Persuasion." *Encyclopedia of Rhetoric and Composition: Communication from Ancient Times to the Information Age.* Ed. Theresa Enos. New York: Garland, 1996. 505–12.

Oblinger, Diana G., and Anne-Lee Verville. "Information Technology as a Change Agent." *Educom Review* 34 (1999): 46–55.

Olsen, Florence. "Faculty Wariness of Technology Remains a Challenge, Computing Survey Finds." *Chronicle of Higher Education* 29 Oct. 1999: A65.

Ormiston, Gayle E. "Introduction." *From Artifact to Habitat: Studies in the Critical Engagement of Technology.* Ed. Gayle E. Ormiston. Bethlehem: Lehigh UP, 1990. 13–27.

Orr, David W. "The Liberal Arts, the Campus, and the Biosphere." *Harvard Educational Review* 60 (1990): 205–16.

Papert, Seymour. *The Connected Family: Bridging the Digital Generation Gap.* Atlanta: Longstreet, 1996.

———. *Mindstorms: Children, Computers, and Powerful Ideas.* New York: Basic, 1980.

Parasuraman, Saroj, and Magid Igbaria. "An Examination of Gender Differences in the Determinants of Computer Anxiety and Attitudes Toward Microcomputers among Managers." *International Journal of Man-Machine Studies* 32 (1990): 327–40.

Parker, Angie. "From Puppets to Problem Solvers: A Constructivistic Approach to Computer Literacy." *International Journal of Instructional Media* 22 (1995): 233–39.

Parunak, H. Van Dyke. "Ordering the Information Graph." *Hypertext/Hypermedia Handbook.* Ed. Emily Berk and Joseph Devlin. New York: McGraw, 1991. 299–325.

Peckham, Irvin. "Capturing the Evolution of Corporate E-mail: An Ethnographic Case Study." *Computers and Composition* 14 (1997): 343–60.

Pfaffenberger, Bryan. "Technological Dramas." *Science, Technology, and Human Values* 17 (1992): 282–312.

Poster, Mark. *The Second Media Age.* Cambridge: Polity, 1995.

Postman, Neil. *The End of Education: Redefining the Value of School.* New York: Knopf, 1995.

Prawat, Richard S. "Constructivisms, Modern and Postmodern." *Educational Psychologist* 31 (1996): 215–25.

Press, Larry. "Before the Altair: The History of Personal Computing." *Communications of the ACM* 36 (1993): 27–33.

Ratan, Suneel. "A New Divide Between Haves and Have-Nots?" *Welcome to Cyberspace.* Spec. issue of *Time* 145.12 (spring 1995): 25–26.

Redish, Janice C. "Understanding Readers." *Techniques for Technical Communicators.* Ed. Carol M. Barnum and Saul Carliner. New York: Macmillan, 1993. 14–41.

Reeves, Brent, and Frank Shipman. "Supporting Communication Between Designers with Artifact-Centered Evolving Information Spaces." *ACM Conference Proceedings on Computer Supported Cooperative Work, Toronto, 1–4 November 1992.* New York: ACM, 1992. 394–401.

Reich, Robert B. *The Work of Nations: Preparing Ourselves for Twenty-First-Century Capitalism.* New York: Vintage, 1992.

Reiss, Levi. *Computer Literacy.* Boston: PWS, 1984.

Rheingold, Howard. *Tools for Thought: The People and Ideas Behind the Next Computer Revolution.* New York: Simon, 1985.

Richards, I. A. *The Philosophy of Rhetoric.* New York: Oxford UP, 1936.

Rickly, Rebecca J. "Making Technology Count: Incentives, Rewards, and Evaluations." *Electronic Networks: Crossing Boundaries/Creating Communities.* Ed. Tharon Howard and Chris Benson. Portsmouth: Boynton, 1999. 225–39.

Rittel, Horst W., and Melvin M. Webber. "Dilemmas in a General Theory of Planning." *Policy Sciences* 4 (1973): 155–69.

Rockman, Saul. "In School or Out: Technology, Equity, and the Future of Our Kids." *Communications of the ACM* 38 (1995): 25–29.

Rose, Mike. *Writer's Block: The Cognitive Dimension.* Carbondale: Southern Illinois UP, 1984.

Rosenberg, Martin. "Contingency, Liberation, and the Seduction of Geometry: Hypertext as an Avant-Garde Medium." *Perforations* 2.3 (1992): 1–12.

Rosenberg, Richard S. "Beyond the Code of Ethics: The Responsibility of Professional Societies." *ACM Proceedings of the Ethics and Social Impact Component on Shaping Policy in the Information Age, Washington, DC., 10–12 May 1998.* New York: ACM, 1998. 18–25.

Roszak, Theodore. *The Cult of Information: A Neo-Luddite Treatise on High-Tech, Artificial Intelligence, and the True Art of Thinking.* Berkeley: U of California P, 1994.

Rust, Val D. "From Modern to Postmodern Ways of Seeing Social and Educational Change." *Social Cartography: Mapping Ways of Seeing Social and*

*Educational Change.* Ed. Rolland G. Paulston. New York: Garland, 1996. 29–51.

Sargent, Randy, Mitchel Resnick, Fred Martin, and Brian Silverman. "Building and Learning with Programmable Bricks." *Constructionism in Practice: Designing, Thinking, and Learning in a Digital World.* Ed. Yasmin Kafai and Mitchel Resnick. Mahwah: Erlbaum, 1996. 161–73.

Saussure, Ferdinand de. *Course in General Linguistics.* New York: McGraw, 1959.

Savery, John R., and Thomas M. Duffy. "Problem Based Learning: An Instructional Model and Its Constructivist Framework." *Constructivist Learning Environments: Case Studies in Instructional Design.* Ed. Brent G. Wilson. Englewood Cliffs: Educational Technology Pub., 1996. 135–48.

Schmitt, Maribeth Cassidy, and Timothy J. Newby. "Metacognition: Relevance to Instructional Design." *Journal of Instructional Development* 9 (1986): 29–33.

Schön, Donald. *The Reflective Practitioner: How Professionals Think in Action.* New York: Basic, 1983.

Schrage, Michael. *Shared Minds: The New Technologies of Collaboration.* New York: Random, 1990.

Schwartz, Helen J. "'Dominion Everywhere': Computers as Cultural Artifacts." *Literacy Online: The Promise (and Peril) of Reading and Writing with Computers.* Ed. Myron C. Tuman. Pittsburgh: U of Pittsburgh P, 1992. 95–108.

Scribner, Sylvia. "Literacy in Three Metaphors." *Perspectives on Literacy.* Ed. Barry M. Kroll, Eugene R. Kintgen, and Mike Rose. Carbondale: Southern Illinois UP, 1988. 71–81.

Seesing, Paul R., and Mark P. Haselkorn. "Communicating Technology Risk to the Public: The Year 2000 Example." *Proceedings of the 1998 IEEE Professional Communication Conference, Quebec City, 23–25 September 1998.* Piscataway: IEEE, 1998. 349–59.

Selber, Stuart A. "Hypertext Spheres of Influence in Technical Communication Instructional Contexts." *Computers and Technical Communication: Pedagogical and Programmatic Perspectives.* Ed. Stuart A. Selber. Greenwich: Ablex, 1997. 17–43.

Selber, Stuart A., Johndan Johnson-Eilola, and Brad Mehlenbacher. "Online Support Systems: Tutorials, Documentation, and Help." *Handbook for Computer Science and Engineering.* Ed. Allen B. Tucker. Boca Raton: CRC, 1997. 1619–43.

Selber, Stuart A., Johndan Johnson-Eilola, and Cynthia L. Selfe. "Contexts for Faculty Professional Development in the Age of Electronic Writing and Communication." *Technical Communication* 42 (1995): 581–84.

Selber, Stuart A., Dan McGavin, William Klein, and Johndan Johnson-Eilola. "Key Issues in Hypertext-Supported Collaborative Writing." *Nonacademic*

*Writing: Social Theory and Technology.* Ed. Ann Hill Duin and Craig J. Hansen. Hillsdale: Erlbaum, 1996. 257–80.

Selfe, Cynthia L. "Preparing English Teachers for the Virtual Age: The Case for Technology Critics." *Re-Imagining Computers and Composition: Teaching and Research in the Virtual Age.* Ed. Gail E. Hawisher and Paul LeBlanc. Portsmouth: Boynton, 1992. 24–42.

——. *Technology and Literacy in the Twenty-First Century: The Importance of Paying Attention.* Carbondale: Southern Illinois UP, 1999.

Selfe, Cynthia L., and Paul R. Meyer. "Testing the Claims for On-Line Conferences." *Written Communication* 8 (1991): 163–92.

Selfe, Cynthia L., and Richard J. Selfe. "The Politics of the Interface: Power and Its Exercise in Electronic Contact Zones." *College Composition and Communication* 45 (1994): 480–504.

Shaiken, Harley. *Work Transformed: Automation and Labor in the Computer Age.* Lexington: Lexington, 1986.

Shenk, David. *Data Smog: Surviving the Information Glut.* New York: Harper, 1997.

Shirk, Henrietta Nickels. "Technical Writing's Roots in Computer Science: The Evolution from Technician to Technical Writers." *Journal of Technical Writing and Communication* 18 (1988): 305–23.

Shneiderman, Ben. *Designing the User Interface: Strategies for Effective Human-Computer Interaction.* Reading: Addison, 1987.

Shor, Ira. "What Is Critical Literacy?" *Critical Literacy in Action: Writing Words, Changing Worlds.* Ed. Ira Shor and Caroline Pari. Portsmouth: Boynton, 1999. 1–30.

Simon, Herbert A. "The Consequences of Computers for Centralization and Decentralization." *The Computer Age: A Twenty-Year View.* Ed. Michael L. Dertouzos and Joel Moses. Cambridge: MIT P, 1980. 212–28.

Simons, P. Robert-Jan. "Constructive Learning: The Role of the Learner." *Designing Environments for Constructive Learning.* Ed. Joost Lowyck, Thomas M. Duffy, and David H. Jonassen. New York: Springer, 1993. 291–313.

Sims, Brenda R. "Electronic Mail in Two Corporate Workplaces." *Electronic Literacies in the Workplace: Technologies of Writing.* Ed. Patricia Sullivan and Jennie Dautermann. Urbana: NCTE and *Computers and Composition,* 1996. 41–64.

Singh, Surendra N., and Nikunj P. Dalal. "Web Home Pages as Advertisements." *Communications of the ACM* 42 (1999): 91–98.

Skyttner, Lars. *General Systems Theory: An Introduction.* London: Macmillan, 1996.

Slatin, John M. "The Art of ALT: Toward a More Accessible Web." *Computers and Composition* 18 (2001): 73–81.

————. "Reading Hypertext: Order and Coherence in a New Medium." *College English* 52 (1990): 870–83.

Smith, Catherine. "Reconceiving Hypertext." *Evolving Perspectives on Computers and Composition Studies: Questions for the 1990s.* Ed. Gail E. Hawisher and Cynthia L. Selfe. Urbana: NCTE and *Computers and Composition,* 1991. 224–52.

Smith, John B., and F. Donelson Smith. "ABC: A Hypermedia System for Artifact-Based Collaboration." *Proceedings of the Third ACM Conference on Hypertext, San Antonio, 15–18 December 1991.* New York: ACM, 1991. 179–92.

Smyth, John. "Developing and Sustaining Critical Reflection in Teacher Education." *Journal of Teacher Education* 40 (1989): 2–9.

Soloway, Elliot, Cathleen Norris, Phyllis Blumenfeld, Barry Fishman, Joseph Krajcik, and Ronald Marx. "K–12 and the Internet." *Communications of the ACM* 43 (2000): 19–23.

Sommers, Nancy. "Revision Strategies of Student Writers and Experienced Adult Writers." *College Composition and Communication* 31 (1980): 378–88.

Sorensen, Elsebeth Korsgaard. "Metaphors and the Design of the Human Interface." *Collaborative Learning Through Computer Conferencing: The Najaden Papers.* Ed. Anthony R. Kaye. New York: Springer, 1991. 189–99.

Sosnoski, James. "Hyper-Readers and Their Reading Engines." *Passions, Pedagogies, and Twenty-First Century Technologies.* Ed. Gail E. Hawisher and Cynthia L. Selfe. Logan: Utah State UP and NCTE, 1999. 161–77.

Spender, Dale. *Nattering on the Net: Women, Power and Cyberspace.* North Melbourne: Spinifex, 1995.

Spinuzzi, Clay. "Grappling with Distributed Usability: A Cultural-Historical Examination of Documentation Genres over Four Decades." *Journal of Technical Writing and Communication* 31 (2001): 41–59.

Spiro, Rand J., Paul J. Feltovich, Michael J. Jacobson, and Richard L. Coulson. "Cognitive Flexibility, Constructivism, and Hypertext: Random Access Instruction for Advanced Knowledge Acquisition in Ill-Structured Domains." *Educational Technology* May 1991: 24–33.

Sproull, Lee, and Sara Kiesler. "Reducing Social Context Cues: Electronic Mail in Organization Communication." *Management Science* 32 (1986): 1492–512.

Sterne, Jonathan. "The Computer Race Goes to Class: How Computers in Schools Helped Shape the Racial Topography of the Internet." *Race in Cyberspace.* Ed. Lisa Nakamura, Beth Kolko, and Gilbert B. Rodman. New York: Routledge, 2000. 191–212.

Street, Brian V. *Social Literacies: Critical Approaches to Literacy in Development, Ethnography and Education.* New York: Longman, 1995.

Street, John. *Politics and Technology.* New York: Guilford, 1992.

Stuckey, J. Elspeth. *The Violence of Literacy.* Portsmouth: Boynton, 1991.

Suchman, Lucy. *Plans and Situated Actions: The Problem of Human-Machine Communication.* Cambridge: Cambridge UP, 1987.

Sullivan, Patricia, and James E. Porter. *Opening Spaces: Writing Technologies and Critical Research Practices.* Greenwich: Ablex, 1997.

Taylor, Todd. "The Persistence of Authority: Coercing the Student Body." *Literacy Theory in the Age of the Internet.* Ed. Todd Taylor and Irene Ward. New York: Columbia UP, 1998. 109–21.

Thompson, Patrick W. "Constructivism, Cybernetics, and Information Processing: Implications for Technologies of Research on Learning." *Constructivism in Education.* Ed. Leslie P. Steffe and Jerry Gale. Hillsdale: Erlbaum, 1995. 123–33.

Thralls, Charlotte, and Nancy Roundy Blyler. "The Social Perspective and Professional Communication: Diversity and Directions in Research." *Professional Communication: The Social Perspective.* Newbury Park: Sage, 1993. 3–34.

Tomei, Lawrence A. "The Technology Facade." *Syllabus: New Directions in Education Technology* 13 (1999): 32–34.

Trimbur, John. "Consensus and Difference in Collaborative Learning." *College English* 51 (1989): 602–16.

Tseng, Shawn, and B. J. Fogg. "Credibility and Computing Technology." *Communications of the ACM* 42 (1999): 39–44.

Tuman, Myron C. *Word Perfect: Literacy in the Computer Age.* Pittsburgh: U of Pittsburgh P, 1992.

Turkle, Sherry. *Life on the Screen: Identity in the Age of the Internet.* New York: Simon, 1995.

———. *The Second Self: Computers and the Human Spirit.* New York: Simon, 1984.

Turkle, Sherry, and Seymour Papert. "Epistemological Pluralism: Styles and Voices Within the Computer Culture." *Signs: Journal of Women in Culture and Society* 16 (1990): 128–57.

Ummelen, Nicole. "Procedural and Declarative Knowledge: A Closer Examination of the Distinction." *Quality of Technical Documentation.* Ed. Carel Jansen, Michael Steehouder, Pieter van der Poort, and Ron Verheijen. Atlanta: Rodopi, 1994. 115–30.

Unsworth, John. "Electronic Scholarship; or, Scholarly Publishing and the Public." *The Literary Text in the Digital Age.* Ed. Richard J. Finneran. Ann Arbor: U of Michigan P, 1996. 233–43.

Van Dyke, Carolynn. "Taking 'Computer Literacy' Literally." *Communications of the ACM* 30 (1987): 366–74.

Venezky, Richard L. "Gathering Up, Looking Ahead." *Toward Defining Literacy.* Ed. Richard L. Venezky, Daniel A. Wagner, and Barrie S. Ciliberti. Newark: International Reading Assoc. 70–74.

Vernon, Alex. "Computerized Grammar Checkers 2000: Capabilities, Limitations, and Pedagogical Possibilities." *Computers and Composition* 17 (2000): 329–49.

Vitanza, Victor J. *CyberReader.* Boston: Allyn, 1999.

Walker, Decker F. "Reflections on the Educational Potential and Limitations of Microcomputers." *The Information Age Classroom: Using the Computer as a Tool.* Ed. Terence R. Cannings and Stephen W. Brown. Irvine: Franklin, 1986. 244–50.

Walker, Janice R., and John Ruszkiewicz. *Writing@online.edu.* New York: Longman, 2000.

Warnock, Mary. "Good Teaching." *Beyond Liberal Education: Essays in Honour of Paul H. Hirst.* Ed. Robin Barrow and Patricia White. New York: Routledge, 1993. 16–29.

Weiser, Mark. "The Computer for the Twenty-First Century." *Scientific American* July 1991: 94–104.

Weizenbaum, Joseph. *Computer Power and Human Reason: From Judgment to Calculation.* New York: Freeman, 1976.

Welch, Kathleen E. *Electric Rhetoric: Classical Rhetoric, Oralism, and a New Literacy.* Cambridge: MIT P, 1999.

Wiedenbeck, Susan, and Patti L. Zila. "Hands-On Practice in Learning to Use Software: A Comparison of Exercise, Exploration, and Combined Formats." *ACM Transactions on Computer-Human Interaction* 4 (1997): 169–96.

Wiggam, Lee. "Expanding the Sphere: The Importance of Effective Communication in Change." *Systemic Change in Education.* Ed. Charles M. Reigeluth and Robert J. Garfinkle. Englewood Cliffs: Educational Technology Pub., 1994. 155–61.

Wiklund, Michael E., ed. *Usability in Practice: How Companies Develop User-Friendly Products.* Boston: AP Professional, 1994.

Williams, Robin. *The PC Is Not a Typewriter.* Berkeley: Peachpit, 1992.

Williams, Sean D. "Part 1: Thinking out of the Pro-Verbal Box." *Computers and Composition* 18 (2001): 21–32.

Winner, Langdon. *The Whale and the Reactor: A Search for Limits in an Age of High Technology.* Chicago: U of Chicago P, 1986.

Winograd, Terry, ed. *Bringing Design to Software.* New York: ACM, 1996.

———. "Frame Representations and the Declarative/Procedural Controversy." *Representation and Understanding: Studies in Cognitive Science.* Ed. Daniel G. Borrow and Allan Collins. New York: Academic, 1975. 185–210.

Winograd, Terry, and Fernando Flores. *Understanding Computers and Cognition: A New Foundation for Design.* Reading: Addison, 1986.

Wixon, Dennis, and Judith Ramey, ed. *Field Methods Casebook for Software Design.* New York: Wiley, 1996.

Wood, Dennis. *The Power of Maps.* New York: Guilford, 1992.

Wurman, Richard Saul. *Information Anxiety.* New York: Doubleday, 1989.

Xia, Weidong, and Gwanhoo Lee. "The Influence of Persuasion, Training, and Experience on User Perceptions and Acceptance of IT Innovations." *Proceedings of the Twenty-First ACM International Conference on Information Systems, Brisbane, 10–13 December 2000.* New York: ACM, 2000. 371–84.

Yagelski, Robert P. *Literacies and Technologies: A Reader for Contemporary Writers.* New York: Longman, 2001.

Yagelski, Robert P., and Jeffrey T. Grabill. "Computer-Mediated Communication in the Undergraduate Writing Classroom: A Study of the Relationship of Online Discourse and Classroom Discourse in Two Writing Classes." *Computers and Composition* 15 (1998): 11–40.

Yancey, Kathleen Blake. *Reflection in the Writing Classroom.* Logan: Utah State UP, 1998.

Young, Richard E., Alton L. Becker, and Kenneth L. Pike. *Rhetoric: Discovery and Change.* New York: Harcourt, 1970.

Zuboff, Shoshana. *In the Age of the Smart Machine: The Future of Work and Power.* New York: Basic, 1988.

Zucchermaglio, Cristina. "Toward a Cognitive Ergonomics of Educational Technology." *Designing Environments for Constructive Learning.* Ed. Joost Lowyck, Thomas M. Duffy, and David H. Jonassen. New York: Springer, 1993. 249–60.

# Index

STUART A. SELBER is an assistant professor of English at Penn State University. The recipient of three national publication awards, he chairs the Conference on College Composition and Communication Committee on Technical Communication and is a past president of the Council for Programs in Technical and Scientific Communication.

*Studies in Writing & Rhetoric*

In 1980 the Conference on College Composition and Communication established the Studies in Writing & Rhetoric (SWR) series as a forum for monograph-length arguments or presentations that engage general compositionists. SWR encourages extended essays or research reports addressing any issue in composition and rhetoric from any theoretical or research perspective as long as the general significance to the field is clear. Previous SWR publications serve as models for prospective authors; in addition, contributors may propose alternate formats and agendas that inform or extend the field's current debates.

SWR is particularly interested in projects that connect the specific research site or theoretical framework to contemporary classroom and institutional contexts of direct concern to compositionists across the nation. Such connections may come from several approaches, including cultural, theoretical, field-based, gendered, historical, and interdisciplinary. SWR especially encourages monographs by scholars early in their careers, by established scholars who wish to share an insight or exhortation with the field, and by scholars of color.

The SWR series editor and editorial board members are committed to working closely with prospective authors and offering significant developmental advice for encouraged manuscripts and prospectuses. Editorships rotate every five years. Prospective authors intending to submit a prospectus during the 2002 to 2007 editorial appointment should obtain submission guidelines from Robert Brooke, SWR editor, University of Nebraska-Lincoln, Department of English, P.O. Box 880337, 202 Andrews Hall, Lincoln, NE 68588-0337.

General inquiries may also be addressed to Sponsoring Editor, Studies in Writing & Rhetoric, Southern Illinois University Press, P.O. Box 3697, Carbondale, IL 62902-3697.